The Ri

Winning More, Losing Less,

w i l l i a m

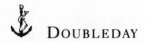
DOUBLEDAY

ght Horse

and Having a Great Time at the Racetrack

murray

New York   London   Toronto   Sydney   Auckland

PUBLISHED BY DOUBLEDAY

a division of Bantam Doubleday Dell Publishing Group, Inc.
1540 Broadway, New York, New York 10036

DOUBLEDAY and the portrayal of an anchor with a dolphin are trademarks of
Doubleday, a division of Bantam Doubleday Dell Publishing Group, Inc.

Excerpts of this book have been published previously in different editions
of the *Daily Racing Form.*

The author would like to thank the *Daily Racing Form* for permission to
reprint the results charts that appear in this book.

Book design by Maria Carella

Library of Congress Cataloging-in-Publication Data
Murray, William, 1926–
    The right horse : winning more, losing less, and having a great
time at the racetrack / William Murray.—1st ed.
      p. cm.
    Includes bibliographical references (p.) and index.
    1. Horse racing—Betting. I. Title.
    SF331.M95   1997
    798.401—dc21   97-3208
                                                 CIP

ISBN 0-385-48353-8

Printed in the United States of America

July 1997

First Edition

10 9 8 7 6 5 4 3 2 1

This book is dedicated to Nick Giovinazzo

—great host, fine cook, and intrepid horseplayer

—and his wife, Lois, who puts up with him.

Contents

Contents

----

x

"The purpose of life is pleasure. Man should not spend life embalmed in static reasonableness."
—my friend Sam Sokol,
in a letter to his father

- - - - - - - - - - - - - -

"You're probably going to waste your life having a good time."
—screenwriter Peter Bellwood's mother,
in a letter to him

Post Time

Last summer, during the course of the Del Mar meet in California, I invited two friends of mine, a married couple, to spend a day at the races. Neither of them knew anything about horse racing and had never been to a racetrack. I got them reservations in the Turf Club, at a nice table with a good view over the racing surfaces and the infield. I gave them detailed information about how and when to get there, where to park, what to wear, what to bring (especially two pairs of good binoculars), what to expect when they got there, and what to buy in the way of documents—programs, the *Daily Racing Form*, tout sheets. I told them approximately what they could expect to spend for parking, food and drink, and other amenities. Most important, I gave them a brief lecture about how to bet.

I love horse racing. One of the reasons I've had a lifelong infatuation with the game is that on my very first day at the track, as a teenager, I won several hundred dollars, a small fortune to me at the time. I wanted my friends to have the same experience, and so I worked very hard to make sure they wouldn't tumble into one of the many pitfalls, financial and otherwise, that await the unwary and the innocent who wander every day onto the grounds of one of this country's and Canada's approximately one hundred and ten Thoroughbred racetracks.

The night before the great day, I spent several hours burrowing into the statistics in the *Daily Racing Form* in an effort to come up with enough potential winners to ensure that my friends would enjoy themselves. By the time I showed up at their table, a half hour before the first race, I had isolated what I thought were the so-called live horses from the ninety-seven animals entered on the program. I had worked so hard for them that I had slept badly and was nursing a small nagging headache from the effort.

I found them already hugely enjoying themselves. They had followed my advice and arrived early enough to avoid the worst of the traffic, then had opted to spend ten dollars for valet parking, so as not to have to walk to the front gate. They were finishing their lunch, while all around them the later arrivals were waiting to be seated or competing for the attention of the staff. They had bought programs, a copy of the *Form*, and were studying the selections made by the public handicappers in the local newspaper. They also told me that they had decided they could afford to wager between them up to ten dollars a race, a total of ninety dollars. If they lost every race, they would have spent about a hundred and fifty dollars, approximately what it would have cost them to go out for dinner and an evening's entertainment in the San Diego area where they lived. They were ecstatic about everything they had experienced so far—the surroundings, the people, the atmosphere—and were looking forward to being able to see the horses up close in the paddock, as well as the races themselves.

I complimented them on their obvious native smarts and then unloaded the fruits of my wisdom and hard work upon them. I gave them three horses in every race in order of preference. I reminded them that in gambling, as in life, value is everything, and that the surest way to lose money at the track is to bet heavily on favorites. I imparted a few more bits of basic advice, told them I'd be back later in the afternoon to take them to the paddock and generally show them around, then left them to their own devices.

As always happens in these situations, only one of the first twelve horses I picked managed to win, and that one, my third choice in a short field of six three-year-old fillies, was an obvious favorite, returning only $5.20 for every two dollars wagered. By the time I showed up at my friends' table again, I fully expected to find them soured by having lost every race and highly dubious of my professed expertise.

I needn't have worried. They had ignored everything I had told them, except about value, and had bet some of their money in the first race on a long shot named Smiling Lass that romped in, returning twenty-four dollars on a two-dollar ticket. (All payoffs at the races are computed on the basis of a two-dollar wager.) They had decided to bet on Smiling Lass because the wife liked the horse's name. They hadn't cashed a ticket since, but it didn't matter. Having noticed that I seemed to be able to bring in horses second and third, they were now planning to bet only to show and also to venture into the far more difficult world of so-called exotic wagering: hooking up horses to one another in combinations and parlay bets such as exactas, quinellas, trifectas, doubles, pick-threes, pick-sixes, etc.

I pulled up a chair and sat down. They could do whatever they wanted, I told them; after all, they weren't planning to come back the next day. As long as they stuck to their budget, they couldn't get hurt. They might even continue to be lucky. But again I stressed the importance of value and suggested that they reserve at least some of their capital to bet *to win only* on any horse I had given them going off at odds of four to one or better. They promised me they would and I told them I'd come back to take them down to the paddock for the feature race, the eighth on the day's card of ten.

Much to my relief, three of my selections won the next three races, paying $13.20, $22.80, and $9.80. By the time we regrouped in the paddock for the Pat O'Brien Handicap, a race for top sprinters competing for a purse of $100,000, we were all winning. When my top two horses won the feature and the ninth race, paying $12.40 and $19.80, my friends had decided I was a genius. It didn't matter at all that we blew the tenth.

They loved the goings-on in the paddock, also known as the walking ring. They were struck by the beauty and power of these top Thoroughbreds seen up close. I pointed out and named some of the trainers and the jockeys; I introduced my friends around. When I whisked them for the last three races into a grandstand box over the finish line, much closer to the action than they had been in the rarefied world of the Turf Club, they were delighted. "This is what I like," the husband said, gazing around with a big grin on his face. "This is where it's at, this is where I want to be." And I knew they'd be back. Why? Because they'd had fun.

WHAT HAPPENS to my friends and how it may affect their view of this great sport is one reason for this book. I want everybody, in fact, to have a great time at the track. What's the best thing in the world? A winning day at the races. What's the second-best thing? A losing day at the races. That's how the regulars feel. But you can't have a good time if you don't know what you're doing, or how the game is played, or who the players are.

Red Smith, the late great sportswriter for the *New York Times*, once observed that, whenever he was at a loss as to how to fill his daily column, all he had to do was visit a racetrack and he'd come away with a dozen good stories. You'll find some of these stories, as well as sayings, bits of track lore, and handed-down wisdom, in this book. They should help to illuminate the information on handicapping and money management that is crucial, even in the short run, to the enjoyment of the scene.

As I was finishing up this manuscript, a woman named Rose Hamburger died in New York at the age of a hundred and five. According to her obituary in the *New York Times*, Mrs. Hamburger had been going to the races since the age of twenty, when her father, on a trip abroad, took her to a track in Germany. She cashed the first bet of her life, on "an adorable jockey in a little green silk shirt," and went home a winner. "I was hooked," she said.

She worked half of her long life as a real estate agent in the Baltimore area, but managed her day so as to leave most afternoons open for forays to Pimlico Race Course, where she became a celebrated and popular fixture. She saw every Preakness Stakes run there from 1915 to 1988, including Man o' War's win in 1920.

In 1975, widowed and living alone, she moved to New York to be close to her two daughters. She began frequenting the New York tracks, Aqueduct and Belmont. On her hundred and second birthday, Aqueduct named a race in her honor and threw a party for her. At the age of a hundred and five, she went to work for the *New York Post* as a public handicapper called Gamblin' Rose. Although the newspaper undoubtedly exploited her for promotional reasons, she took her work seriously and went out a winner, when her last selection before dying came in first at Saratoga.

I like this story, and I know dozens more just like it. Horseplayers don't all die broke, as Damon Runyon once claimed. If you don't allow yourself to be made a fool of at the betting windows, the racetrack can be a nourishing and wonderful place. I've often been asked whether I'm ahead or behind in my action at the track over the years. I always give the same answer: I've written eleven books about racing and dozens of articles, I've made many friends, I met my wife at Santa Anita, and I've had a terrific time. I'm a lifetime winner, and you can be too.

The Tracks:
Would Elizabeth Taylor
Do This?

chapter 2

Somebody suggests an outing to your local racetrack and you agree to go along, if only out of curiosity. You've never been to a racetrack and you know nothing about the sport, though you may have heard about Man o' War, Secretariat, and Cigar. The event is touted to you as a day spent in the open, watching beautiful animals gambol about, so you begin to look forward to it. Your friends have been before you and know something about the game; you'll just tag along, make small wagers on the horses they select, and generally enjoy yourself.

The day arrives and everyone piles into your car to get to the track, which may be an hour or so away from where you live. But it's a nice sunny day and you don't mind, even

----

though the traffic, especially in large cities like New York and Los Angeles, can be ferocious. You don't leave yourself enough time and so you find yourself caught in a traffic jam on some freeway or grubby-looking boulevard. Never mind. You do finally get there and drive up to the gate about twenty minutes before post time for the first race.

To save time, you buy valet parking and watch your car being driven away by some fugitive from a demolition derby. For another six dollars, you buy clubhouse admission, then pay four more dollars for a reserved seat. You buy a program ($1.50), a *Daily Racing Form* ($3.25), and then decide to lay out another eight bucks for a couple of so-called tout sheets, publications in which some presumed expert picks the likely winners for you. You don't have time to eat lunch, so you spring for an overpriced sandwich and soft drink, then look for your seat, which turns out to be a sixteenth of a mile away from the finish line. You have now spent nearly fifty dollars and have yet to make a bet.

You have no idea how to risk your money, so you scan your program for guidance. At the larger tracks you'll be able to find some indication of what to do, but usually only the barest rudiments are explained. The program may tell you what wagers are available on each race and also exactly how to make a bet. What it doesn't tell you is what the chances of your winning such a bet are and whether it's worth making.

One of the members of your party urges you to check your *Racing Form*, so you open it to find yourself confronted by a great mass of statistics. As a neophyte, you have no time to master the intricacies of deciphering all those numbers, so you decide to rely on your tout sheets. What you find out, as the afternoon progresses, is that the professional handicappers usually pick favorites. Two or three of these horses win during the course of the day, but none of them pays much more than a pittance. You take a stab at a few of the exotic wagers, but you immediately discover that bringing in these better-paying combinations is difficult. You try to ask for advice from one of the clerks at the betting windows, but he's too busy to help you. The people behind you in line become impatient and abusive when you show signs of wishing to linger. You slink back to your seat, then you watch your money disappear when the two horses you've selected in an exacta finish one-three.

At the end of the day, as you drive glumly back to town, you wonder what you did wrong. (Your friends, for some mysterious reason, seem to have won.) You add up your losses. In addition to the roughly fifty dollars you spent before making a bet, you've lost another couple of hundred through the windows. You admit to yourself that you were moved by the beauty of the racing scene and the spectacle of the horses running their races, but you decide that the game is too expensive to play on a regular basis. You have not had $250 worth of fun. You wish you had spent the money either on some other sporting event or on a play with a nice dinner out. It will be many months, if ever, before anyone is able to persuade you to come to the races again.

You may, of course, have gotten lucky. Most of the dedicated horseplayers I know had wonderful experiences the first time they went to the track. Without knowing anything about the sport or how to bet, they came away with fresh money in their pockets and were instantly hooked. I was sixteen when I went to the track for the first time, with a man who had married my older cousin and knew what to do. He handed me the money to bet and selected the first five winners on the card, by which time we were awash in loot. Then he asked me to pick a horse in a field of two-year-old fillies, none of whom had ever competed before. I selected a name I liked, Qué Hora, and we watched her romp home first at the delicious odds of nineteen to one. By this time we had accumulated a dedicated entourage of enthusiasts who followed us about, wanting to know what horse we were going to bet on in the last contest on the card. But we had decided not to push our luck and went home to squander a small portion of our winnings on tickets to a hit Broadway musical and a lavish repast at one of the best restaurants in town.

That sort of success can turn anyone's head. I've been a fervent fan ever since, but it was many years before I felt I knew what I was doing at the track. I learned the hard way, by losing money, that becoming a good handicapper is only one step on the road to enjoying the races. If I had lost too big a chunk of my own capital that first day and had had no one to guide me through it, I might never have come back. Winning money will compensate for any amount of discomfort and inconvenience at the track, but you soon find out that it's much easier to lose than to win. The canny regulars, people who go frequently to either the racetrack or a betting facility, know that survival requires knowledge, discipline, and, above all, patience. Even as a casual player, you have to accept that reality. Then, if you lose, you can take comfort in the fact that there are days when, no matter what you do, the horses will perform erratically. At least you will not be out of pocket because you weren't prepared, but because it simply wasn't your day. Bad luck is something you can't do much about, but for most people luck evens out in the end. The photo finish you lose today will be compensated for by the one you will win tomorrow; the horse that gets disqualified and placed last will later be erased from your memory by one moved up to first at somebody else's expense. At the racetrack, it's always tomorrow.

THE FIRST STEP in beating the races is to master the art of not allowing the track's often misguided management and indifferent employees to treat you cavalierly, as if you should be grateful for their allowing you onto the premises in the first place. Thoroughbred horse racing began in England as a rich man's game, under the guise of improving the breed. Aristocrats were supposed to be indifferent to the outcomes of their wagers; it was the sporting aspect of the scene that counted. The public was tolerated at these race meets and allowed to make bets on their favorites, but the common herd was excluded from the inner circles. Jockey clubs and turf clubs and private boxes were created to be the exclusive domain of the wealthy and the powerful. The race meets were held out in the countryside and people had to travel for miles to get to them. When they arrived, they were regarded as minor nuisances whose sole contribution to the goings-on was to enrich the local bookies. They were provided with little information and relegated to enclosures from which the racing could hardly be seen, even with the aid of powerful binoculars.

The scene today, at least here in the United States, is a vastly different one. The owners and the breeders no longer provide the juice that keeps the enterprise going. It is the betting public that pays all the bills. People pour tens of millions of dollars a day through the betting windows. A percentage of this money, ranging usually from fifteen to twenty percent, is cut out of the pools to provide financing for all the activities of the various racing associations, as well as the inevitable tax payments to the federal and state governments. In other words, it costs you a minimum of fifteen cents out of every dollar you wager to play this game. That percentage, what gamblers call the vigorish, is enormous compared to other gambling activities. In Las Vegas, for instance, a smart player can reduce the casino's take to under two percent at craps and to less than five percent on many other betting propositions. If you go strictly by these numbers, the average horseplayer is essentially a sucker whose devotion to the sport should be exalted by the racetracks; his well-being should be the first priority of everyone connected with the sport.

It's only recently, however, that the people who run this enterprise have begun to take care of the needs of their patrons. The betting public has always had to garner even the most basic information about the contestants from independently owned publications, most notably the *Daily Racing Form*. The tracks never bothered to provide the players with the information without which no one can make an informed guess as to the outcome of a race. They overcharged, as they still do, for admission, parking, reserved seats, and especially food and drink. They continued to deny access to the innermost circles, reserving the best seating and recreational facilities for the privileged and the wealthy. They resisted like cornered wolverines having to ensure the honesty of their clockers, the people who time early morning workouts and make the information public, and still refuse to disclose the full extent of the various medications used to keep horses running. Old concepts and traditions die hard. The ancient attitude that the betting public ought to be barely tolerated and that horseplayers are the scum of the earth still persists in some quarters. I used to have the feeling that the tracks would have liked us to wear bells around our necks, like medieval lepers, so that the folks who run the game could avoid us, crying "Unclean, unclean" as they fled to the sanctity of their turf clubs and private boxes.

Those of us who spent a lot of time at the races soon

learned what we had to do to survive and how to make the experience a pleasurable one. Racetracks are awash in wiseguys who have found ways to circumvent most of life's minor roadblocks. It's another way of beating the odds, as exemplified by an old gambling maxim that in life "everything is six to five against."

Wiseguys know all about the odds and the vigorish. They may not always come away winners, but it won't be because they've been hobbled by ancient prejudices, by society's often senseless rules and customs, or the abuses of power in high and low places. Wiseguys know the score. "What I always ask myself is, would Elizabeth Taylor do this?" a friend of mine commented a few years ago, as we stood crushed together in a mass of people pushing through customs lines on our way back from a Sunday afternoon of racing at the old Agua Caliente racetrack, now closed to live racing, in Tijuana, Mexico. We always drove back across the border after that, late at night after a few *cervezas*, a good dinner, and a pleasant hour or two spent at the jai alai palace downtown.

I first learned about the wiseguy approach in the military, during an inglorious tour of duty in my late teens. I had begun to serve under the misapprehension that honor, truth, and selfless commitment to a worthy cause were the basic criteria for advancement. The first time I behaved honorably and told the truth about a minor evasion of rules I was involved in resulted in a week of KP. I soon wised up and learned how to survive. In this respect, the army is not unlike the racetrack. Both are great places to acquire an education about how the world really works—not at all what I was taught to believe in the fancy prep schools and Ivy League college I attended.

Wiseguys know, for instance, that the most direct way to get to a racetrack is almost never the best one. They have figured out that parking attendants and ushers should be lightly greased to provide more convenient access and better seats. They cultivate powerful acquaintances who can supply parking stickers and invitations to the Turf Club, where they can mingle with the swells.

They never become trapped in betting lines behind uncertain neophytes, system players, and women with large handbags. Above all, they cling to the saving knowledge that things are seldom what they seem and that the best defense against racing's multitudinous pitfalls is never to trust anybody completely—management, employees, jockeys, trainers, tipsters, or, above all, members of the press.

The latter, of course, are the ultimate wiseguys. America's guests, they never have to shell out for anything. In fact, they are actually paid for being where they want to be and doing what they want to do. How's that for beating the odds? You may never achieve their privileged eminence, but you can profit by emulating them. Here's how:

Be sure to arrive at the track early enough to make yourself comfortable and find out what they're giving away free that day. The better tracks now all have programs in place to please their customers. At last they're making an effort; profit by it. Get to know who the efficient employees are and tip the ushers and the parking attendants for better spots. Find and cultivate the veterans of the game. They know who the best parimutuel clerks are and can show you how to work the betting machines. Chat with anybody, keep your ears open, and don't be afraid to ask for advice and favors. Most horseplayers are generous souls who see life at the track as a long voyage on which you are all embarked facing fearful odds. Helping hands are readily available, if you know where to look and what to ask. *Carpe diem.*

TRAINERS:
BAD NEWS, GOOD NEWS,
HORSESPEAK

The single most important person who will affect your life at the racetrack is the trainer. He's the one who makes all the decisions regarding the horses in his charge, and what he does with them ultimately affects you, because you are the one risking your money on his animals. In his own circumscribed little world, the trainer reigns supreme, with all the power and perks of a Balkan warlord. His talent can enrich you, his mistakes disastrously affect your well-being.

Every trainer has a different style, and statistics on their overall performances are readily available. It is important for you to get some sense of how they operate, because even the best ones have weaknesses that can pose a hazard to your wallet. Some trainers work their horses fast; others prefer a more leisurely approach. Some trainers are good with young horses that have never run before; others prefer to use these early races as conditioners for contests down the line. There are trainers who are excellent with speed horses in sprints, races of seven furlongs or less; others who use speed to prepare their charges for the longer distances. A few trainers specialize in certain kinds of races; some, for instance, favor pointing their animals for the turf (or grass) courses, where the average purses are larger. There are all sorts of gradations, many different approaches and techniques. The only easy task you will have as a handicapper is isolating the incompetents and eliminating them from your calculations. They win so seldom that by throwing them out you can save yourself a ton of money.

Then, still on the bad news side, there is the problem of what is euphemistically called medication. Everyone who goes to the races regularly knows that there are a few unscrupulous conditioners who rely almost exclusively on drugs to keep their horses running. Some of these people win a lot of races and can be found near the top of the trainer standings at every meet. As a bettor, you would do well to be wary of them, because you could find yourself wagering on animals too sore to run at all.

The irony is that quite a few of the medications used on horses today are not only legal but necessary. You will note from your *Racing Form* that most horses today are given Lasix, a diuretic that helps them breathe more easily by keeping their lungs free of fluids, and Butazolidin, a drug to ease pain in joints and muscle soreness. But horses are also treated routinely with cortisone, anabolic steroids, and various analgesics. Fluid is drained out of swollen joints, nerves are deadened to mask pain. Without such procedures it would be impossible to fill the daily racing programs, because all over this country we race an average of five days a week, eight to ten races a day, year round.

A lot of good people in the industry, including the better trainers, would like to cut down on the number of races offered and give their athletes a rest. The game, however, has become a moneymaking machine that feeds the state and federal tax coffers, so it's unlikely that anything significant will be done soon to reduce the number of live racing days a year. Asking a politician to take the long view by cutting back on an immediate source of income is equivalent to begging for mercy from a Serbian general.

Then there are conditioners, luckily not many, who will also use drugs that are not approved. It won't take you long to isolate these so-called juice trainers from the pack. You will note that most of them win races in streaks that may last several weeks. Then, for some mysterious reason, their horses will stop running well and they will undergo long periods when their entries fail to perform. There are two main reasons for such reversals of form. Thoroughbreds are powerful but fragile; the best ones are not asked to run more than a few times a year. A juice trainer will run his horses every week or ten days at least without pause. After a while the animals break down. The second reason often has to do with a clamping down on their practices by the racetracks. The drug tests periodically administered to some horses show positive results and investigations are launched.

A trainer who is being investigated stops using his excess and illegal medications, so his horses stop running well. He will remain in the shadows for as long as he feels he's being watched and you can safely toss his horses out as contenders. The moment he starts winning again, however, he will win often, sometimes at a thirty or even a forty percent clip for a while. The best time to bet on a juice trainer's horse is immediately after he has acquired the animal from someone else. Loaded to the ears on drugs, the trainer's new charge will often perform way beyond his usual form. In New York, not too long ago, there was a conditioner who became famous for acquiring cheap horses and immediately moving them up in class, where they performed like stakes winners. A friend of mine wanted to propose him for the Nobel Prize in chemistry. His operation became so blatant that it compelled the racing establishment to turn the screws on him. His horses stopped winning and he was all but driven out of the sport.

It's difficult to control this unsavory aspect of the game. One reason is that the racing establishment is terrified of scandal and is also afraid of coming under fire from the animal-rights groups, some of which have already campaigned against racing. (Don't fret: at the big tracks the horses are treated very well, better than the humans who care for them.) The industry thus tends to cover up and pretend that nothing serious is amiss. The argument goes that there are unscrupulous people in every walk of life and that rooting them out is all that is required. The second reason is the incredible proliferation of drugs readily available on the market, far more than can easily be tested for, and new ones are developed every day. All that the racing associations can do is their best to control the problem by handing out stiff punishments to the transgressors they catch.

Now for the good news. Trainers, as a group, are among the best people you will meet in the sport. Most of them have become trainers because they love the game and they care deeply about their animals. One of the best times to be around a racetrack is in the early morning, when the real work gets done. Most successful trainers are at their shed rows by dawn, and the conditioning of their charges takes place during the morning hours. In the afternoons, the trainers who have horses running that day will be found at the track, where they hang around the grandstand box area and one or two favorite bars. They tell good stories and they are entertaining raconteurs, though you would not want to discuss politics or international affairs with many of them, especially if you happen to be a Democrat.

Although there's been an influx of women into the profession during the past decade, most trainers are male. They tend to mistake the Bill of Rights for the Communist Manifesto and believe that government programs to aid the poor are plots to subvert the American way of life. The older ones, especially, are throwbacks to a vanished era, when men were men and the known world was run by white Anglo males.

Despite his power, however, the trainer's livelihood is pretty much at the mercy of his owners, which puts him these days in the precarious position of a middle-management executive, apt to be cast adrift at any moment. I happened to be around a trainer's barn one morning when an owner called up to tell him he was taking his horses away from him. The animals represented more than half of the trainer's small string and included his most promising charges. Not only was it a financial blow, it was a moral one as well, because, in effect, the owner was saying to him, "You're not doing a good enough job and I'm firing you."

The trainer wasn't surprised; in fact, he'd been expecting it. The horses hadn't been running well for him recently and too many owners these days, especially the newcomers to the sport, are an impatient lot. Imams of industry, they are the sort of people who have become used to instant success. They've piled up their loot elsewhere, while being acclaimed as geniuses in the *Wall Street Journal*, and they've gone into racing expecting quick gratification. After all, they reason, a person brilliant enough to acquire a hoard by disfiguring the countryside with shopping malls, playing the money game on Wall Street, or permeating the air with pop ought to be smart enough to succeed in horse racing, which only involves managing some beautiful but dumb beasts to perform on cue.

Unfortunately, these dumb beasts are not only expensive but high-strung and delicate. It takes months, sometimes a year or more, to get the best out of them. It involves dedication, very hard work, the patience of Job, and sometimes even love. The best trainer is the one who will not abuse an animal by rushing him into the starting gate too soon. The owners who can't tell a horse from a mule don't understand that. A few years ago one of them, then very new to the game, confronted Charles Whittingham, a legendary figure in the sport, and suggested that it would be nice if this filly he'd had in training for months could be persuaded to run on his wife's birthday. "When's her birthday?" Charlie asked. The owner named a date in August, only a few weeks away. "It would be better if it was in December," Charlie replied.

An owner, of course, has every right to take his horses away from a trainer and give them to somebody else. After all, he paid for them and he foots the very considerable monthly bills. If he's unhappy, why shouldn't he be able to go elsewhere? The fact that the trainer has a proven record as a winner and may have put in months of painstaking work and dedicated care on his beasts is immaterial. We're still a two-party democracy in this nation, but the only party we really believe in, as Gore Vidal noted, is the party of property. Loyalty and talent don't figure into this equation.

If you want to know who the successful owners are, take a close look at the statistics and you'll have no trouble identifying them. They're the people who are smart enough to know that they don't know everything. They put in some time at finding themselves a good trainer and they stick with him. They're not interested in becoming overnight celebrities, mouthing off on TV or being sucked up to in the Turf Club. They don't expect their trainers to kiss their feet in gratitude, fawn over their relatives, or coddle their kids. They treat their trainers not as employees but as partners. If they insist on calling all the shots, they are doomed to lose.

On the day he was fired, one of my trainer friend's horses won a nice race for his departing owner. Patience is the name of this game.

ONE TALENT all trainers, good and bad, have mastered is a language of their own. It's as necessary to their survival as camouflage to an herbivore in an African game park. In the old days, before published statistics and when most owners were landed gentry, it didn't matter what you said. "Treat owners like mushrooms," was the word. "Keep them in the dark and feed them lots of shit." Today, however, with an intrusive press, TV coverage, and a betting public clamoring for accurate information, the trainers have had to resort to a lingo that would have charmed George Orwell. I call it Horsespeak:

A trainer, for example, will hardly ever tell an owner that his horse is fit and ready to win. He'll say that his animal "may be a little short," or, "I wish I'd had time to put one more work into him," or, "He may need the race." That way, when he finishes up the track, the trainer will have prepared the ground for the post-race analysis. He'll say, "He didn't like the dirt in his face," or, "He'll do better going long (or short)," or, "He had his head turned (or stumbled) after the gate opened," or, "He got pinched (or fanned) on the turn," or, "He'll like the grass (or the dirt) better," or, "He may need blinkers (or a different bit or goggles or shoes)." One of the best is, "The track was cuppy." The owner won't know what that means and neither will anyone else, but it works. In the history of racing no horse has ever liked a cuppy track.

Above all, the trainer will never admit that the beautiful creature the owner has just paid big bucks for on his recommendation can't run faster than a cow lumbering toward a feed bin. The trainer wants to keep that stall filled at between sixty and a hundred dollars a day, which is the minimum it costs today to keep a Thoroughbred in training. So he'll tell his owner that his untalented champion is "kicking down the barn door," that "he hasn't got a pimple on him," that "he's really on the muscle," that "he's a real doer" (which means only that he eats a lot), and that any day now, as soon as he stops coughing, or running a little fever, or gets over the tiny abscess in his foot, or has his wolf teeth (whatever they are) pulled, or has overcome any other of the thousands of minor ailments you can trot out, he'll be on his way to the Kentucky Derby or the Breeders' Cup.

Eventually, once the horse has run a few times and lost every race by ten or twenty lengths and keeps throwing in those glacially slow works, not even Horsespeak will save him. If the trainer hasn't been able to win a race or two for this owner over the years, the owner may actually decide to dump him. But there's nothing to worry about, providing the trainer happens to have a personable appearance and the gift of gab. The supply of suckers in the Turf Club is inexhaustible.

HORSESPEAK would have bailed out the reputations of a lot of history's great losers. Take General George Armstrong Custer, for instance. There he is at the Little Big Horn in 1876, about to take an arrow in his chest. He could have said, "We'd have won this easy if we didn't go wide around both buttes."

Here's the captain of the *Titanic,* standing on the bridge of his ship as it goes down after hitting an iceberg, with the band playing "Nearer My God to Thee." "It was real deep and holding out there," he'd say, "and then, when we tried to come through on the inside, we got blocked."

Consider the plight of Napoleon in Russia. He has failed to reach Moscow, and now he's retreating through the snows of a Russian winter with his defeated army, his hopes of empire permanently smashed. "The ground was really cuppy," he'd declare, "and we couldn't handle it at all. My boys like to hear their feet rattle."

King Priam of Troy is poised on the walls of his besieged city, watching the chariot of the Greek hero, Achilles, drag the corpse of his defeated son Hector in the dust. Instead of wailing and tearing his hair out by the roots, he'd say, "We never lose if we don't jump the boy up in class too quick."

General George McClellan, in command of the Army of the Potomac, squats glumly in his tent after the Battle of Antietam, in which his Union forces have been mangled by the Confederates. "I knew we was a little short," he'd complain, "but my owner got tired of waiting. We needed at least one more work."

Hannibal is having a hell of a time getting his invading army across the Alps. His elephants keep falling off cliffs. He's wondering if he's ever going to reach the fertile plains below, where the Roman legions await him. "If I'd known what poor

shippers these big suckers are, we'd have stayed in the barn,"
he'd say, "but the owners insisted."

Lucrezia Borgia, accused along with her brother Cesare
of having poisoned her kinsman, Pope Alexander VI, would
have pleaded, "Either the lab screwed up or it was something
in the feed."

Job, the Old Testament patriarch who has been forced to
endure a series of terrible afflictions, could have cried out in
his anguish, "How come I always get taken down? The Big
Steward up there is blind!"

How much easier life would be if we could spend it all
at the racetrack. In that enchanted land, no one ever screws
up; it's always either bad luck or somebody else's fault. If
you're planning to spend any time at the track, you'll be fed
lots of Horsespeak. Ignore it.

Instead, check out the trainer's statistics, study his relationships with various riders, make notes on what kind of races
he wins. It's the only way you can get some idea about his methods. A good trainer will win between ten and twenty percent of
his races meet after meet, year in and year out, regardless of the
quality of his stock. At the top of the game you'll find the stars
like Bill Mott, who trained Cigar, and D. Wayne Lukas, the
greatest salesman in the history of the sport. Their owners spend
millions buying them the expensive yearlings who grow up to
win most of the classic contests. But below these glamorous figures you'll also soon spot the good horsemen who know how to
win and get the best out of mediocre animals—a Tom Roberts
in San Francisco, a Brian Mayberry in Los Angeles, a Leo
O'Brien in New York. The list is a long one, but worth compil-
ing. Sometimes a good horse will overcome an untalented trainer
and win anyway, but not often and not for long. Keep yourself
solvent and happy at the races by paying attention.

Jockeys: Little Shakespearean Actors

A lot of people at the racetrack bet on jockeys. You can always tell who they are by the way they root. When the horses turn into the stretch, you can hear them shout, "Come on, Corey (or Jerry or Mike or Julie or Gary or Eddie), let him run, cut the corner, set him down, bring him home," etc., etc. When their riders win, the fans heap encomiums on their heads; when they lose, it's always because they blew it. For these horseplayers it's never the horse's or the trainer's fault; it's as if the riders are out there on their own, competing with one another like track stars.

I have a friend whom I'll call Walter, an aging curmudgeon who frequents the off-track betting facility in Del Mar. Walter has convinced himself that every race is fixed.

Well, not fixed, exactly. He believes it's a game the jockeys manipulate for their own benefit. "Look at him stiff that horse," Walter will say, watching a top rider like Chris McCarron steady some animal blocked behind a wall of fading speed horses. "Solis in a sprint from the inside post?" he'll comment before the race. "You got two chances—little and none." When the rider fails to win, which is what usually happens, Walter considers the outcome a confirmation of his jaundiced view. "Oh, that was great," he'll say sarcastically. "Did you see that? He could have won by ten. That was an Academy Award performance."

The only jockeys Walter doesn't castigate are the ones he's recently cashed tickets on, but it's only a matter of time before he loses a couple of bets and his most recent heroes find themselves enshrined in Walter's personal Hall of Shame, a pantheon from which no rider is permanently excluded. "Little Shakespearean actors, that's what they are," he says. "Their pictures should be up on every post office wall."

It's amazing how many people who go to the races every day share Walter's assessment. The horses themselves and their trainers never figure in their calculations at all; when these bettors lose their money, it's always the rider's fault. Shortly after R. D. Hubbard, the chairman and CEO of Hollywood Park, acquired control of The Woodlands, a track in Kansas City that offered both Thoroughbred and greyhound racing, he began to wonder why his customers clearly preferred the dogs over the ponies. He took a survey and discovered that sixty-five percent of his patrons favored the greyhounds because they didn't have riders on their backs, a touching confirmation of the public's trust in its fellow human beings.

Some people, including many big bettors and a number

of well-known handicappers, actually hate jockeys. One of them once suggested to me that racing would be better off if the horses were allowed to run on their own. Thoroughbreds are trained to run around a track and, like all horses, have a natural herding instinct. They also love to run and the good ones are highly competitive. They know what's expected of them and where the finish line is. "Horses aren't as dumb as some folks think they are," my friend maintains. "You can train a horse to do almost anything except vote, which shows a horse is a lot smarter than we are. Even the bums can be made to run." How? "We load them into the starting gate," he continues. "Then, when the gate opens, you have all these loudspeakers behind them with lions roaring. That gets their attention and they're out of there. When they get to the turns, you have more loudspeakers and more lions roaring. They'll run their eyeballs out." To prove his theory about how much fairer the racing would be, he points out that in the wild you never see horses run up on one another's heels, or get blocked or fanned on the turns, or have to take up because some other horse has cut in front of them. "Get rid of the damn jockeys," he concludes, "and every race will be a fair one in which the best horse will always win."

What the Woodlands survey proved is that most people who go to racetracks still haven't much of a clue as to what the game is all about. Too ignorant or too lazy to learn what criteria really apply to picking winners, the players who bet on jockeys instead of the major athletes themselves (the horses) are doomed to remain losers. Which is nice for the rest of us and essential to the wiseguys, who couldn't possibly survive at the track, with its hideous vigorish, if all the bettors knew what they were doing.

The only successful players I know are the ones for

whom the jockey is a secondary handicapping factor. Far more important to them are what they call the numbers (workouts, speed ratings, track variants) concerning the animals themselves and their trainers. For them the importance of the jockey relates directly to his relationship with the trainer who engages his services and they keep statistics reflecting that conviction. The performance records of individual riders are recorded in the *Racing Form* and in some programs but, for jockey-trainer relationships, you either have to keep your own stats or acquire them from others. Many trainers favor particular riders. As of this writing, in Southern California, for instance, Vladimir Cerin will give first call on most of his horses to Chris Antley; Bill Spawr favors Laffit Pincay, Jr.; Brian Mayberry wants Martin Pedroza or Eddie Delahoussaye on his stock; Ron McAnally favors Chris McCarron. If you love horse racing and you plan to go often, you should take the trouble to find out what you can about these relationships. Some are more successful than others and they are constantly shifting, but no wily veteran of the racetrack I know believes that jockeys dictate the outcome of most races.

At the major racetracks the riders are all so skillful that there is very little to choose among them. At Del Mar, every summer, the track puts on an exhibition race for retired riders called the Rocking Chair Derby. It's a nonwagering event in which the riders, of various advanced ages and skills, are assigned to their mounts by drawing lots. Invariably, the best horse wins, with the out-of-shape old jocks hanging on as best they can. The horses perform just about as well at this sprint distance as they would have with top riders on their backs.

It is a fact, however, that the most successful jockeys get the pick of the mounts. An argument can be made, therefore, that by handicapping jockeys a horseplayer will automatically wind up wagering on the best animals. They will also usually be the ones at the lowest odds, not necessarily a good way to go at the parimutuel windows. And there are inherent dangers in this method. To get on a top horse, a rider will often take assignments on the trainer's other entries that day, none of whom may be able to run a step. On the whole, betting on jockeys is a risky proposition; it's the horse that does the running.

That said, I have to confess that I have a few personal biases in favor of certain jockeys. First of all, give me Laffit Pincay on anything. He's the ultimate class act, a rider who tries from start to finish, who never gives up on a horse unless he's hopelessly beaten, and who can be counted on to fight for any part of the purse money, right down to fifth place. He's an owner's dream. In sprints, I want Pat Valenzuela or Martin Pedroza, who are superb at getting horses to break fast out of the gate. Then who's better than Eddie Delahoussaye at finishing a race? Pat Day is the finest judge of pace in the game; his horses always have something left for the drive. On the turf, give me Chris McCarron or Gary Stevens, who are superb at rating an animal and finding the right moment to make their moves. On class horses at any distance, you would always want a leading rider—a Nakatani, a Bailey, a Solis, a Perret, a Mike Smith—athletes who know how to coax the best out of their mounts.

Feminists will note that I have not mentioned a single woman. Obviously, Julie Krone, a terrific rider on the New York and Florida circuits, cannot be left off a list of anybody's top riders. And there are other women jockeys all over the country who can almost certainly ride as well as any man. The problem is that I go to the races mainly in Southern California, where the sport features very few female race riders. The argument out here is that, on the tighter, narrower Western tracks that favor speed and where "bootin' and scootin' " out of the gate is the surest route to the winner's circle, women don't have the physical strength to get the job done. We've all heard that kind of argument before, haven't we? So now let me give you a useful betting tip. At the moment, we have a rider out here named Joy Scott. Because she's a woman, she gets on very few "live" horses, ones with a real chance to win. Almost always her horses go off at high odds. When she does happen to get up on one that can run a little bit, she'll get the best out of him. I've cashed some very nice tickets on her. Women riders are usually underrated; take advantage of it.

THERE WAS a period of my betting life when I thought about moving to San Francisco. Why not? I asked myself. It's by far America's most beautiful city, with dozens of the country's finest restaurants, an excellent professional football team, a lively night life, a good opera season, and it's within easy driving distance of some of the most spectacular scenery in the world. And although it rains a lot, it never gets too cold. Besides, who wants to see the sun all the time? Horseplayers need bad weather. A bright blue sky is hard to cope with after a bad losing day.

My theory (and the real reason I thought about moving) is that I could never have a long losing streak in San Francisco. Not like one I once had at Del Mar, where I came up with thirty-three consecutive losers. I had the ATM machines humming all week long. I live near Del Mar, I love the place, but losers? Del Mar has killed more people than the bubonic plague; even Cigar lost here. And tracks everywhere are potentially losing environments; like casinos or the stock market, gamble in them and you *will* have a losing streak. Count on it. I've never found any sure way to stop one except in San Francisco.

The answer to this puzzle is a jockey named Russell Baze. He is the one exception to my rule about betting on jockeys. If there's a better or more honest one anywhere in the country, I'd like to know who he is. Whether I'm at one of the San Francisco tracks or watching the races from there on a TV monitor at the Del Mar satellite wagering facility, I see Russell Baze win on horses that simply don't figure to do so.

If you open your *Racing Form*, you will note that Russell Baze wins about thirty percent of the time, and not just on odds-on favorites either. There must be horseplayers who don't like him, the usual paranoids who expect their jockeys to win every race, with or without horses under them. Then there are the people who claim that Russell Baze wins so often only because he's riding in Northern California where the competition is easier; if he were riding against the best, he wouldn't be in the top ten. That may be, but then, as a bettor, why not take advantage of it? Anyway, I never see Russell Baze take up out of the gate, or not come through on the inside, or swing too wide on the turns, or move too early or too late, or, most important, stop trying for the minor awards when his horse is clearly beaten for first. In Southern California, the only jockey for whom I can make a similar claim is Laffit Pincay. But Pincay is in the twilight of his illustrious career and doesn't get the good mounts he deserves anymore; Russell Baze does.

The fans who go to the races regularly form their own opinions regarding the talents of the riders on hand. Everyone, too, develops pet peeves concerning the abilities and styles of certain jockeys. Little consideration is given to the fact that they are risking their lives every day on the backs of large, powerful, skittish, and often willful beasts. More jockeys are seriously injured and killed every year than in any other sport. Even trainers, who ought to know better, sometimes fail to appreciate their talents and the risks they run. I once heard a conditioner named Willis Reavis complain bitterly about the bad rides he had been getting from a jockey he persisted in putting up on a particular horse. When I asked him why he didn't try another rider, he said, "I figure eventually this guy will run out of mistakes."

As FOR the aspect of cheating, it is rarer these days than it used to be, especially at the bigger racetracks where the purses are large and even a mediocre rider can make a decent living. Also, the races there are closely monitored and suspicious behavior is usually quickly investigated. Not so long ago, before the advent of television, it was easier to fool around. Eddie Arcaro, one of the greatest riders in history and a dominant figure on the New York racing scene well into the 1950s, likes to tell of a little coup he and some of his colleagues put over on a hot apprentice rider named Bobby Ussery. Arcaro was up on the favorite in a short field of six or seven horses going at the sprint distance of six furlongs. Ussery was up on the second choice. In the jockeys' room before the race, Ussery noticed the other riders gathered in a group around Arcaro. They were whispering together and occasionally casting glances over at him, as he sat alone, preparing for the race. Nobody spoke to him, but they nodded and grinned at one another as they headed out to the paddock.

When the race went off, all the other riders took a firm

hold on their mounts and allowed Arcaro to break alone on the lead. Ussery spurred his mount in pursuit. He closed steadily on Arcaro. At the head of the stretch he came alongside and together, whipping and pumping, the two riders urged their steeds toward the finish line. A sixteenth of a mile from home, Ussery's horse began slowly to pull away from the favorite. Ussery glanced over at Arcaro. "Up yours, you guinea bastard!" he shouted in triumph as he drove for the wire. Only to hear Arcaro's voice call after him, "Go get 'em, kid! We're all bettin' on you!"

This account may be apocryphal; Arcaro loves to tell a good story. Occasionally, however, even at the richer tracks, riders will cheat. Wherever money moves, dishonesty is present. We all have vivid memories of horses being "armed" (held back) out of the gate or "given a race" by Hall of Fame jockeys and we know that at the smaller tracks and on the cheap fair circuits bizarre events occur far too frequently. But even there the trainers are more often to blame than the jockeys, whose lives are on the line, especially on the backs of unsound, overly medicated steeds.

Jockeys do make mistakes, lots of them. In fact, it can be argued that the best of them, like the best generals, are the ones who make the fewest errors. One of my favorite racetrack stories has to do with the instructions given by a trainer before the race to a rider who had recently been making mistakes. On this occasion, as the horses circled the paddock and the jockey waited for instructions about a horse he had never ridden before, the trainer kept silent. Finally, just before it was time to mount up and head for the track, the jockey asked if there was anything special he should know about the horse and how he should ride him. "Oh, yeah," the trainer said, as if he had somehow forgotten to inform him. "This horse'll break good for you and he's got some speed, so you ought to have a good position by the turn. Try to keep him close to the pace and not too wide, but keep a hold on him. Try not to get boxed in either and be patient. Then, when you get to the three-eighths pole, fuck up like you always do."

As a bettor, one of the most important things you must remember about jockeys in general is that they don't know as much as they think they do. Most of them don't handicap even their own races and, in the cheaper contests, they often have only a vague idea what to expect from the animal they've been engaged to ride, especially if it's for the first time. They have to rely on what the trainer tells them, their own instincts, and how the race itself develops. This doesn't prevent some of them from having strong opinions, which they air in public or confide to their acquaintances, and which often reach the ears of members of the betting public. Discount them. Eddie Arcaro reportedly once told an interviewer that he could have made more money booking the wagering action from the jockeys' room than by riding.

OWNERS:
CHASING THE DREAM

chapter 5

At some point in your racegoing career someone is going to suggest that you buy into the game by becoming an owner, either by yourself or as a member of a partnership or a syndicate of investors. It may never have occurred to you to do so, but you will be tempted. After all, wouldn't you like to have your picture taken in the winner's circle and bask in the reflected glory of your very own champion?

Several summers ago a retired businessman I know called me up to ask me if I thought he should invest sixteen thousand dollars to acquire a half interest in an unraced two-year-old filly about to make her debut at Del Mar. I did a little research and found out that the filly was sired by an undistinguished stallion and was out of an even less distinguished mare. She was a California homebred, which meant that my friend's money would bail her owner-trainer out of his expenses in getting her to the races and leave him still owning half of her, while retaining control of her future. That was part of the deal, as it was presented to me. On the plus side, the filly had shown enough speed in her workouts to attract Kent Desormeaux, a top jockey, as her rider and was picked to win the race by the newspaper handicappers.

I told my acquaintance not to think of the deal as an investment but as a high-risk gambling venture that might provide some entertainment and a few thrills for him. He had come into the deal through having met the owner-trainer's wife on a golf course and knew nothing about him. I told him the man was a well-established public trainer who had been around for years, raced mostly cheap stock, and had a reputation for being good with two-year-olds. I suggested he offer eight thousand dollars for a quarter interest, get ready to have some fun, and prepare to kiss his money goodbye.

I don't know what he decided to do. As for the filly, she broke poorly in her debut, was shuffled around between horses until Desormeaux got her to the outside, after which she put in a good run to finish second, beaten by about two lengths. She went on from there to win a couple of races but soon sank into oblivion and was last heard from running at the Northern California tracks in the cheapest contests on the daily programs. Owning a racehorse is a risky business venture that can only be justified by passion.

The first Thoroughbred I ever owned, in partnership with four friends, was named War Flag and he won the first race he ever ran for us, at Del Mar in the fall of 1968. I remember every moment of that event: the way War Flag looked in the paddock before the race, on his toes, prancing, full of himself and the power that would propel him to victory; the way he galloped out on the track, his neck bowed, head down, the rider hunched over him, keeping a tight hold on the reins; how easily he burst out of the starting gate across the infield from where we sat, tense with expectation; the long sweep of his stride as he moved past the rest of the field on the turn toward the finish line directly in front of us. I remember jumping up and down. Somehow I smashed the unbreakable crystal on my wristwatch and my wallet flew out of my inside jacket pocket. I retrieved it and we rushed down to the winner's circle to stand in a group, our arms around one another, while the horse, his rider still up in the saddle, posed beside us for the obligatory picture.

The intensity of the exhilaration I experienced that day is almost impossible to describe. It lasted through a long, riotous dinner with my colleagues and family and extended through the weeks preceding War Flag's next race, at Santa Anita early in the winter meet. I regarded that event as merely the second step on the golden road leading us to the Kentucky Derby in the spring.

That dream ended abruptly when War Flag, for some mysterious reason, failed to raise a gallop in his second effort. He never won again for us and eventually vanished from view. The last time I saw him was two years later, in the barn area at Pomona. He had passed on from us to other owners and was running in cheap races with a right knee that looked like a cantaloupe. He had won a few more times since his first glorious day, but nothing of importance, and had sunk into the mediocrity that afflicts most racehorses. I felt badly for him and for us, for the dream we had invested in him, but by that time I was no longer a neophyte in the ways of ownership and

I had learned not to expect too much from any horse, mine or anyone else's. The Thoroughbred is a beautiful, enchanting, but frustrating creature. He will raise you up to undreamed-of heights one moment, then drop you into a slough of despair the next. Even the best of them will disappoint you in the end, if only because most of them, sooner or later, wind up, as a trainer friend of mine once put it, "standing on three legs."

Racehorses are oddly frangible animals, roughly a thousand pounds of bone and muscle perched precariously on ankles no larger than a man's wrist. They are all descended from three stallions imported into England late in the seventeenth and early in the eighteenth century to improve the breed in a country where racing had already been an upper-class pastime for several hundred years. One of these stallions, the Darley Arabian, was the progenitor of a great champion named Eclipse, foaled in 1764, from whom most of today's Thoroughbreds are descended. The other two important stallions, the Godolphin Barb and the Byerly Turk, have also produced long lines of winners, but Eclipse's descendants dominate today's Thoroughbred panorama, in this country as well as abroad. The inbreeding that has produced the modern Thoroughbred undoubtedly accounts for the genetic fragility that causes so many racehorses to break down, sometimes fatally, in mid-career.

Horses can also injure themselves in an endless variety of ways. They kick the walls of their stalls, they step into holes, they bruise their hooves on pebbles, they try to jump fences that are too high for them. If there's a nail or a jagged edge protruding anywhere, they will rub up against it. They also have primitive digestive systems that prevent them from expelling anything through their mouths and often die of a disease called colic, which bloats them up with gas and ruptures their intestines. And they suffer from many of the same ailments that afflict humans, including the flu, pneumonia, and various infections that can only be cured by massive doses of antibiotics. They develop wracking coughs that they pass on to one another and that can last for weeks, sometimes months. The people who want to sell you racehorses refer to the prospect as an investment, but you'd probably do better buying penny stocks across the counter.

Why, then, would anybody want to own one of these beasts? The answer is very simple. They are among the most beautiful of nature's creations and, as competing athletes, they become totally identified with their masters. I've been lucky enough to have owned small pieces of two horses who won minor stakes races, and the thrill of seeing your animal compete successfully in a quality event is akin to having done so yourself. The Thoroughbred becomes an extension of his owner, a living dream come true.

You will be warned by people like me, who have been around the racing scene for a long time and know better, not to fall in love with your horse, if only to spare yourself too much grief. Many owners couldn't care less about their animals, but regard them only as extensions of themselves. When they're through with them, they get rid of them with no more regret or care for their future well-being than they would feel for a broken toy or a worn-out sofa. A pox on them. If you decide at some point in your racegoing career to buy a slice, however small, of this pie in the sky, then my advice would be to ignore all cold-hearted admonitions. Fall in love, identify with your champion, and so try to grab at least a small piece of immortality for yourself.

As I write these words, a very rich man named Allen Paulson is the owner of the world's best racehorse on a dirt surface. His champion's name is Cigar, an unglamorous moniker for an athlete of such glorious accomplishments. Paulson has poured millions into the game, has owned many winners, but nothing as spectacular as this animal. Cigar doesn't seem to run like an ordinary horse. He glides to the front, moving with seemingly effortless grace into contention, then moves toward the finish line as if dancing on clouds. The great athletes always make it look easy: Joe DiMaggio catching a fly ball, Carl Lewis running, Wayne Gretzsky moving with the puck, Michael Jordan doing anything with a basketball.

The miracle of Cigar is that he began his career as a mediocre performer on turf, a surface that his breeding seemed to suit him for. He did not achieve greatness until he was transferred to the main course, the dark brown dirt ovals on which most American horses perform. He then proceeded to win sixteen consecutive races against the best competition available, thus tying the modern-day record held by Citation, a legendary colt of two generations back. By that time Paulson had already experienced a full gamut of emotions with his star, from initial disappointment to ultimate triumph. The millions of dollars Cigar had earned meant relatively little to him, because Paulson's career is typically littered with disappointments and failures, promising yearlings and two-year-olds who either never made it to the races or never lived up to their sales tags. (A well-bred colt can cost as high as a million dollars at the better auction sales.) Frustration is a dominant theme in any tale of ownership. But when Cigar began to achieve his spectacular feats, humbling and leaving in his wake the best competitors the opposition, here and abroad, could bring against him, it compensated for everything else—all the losses, all the disappointments, all the heartaches that owning a Thoroughbred can bring.

Cigar, however, had at least one more trial to put Paulson through. On August 11, 1996, he was sent to Del Mar to run in the Pacific Classic, a race he was supposed to win easily to break Citation's record. Forty-four thousand people showed up to watch him do it and millions more watched it on television. Cigar ran second, a victim of overconfidence and bad strategy by his trainer and jockey. But maybe not. "Stick around long enough and they all get beat," is one of the oldest maxims in racing. (Citation was humbled twice by an unsung animal named Noor, Secretariat lost five times, even Man o' War failed once.) Paulson and his connections looked that day as if somebody had dropped little marbles on their heads from the observation platform of the Eiffel Tower.

Five weeks later, at Belmont Park in New York, Cigar proved himself again the great competitor that he was by crushing his opposition in the Woodward Stakes. Paulson was once again shot off on a rocket to the stars. He rushed down to the track to greet his returning champion and personally escorted him into the winner's circle, while the crowd cheered and the media surged toward him. He took the occasion to assure everybody that, although Cigar would be retired to stud at the end of the year, he would always remain America's horse. This despite the fact that the Japanese, who have been buying up America's best for several years, had offered him thirty million dollars. That's the mind-numbing effect owning a good horse can have on the human brain.

At a lower level, anyone can participate in this saga. You do not walk into it blindly. There are syndicators, bloodstock agents, and trainers in the game to whom you represent a fat chicken ready for plucking. Do a little homework. Ask questions. The industry now runs seminars for prospective buyers. Don't rush into it. Ultimately, you have to rely on someone you can trust, most often a trainer, to find you the right horse and put you into the game at a level you can afford. You will need luck, lots of it. When your horse does win, however, the rapture you feel will in every way rival that of Allen Paulson watching Cigar.

There's enough glory to go around for everyone. If the sight of your horse, sporting your own colorful silks, does not at least thrill you when you first see him in the paddock or the post parade; if the race itself does not excite you; if the spectacle of your champion charging down the stretch toward the finish line does not move you; if the sight of him hitting the invisible wire first does not enchant you, then perhaps you are spiritually dead. William Faulkner once compared screen writing to picking potato bugs off plants. It wasn't accomplishing something important, like winning the Kentucky Derby, he assured a friend of his. The man knew what he was talking about; he had his priorities straight. An English sportsman named Robert Bontine Cunninghame-Graham declared, "God forbid I should go to any heaven in which there are no horses." As sensible a statement regarding human aspirations as I've ever heard.

WHETHER you ever decide to become an owner or not, the fact of ownership will affect your betting action at the track. As an owner, for example, you are legally not allowed to bet on any horse but yours in the race you've entered. The rule is impossible to enforce and some people pay no attention to it, but it's there. The chances are you will not want to bet on any other animal in the race. Placing a wager on someone else's horse to beat yours, even if you know your contender can't win, is morally repugnant, as if Ben Hur were to throw the chariot race. That doesn't mean, however, that you have to float a second mortgage to back your colorbearer in a race he can't win. You don't have to bet on him at all. Remember, you are also competing for a piece of the purse, which at the bigger tracks can be considerable.

Wisdom and caution are usually wasted on owners. They become blinded by their loyalties and enthusiasms and all the Horsespeak they've been fed. You will be, too, but you will learn. One of the surest ways to lose money at the racetrack is to listen to any owner about his charge's abilities. He almost certainly knows even less than the jockey, who may never have been on his horse's back before. Ignore whatever information you may receive from an owner. Even if he does actually know something, does he know more than you do about all the other horses in the race? Perhaps, if the animal has never run before and is going off at a decent price and the owner's a friend of yours, you might risk a few bucks. For every one of these tickets you'll cash, though, there will be dozens that you won't. Listen to the owner's stories, exult in his optimism, smile and nod sympathetically at his tales of woe and excuses, then bet what you want to bet.

If you happen to be the owner, however, no one can help you.

People:
Damon Runyon Is
Not Dead

chapter 6

Apart from the pure sporting aspect of the game, there are two main reasons I love going to the races. First, the racetrack is a great leveler of rank. No one there cares who you are or what you've done; all that matters is what is going to happen to you next. Second, the track is a setting for undiminished hope. "No owner, trainer, or groom ever committed suicide who had a good two-year-old in the barn" is an old racetrack saw. Never mind last year's disaster or last week's losing streak; that is all going to change today. And don't worry about where the money's coming from either; there's always fresh, as they say.

The regulars, you will find out, have their own peculiar sets of priorities, especially about money. Eddie, an old horseplayer who hasn't been doing too well lately, approaches a crony of his before the first race. "Hey, Frank, I hear you've been doing good," he says. "Are you holding?" "Yeah, I've been doing okay," Frank says warily. "What's up?" "Can you loan me five hundred?" Eddie asks. "The wife's real sick and needs an operation. She may die if she don't get it." "Sure, Eddie, I can loan you the five hundred," Frank says, "but I've got a problem." "What's that?" "Well, if I loan you the five hundred," Frank tells him, "I know you're going to blow it at the track." "No, you don't understand," Eddie says. "I've *got* the track money."

The Eddies of this world are a fixture at every racetrack. They seem to have no visible source of income, but they are always there, betting with both hands. The late Damon Runyon knew many of them and wrote about them. Later, some of them were immortalized in *Guys and Dolls*, the great musical based on his work. That world, populated by hustlers, grifters, loudmouths, pimps, touts, con men, wiseguys, hooked gamblers, flashy ladies, and other eccentric characters, is supposed to have passed from the scene.

A few years ago I participated in a seminar on handicapping and betting conducted by some racetrack friends of mine at a downtown Los Angeles hotel. The keynote speaker was a well-known newspaper columnist and author of handicapping books, who began his lecture by stressing the fact that the era of Damon Runyon was dead. Betting on horses was now a respectable profession, he continued, participated in by upstanding pillars of the community and no different from any other sort of business. I happened to be on the dais with him, and, as he spoke, my gaze traveled idly about the room. There before me were some of the greatest characters I'd ever met, people from all walks of life but united in this one quixotic endeavor—betting the horses. I glanced at the speaker, who at that moment had roused himself to a pitch of enthusiasm for his message that made him sound a bit like a fire-and-brimstone revivalist. His face was flushed, he was sweating, his wispy hair standing straight up in back, and he was dressed in wrinkled khaki pants, an open-necked shirt, and scuffed brown loafers. As he spoke, his rimless eyeglasses persisted in slipping down his nose. He looked like a demented high school math teacher addressing an adult education class recruited from a traveling road show. Runyon could have incorporated the scene intact into one of his short stories.

I don't want to give the impression, however, that most of the people you will meet at the track are oddballs. Most of my racetrack friends are indeed respectable citizens. In addition to my wife, I've met lawyers, doctors, stockbrokers, bankers, politicians, musicians, opera singers, psychologists, police officers, priests, actors, directors, writers, artists, teachers, civil servants, producers, business people, and, of course, celebrities. I can't think of a category of human endeavor that is not represented at the racetrack. And I've bumped into people everywhere who are as fascinated by the game as I am; we are a great confraternity of secret sharers. The only division I make there is one I apply to people I meet anywhere. "The human race is divided into two," my friend Adriano Panatta, the great Italian tennis player, told me twenty years ago, when I was covering a tournament in Stockholm, Sweden. "There are *i bravi*, the good people, and the squalids."

Even the squalids can be fun. Try spending some time with Larry the Loser, who happens to be a living refutation of the maxim that in the end the luck will even out. Larry just can't seem to win, no matter what he does. He's become like the character in an old comic strip who walked around with a small cloud perpetually raining on him even in bright sunshine.

"We've all been through losing streaks. The racetrack can be an extremely unforgiving place," says Gerry Okuneff, a professional handicapper with whom I've been going racing for many years. "A mistake is rarely overcome." Gerry defines a mistake as not finding out something significant about a horse *before* a race is run. "If you haven't done your homework, the chances are you'll lose. That's not bad luck. But no matter how good you are, you will have bad streaks. Racing is a game of inches. Ultimately, you break even on luck."

Unless you're Larry the Loser. I've been watching his action for years and I can't account for what happens to him. He's a serious handicapper, a true student of the game, and a careful money manager, but wherever he goes it's raining all the time. He loses every photo and every stewards' inquiry, most of his exactas finish one-three, every speed horse tires in the stretch, every closer comes up short. Like Job, there's just something about Larry that pisses off the Man Upstairs. If he buys a wrong number at the window, it's a losing one. If he gets shut out, the horse he would have bet on wins. His horses get fanned wide on the turns or left in the gate. The solid favorite that he needs to complete a parlay wager never makes it. His long shot, locked in a head-to-head duel down the stretch with the favorite, always loses. On the days he can't attend, every horse he would have bet on romps in at high prices. After a particularly painful loss some heartless clown will always show up to gloat over having cashed a tiny ticket on the horse that has just beaten him out of thousands by a lip. Every time he wheels a race, the odds-on favorite wins. On the days he bets three key horses breaking from the inside posts, there's a huge bias favoring animals running outside. In a crucial race on the grass, where the riders' skills count far more than on the main oval, his top jockey takes off at the last moment for some reason and is replaced by a bum who is zero for fifty-three starts on the turf. When his show parlay goes down, the horse he needed to complete it always comes in fourth. On one such memorable day, when everything had gone even worse than usual, Larry went out to the parking lot to find that somebody had sideswiped his car.

What I admire about Larry, however, is that he keeps showing up, hopes undiminished. And someday, maybe, his luck will turn. Even Vince Edwards, the late TV actor who was one of the most dedicated losers I've ever met, had a few big winning days before he cashed in his chips. Edwards, however, was a surly and meanspirited bettor, who was unfailingly ungracious in defeat. Larry remains resolutely cheerful.

He reminds me of an old comedian named Joe Frisco, a legendary loser from the 1940s and '50s. Frisco once told an audience that he had gone to the track that day to find it closed, so he had just put his money in an envelope and shoved it under the door. Once, on location in San Francisco for a movie, he telephoned his friend, crooner Bing Crosby, for a loan. Crosby agreed to send him a couple of hundred dollars, then said, "But, Joe, how can you be broke already? It's only ten-thirty in the morning." "I was betting on the workouts," Frisco answered. The comedian, who didn't drive, never took an engagement that was more than a half-hour bus ride from a racetrack.

It's this persistent gallantry in the face of adversity that enchants me. My wife, who was then working as a nurse in a Beverly Hills medical practice, took care of Walter (Whitey) Robertson, a well-known public handicapper for a local newspaper. Whitey had been ill for some time with heart disease and had been advised by his doctors not to attend the races, because of the stress it might impose on him. I remember seeing him during the last months of his life up in the Santa Anita press box. When the race went off, Whitey would turn his back to it to keep himself from rooting too hard. Finally, one sad day, he lay on a stretcher in my wife's office, waiting for an ambulance to take him to the hospital. He knew he wasn't going to make it this time. My wife sat beside him, keeping him company. "Honey, here's some money," he said, pulling a wad of bills out of his pocket. "Get us some exactas."

Every time I go to the track, or to one of the offtrack wagering facilities in my area, I'm sure to bump into at least several of that vast company of gallant souls tilting at the windmills of chance. Maybe it will be Big John, even though a losing photo finish once caused him to suffer a heart attack. As he was being wheeled away on a gurney, he shoved a fifty-dollar bill into a friend's hand. "Bet it for me on the six horse in the next race," he instructed him before they clamped an oxygen mask over his face. Also on hand may be Jimmy the Mouth, Fingers, Tony Large, Lucky Bucks, Whodoyalike, Fat Eddie, Gino the Hippie, Pinhead, One Way, the House of Fear, Del Mar Man, and Joe the Broom, who claims he came by his nickname from having once swept the card. Only their friends know what these characters' real names are and no one else cares.

James Quinn, the author of several of the best handicapping books available, sat for years at Santa Anita in a box with a racetrack acquaintance known to all as Bob the Painter. Quinn had naturally assumed that Bob had acquired his nickname because he was a house painter. He found out one day, quite by accident, that Bob's real name was Robert Irwin, one of our leading conceptual artists. I once bumped into Irwin on a crowded Manhattan bus on a hot summer day. "On the whole, wouldn't you rather be in Del Mar?" I asked him, even though we had never met. "Sure," he replied, "wouldn't you?"

MY FAVORITE of all the characters I've encountered at the track is a man known to many of us as the Desperado. He has lost even more races than Larry but somehow manages to survive. He looks to be in his fifties, of medium height, and overweight. For a time he dyed his hair blond, perhaps to make himself look younger, but his habitual expression at the races is one of disbelief. Nothing seems to go right for him. Somewhere, sometime he must have had a winning day, but never when I've been around.

I first became aware of the Desperado some years ago at Santa Anita. Having just gotten my bet in as the starting gate opened, I was watching the race on a TV monitor. My horse failed to do any running, but two others, one of them the odds-on favorite, were locked in a ferocious struggle down the stretch. The Desperado and a tiny elegant old lady were next to me, rooting their horses home. The old lady's two dollars were on the favorite, which at the last jump just managed to nose out the long shot. "Oh, oh," the little old lady said, jumping up and down with joy, "I won, I won!" The Desperado turned on her in a fury, a stream of foulmouthed expletives pouring from his mouth. "You dumb bitch," he screamed, "I had two hundred dollars on my horse!"

Periodically, the Desperado becomes so vocally deranged by his misfortunes that he has to be escorted from the premises and, occasionally, he's banished from them for a time. He's been set down more often than any jockey I know. During one of these periods of exile he continued to show up at the track. He would stand in the Santa Anita parking lot, just outside the main entrance, and let his friends run his bets for him. Toward the end of one typical losing day, he was observed clutching the iron bars of the fence and shaking it. "I hate this fuckin' place, I hate this fuckin' place!" he bellowed. "And when they let me back in, I'm not coming!"

One early fall I found myself sitting in the stands at Fairplex Park in Pomona, a row behind him. Once again he was beaten in a photo, this time by a long shot he had earlier dismissed as an impossibility. As he was bewailing his fate, an elderly woman in his party held up her winning ticket. "I bet on him," she said. "Oh, you bet on him, did you?" the Desperado said, whirling on her in a rage. "You bet on him! Well, isn't that wonderful! You bet on him!" And he stormed away, shouting, "She bet on him! Oh, my God! She bet on him!" The woman turned to her friends and smiled sadly. "Poor boy," she said. "This is the first time in years I've been to the track with my son. He just can't win." Then she proceeded to tell a story about how, as a child, her boy had rushed out of their house and dived into their swimming pool. "There wasn't any water in it," she concluded.

My favorite story about the Desperado took place just before the last race at the Oak Tree meet in the fall at Santa Anita, some years ago. He came up behind a hard-nosed clocker I know, who was studying the exacta payoffs on a TV monitor in the grandstand. "I got the winner of the ninth," the Desperado whispered. No reaction from the clocker. The Desperado then came around to confront him. "I got the winner of the ninth," he said. The clocker gazed impassively back at him out of a pair of cold blue eyes. "I don't want to know," he said. A pause. "Give me ten bucks," the Desperado said, "and I won't tell you."

IT WILL NOT have escaped your notice that once again this would seem to be a man's world. I know a number of women who are devoted habitués of the racing scene, but few are as eccentric as their male counterparts and none as desperately involved. My own entirely unproven theory about this is that women are far too shrewd to become hooked completely by a pastime as loaded with hazards and frustrations as the racetrack. They are not going to spend all of their time trying to make a living in an occupation as ruinously chancy as gambling, even on horses, and one that offers no secondary benefits, such as Social Security, pension plans, medical care, profit sharing, or unemployment insurance. They understand that the racetrack can be a wonderful place to enjoy themselves, but not to build a life on.

During a time when nothing was working out well for her, my wife began going regularly to the racetrack. Two of the doctors she worked for owned racehorses. The track provided relief from the harsh realities of a failing marriage and the burden of having to work at two jobs to support herself and her unemployed husband. She immediately made new friends at the races and learned how to bet intelligently. Within a year and a half she had bailed herself out of both her marriage and their debts. She never made the mistake, however, of deluding herself that playing the ponies was a viable way to build a future for herself. By the time I met her she was still attending on a regular basis, but only for fun and because she hadn't yet figured out a more fulfilling avocation. She still goes to the races, but infrequently now and mainly to be with me and our friends. She regards my own misadventures with the tolerant forgiving eye of someone who has been there and knows what it's about. Meanwhile, she is, as Voltaire would have put it, cultivating her garden.

A garden is no place for the Desperado and his cronies. You can't bet on roses or whether the mulch will arrive in time to save the petunias. What the boys want is to be in action. I'm glad I'm not one of them, but I love them for it. I once asked the novelist Jim Salter about the fortunes of a mutual friend I hadn't heard from in a long time. "He's listing heavily to starboard," Jim said, "but it's full speed ahead." An epitaph for a horseplayer, if ever I've heard one.

WINNING AND LOSING:
THE MYSTERY FACTOR

No one really knows for sure exactly how many horseplayers actually do manage to win consistently, but the best guess would be no more than two or three out of every hundred who attend regularly. There's that vigorish to contend with. So if horse racing were merely a gambling proposition and not also a great spectacle, who would go? The casinos offer the casual players better odds. Even the lottery, a sanctioned numbers racket, provides bigger payoffs, at least until you read the small print. What could be the attraction to the professional gamblers and who are these few consistent winners?

The lure to gamblers is easy to explain. No matter how low the percentages against you at craps and other games, the casinos will beat you in the end. You may make a giant hit or have a tremendous winning streak, but sooner or later the casinos will be deep into your pockets. This is because, no matter how skillful you may be, the casino games are essentially ones of pure chance. The casino owners want a few people to make big scores, so they can publicize the fact and keep you coming back again and again. Remember, there is nothing you can do to control the spin of the wheels, the cast of the dice, the way the cards will fall. Abracadabra, you lose!

In horse racing, skill is the key to winning, along with a requisite amount of discipline devoted to money management. The vigorish against you is the result of a system invented in Paris, France, in 1865 by a man named Pierre Oller. He suggested that the odds on horses running in a race should be established by the amount of money bet on each horse in relation to the total pool, but *after* the people running the game had cut enough money out of that pot to ensure a profit for themselves. That procedure, now known as the parimutuel (Paris mutuel) system, is the one in use at every racetrack today. The bad news is that the money being cut out of the pools is too high and should be reduced, but probably won't be, if only because the politicians are too greedy and too short-sighted to understand that a reduction in the takeout would soon increase revenues by bringing more big money into the game. The good news is that you are not playing against the house; the racetrack remains indifferent to the outcome, having already been guaranteed a share of the loot. You are engaged, essentially, in a struggle with the other players, most of whom are ill prepared and/or too lazy to pose a serious threat to any disciplined bettor.

This is the aspect of the game that the smarter regulars are out to exploit. Some of them spend an amazing amount of time doing so. "Everybody starts out in kindergarten and some people go on to college, some don't," maintains Gerry Okuneff, who was once the subject of a segment on "60 Minutes." "There's always something still to learn. And you have to work at it. The happy jack squirrels can bet hunches or tips or play favorite jockeys or horses with long tails. If you want to win consistently, however, you have to do your homework."

This can be grueling. By the time Gerry is ready to make a bet he has spent at least seven or eight hours hacking through a dense underbrush of statistics to arrive at what he hopes will be a tidy solution, in the form of a winning ticket. Nothing makes him happier, as he walks into the track or the betting facility near his home, than to see people buying the *Racing Form* and tout sheets at the last minute. He believes that by the end of the day some of their money will be in his pockets.

The racetrack is the only public gambling proposition that does reward hard work, self-discipline, courage, and astute money management. The casinos grind you down and the lottery is a swindle. Today, with the wealth of information available, both in the *Form* and a number of excellent handicapping tomes, some of which are listed in the back of this book, any reasonably intelligent student of the game can convert himself into a potential winner—if not overnight, at least within a few weeks.

The canny, well-prepared players like Gerry will sit out races on every card. They are waiting for the ones that will reward their expertise, even though they know that you can't be sure of beating any particular race. What they expect to do is beat enough selected races to win in the long run. Impervious to tips, rumors, or other people's opinions, they put their trust in their hard-earned knowledge.

Nor is the amount of their bets of any real significance. There are people at the track who risk thousands every day and sometimes earn monster amounts of money. "Those guys bet to impress bimbos and beginners," Gerry Okuneff says. "I have more respect for the person who shows up with a couple of hundred dollars on any given day and can turn it over ten times. If you can do that, you're a player." And nestled safely among the elect.

I once showed up at Santa Anita with only eleven dollars in my pockets, mostly in the form of the quarters that I keep in my car for parking meters and phone calls. I had forgotten my wallet. Because I make it a firm rule never to borrow (or to lend) money at the track, I was forced to go into action with what I had. I invested four dollars in a daily double and hit for over a hundred, then went on to win another four hundred before the day was over. All the more gratifying because I had been on a three-day losing streak.

If you bet always with both hands, the monster hits will carry you along for a while and provide an illusion of prosperity, but you'll give it all back and then some. The actor Mickey Rooney once said that he lost the first five-dollar bill he ever risked on a horse and then spent millions trying to recoup it.

NO MATTER what your skills, however, the racetrack is at least as unforgiving a milieu as the theater, where, as playwright Neil Simon once put it, you can make a killing but not a living. I do know a couple of dozen bettors who make money consistently at the track, but most of them have other or related sources of income. Some of them write columns and books on handicapping and betting strategies, hold seminars, invest in phone lines servicing bettors who call in and pay for their selections. One friend defines his strategy as "OPM"—other people's money. He doesn't sell his talents directly but receives a percentage of any profits made by his friends and clients. His own action is modest, so that, in effect, he stands to lose little and to earn tidily if his selections win, a tactic that eliminates the vigorish. And when he does make a big score, it's not likely the IRS will ever hear about it.

Stripped of its glamour and excitement, and considered solely as a way to make a living, horse racing can become as dreary a pastime as playing the stock market on a daily basis. Most of the people I know who claim to rely solely on their own resources at the track are a seedy bunch, glum older men who sit hour after hour, day after day, passing race after race until they see an opportunity to make a small coup, usually by betting several hundred dollars on an animal to show. The average rate of return on their action is comparable to what they could have made investing in long-term Treasury bonds. Why not just go out and get a job?

On the other hand, simply betting recklessly can cost you too much money. First, set yourself a firm limit on what you can afford to lose, then keep track of your winnings and losses, day by day, year after year. Keep records and you'll know, at least, where you stand and what to do, how to alter strategies if the losses pile up. Make notes and don't lie to yourself. As you will see later on in this book, the statistics and general information that can help you to become a winner are now available to anyone willing to put in a minimum amount of time to analyze them intelligently. And I don't mean six or seven hours a day either; there is such a thing, in racing and in life, as too much merely factual knowledge.

The hardest thing to tolerate in any form of gambling is

a losing streak. No matter how good a handicapper you become or how skillful a bettor, there will come a time when the horses you pick run like pregnant goats. Or, worse, lose by a head bob or a nose at the wire, or—unkindest cut of all—are disqualified by the stewards, those often fickle arbiters of our fate. The stewards, normally three in number, function like referees or umpires; they can "take down" a horse for various reasons, usually for interfering with some other contender in the race. Jockeys on these offending mounts are often "given days," meaning they are suspended from competing anywhere from three days to a week or more, depending upon the severity of the infraction. Like other sporting arbiters, the stewards' rulings frequently appear to be capricious, either too lenient or totally misguided, depending upon where your money happens to be placed. (It's astonishing how subjective we can become in our judgments when our financial health is at stake.) The stewards' rulings can be appealed or challenged in court, but never in time to do you any good as a bettor. The stewards are merely another factor in your survival at the track, but not one you can do anything about.

Shortly before I sat down to write this book, two consecutive disqualifications by the stewards started me off on one of the worst losing streaks of my life, twenty-four losing days out of twenty-six over a period of about two and a half months. I went back over my records and notes and was immediately consoled by the fact that, despite my recent losses, I was still showing a profit of a couple of thousand dollars for the year. My second discovery was even more important: I had been betting too much money. Having found myself so comfortably in the black, I had been confidently playing as if I would keep on winning forever, a form of hubris the racetrack never fails to punish.

When in trouble I often seek consolation from the great writers, the only gods I believe in, along with Giuseppe Verdi. And right there, by thumbing through my *Bartlett's Familiar Quotations*, I came across some words spoken by Winston Churchill to his countrymen shortly after the outbreak of the Second World War. "Death and sorrow will be the companions of our journey; hardship our garment; constancy and valor our only shield," he said. "We must be united, we must be undaunted, we must be inflexible." What a horseplayer this guy would have made!

Thus heartened and newly armored with steely resolve, I went out to the Del Mar satellite the next day, cautiously played five races, and again failed to pick a single winner. I did, however, come away with a modest profit of eighty-seven dollars, because two of my key horses ran second in exacta boxes. So I was still not picking winners, but at least I had broken my streak and I was ahead for the year. To paraphrase another great Churchill quote, the one on Russia, no one can consistently forecast the action of a Thoroughbred; it is a riddle wrapped in a mystery inside an enigma.

THERE ARE people, you will discover, who claim they can save you from ever losing at the racetrack. They have devised foolproof systems for beating the races and they're going to share their secrets with you. All you have to do is pay them a relatively modest amount of money, in return for which they'll speed on to you the fruits of their wisdom. You won't have to do any work yourself to win consistently at the races. You just plug in their system and the computer does the rest. Your job is to cash the tickets.

What's wrong with this picture? Why are all these experts so eager to enrich you? Don't they know that the tote board is directly affected by the ebb and flow of capital? A couple of years ago I was at Santa Anita with a friend of mine who has written several books on handicapping and who picks horses for wealthy clients. He had come out that day to bet on a particular animal that should have gone off at odds of no less than five to one. The horse won but paid only even money, mainly because one of my friend's clients had talked up the animal all over the track and hammered him personally at the betting windows. My friend was distraught, but whose fault was it?

The reason the experts want to sell you their expertise is that they can't make it on their own. It's because of what I call the mystery factor. Every day at the track there are races that defy rational analysis, and occasionally there are whole cards in which the horses run in defiance of logic. Not long ago, at Santa Anita, the lowest winning price of the afternoon was $10.80. If, like some people, you subscribed to a system that depends on trainer or trainer/jockey combinations, you took a bath that day. So did the so-called speed boys, the players who only bet on horses with superior speed ratings; only four of the winners figured to have any chance at all and they were not any speed handicapper's top picks. No methodology dependent in any way on statistics or logic paid off. Blame it on the mystery factor.

Somebody won that day, but who? The long-shot players, the stabbers, the people who bet on hunches, post positions, colors, cute jockeys, handsome trainers, names, astrological forecasts. Everybody at the track has his own way of arriving at a winner and the mystery factor ensures that somewhere, sometime, even the most unprepared innocent is going to cash some big tickets. Wouldn't it be boring if horse racing were as simple to analyze as the municipal bond market?

I was once on a TV interview show in which I was introduced by the falsely cheerful host as an author and "the man who's going to tell us how to win at the races." If I knew how to do that every day, I told this poor soul, why would I have come on his show to blab about it? I don't think he understood, but I know one guy who would have. He's the seedy-looking gent I once spotted by a freeway exit in Del Mar. He was holding up a sign that said, "Will handicap for food."

NOW THAT you've been warned how difficult it is to win consistently at the races and before I proceed to explain what it is you should do to make your betting action at the track at least potentially profitable, let me lay out some ground rules for losing. That's a much easier task. Just do exactly what I tell you and I promise that, within a year, you will be filing for bankruptcy and rising to speak at a meeting of Gamblers Anonymous. Here goes:

The lower the odds on a horse, the more you should bet on it.

No matter how strong an opinion you may have about a race, ignore it. Ask the stranger in line next to you what he thinks and bet on the animal he likes.

Don't bother learning how to handicap or how to bet. Rely entirely upon spontaneous revelation. You won't win, but you may qualify for sainthood.

Always listen to tips, especially ones that start out, "I hear they like . . ." Remember, *they* know everything. Wager only on what *they* like.

Ask the owner of the horse what he thinks of its chances and bet accordingly. If you can't find the owner, ask the trainer. Or the jockey's agent.

Always invite your untutored friends and relations to the track and spend all of your time instructing them, then indulge them by betting only on cute jockeys and horses with long tails.

In your handicapping ignore all horses that show enough speed out of the starting gate to get the lead early. Bet only on plodders that come from out of the clouds.

Always bet on horses that haven't won in a long time or have very low winning percentages. They're due. The same rule applies to trainers and jockeys.

Always bet on the assumption that every race is fixed. Your task is to figure out whose turn it is to win.

Convince yourself that the final time of a race is more important than its fractional time, meaning how long it takes a horse to run a quarter of a mile or half a mile rather than the whole race. Ignore fractional times and bet only on horses that have good final times.

Double the size of your wager after every loss. You're sure to recoup your stash in the end.

Always bet on more than one horse in a race, but in the place and show pools only.

Bet your life savings to show on odds-on favorites in short fields. It's more exciting than bungee jumping or hang gliding. The term in racing for this kind of action is bridge jumping. You'll be doing it, as soon as you find the bridge.

Always bet heavily to break even when you're losing and tighten up when you get ahead. The longer your winning streak, the less you should bet.

Bet only on the basis of workout information, especially

in the case of first-time starters running at a mile or more or breaking from the inside post position in a sprint.

Never bet on a horse stretching out from a sprint to a longer distance or moving up in class after a win.

Bet only on animals dropping into cheap claiming races from graded stakes and handicaps, especially if they are wearing front bandages for the first time.

Always parlay your bets. Don't be content with cashing a single ticket, but risk it all on successive wagers until you lose.

Bring lots of money to the track and bet most of it early.

Always favor the inside posts in sprints and the outside posts in distance races, especially if the start of the long race is close to a turn.

Try to develop a system and stick to it rigidly, day after day, no matter what happens.

Never go to the paddock or look at the post parade. Pay no attention to how the animals look or behave prior to the race. Concentrate on the numbers your computer spits out and bet only on that basis.

Rely religiously on the information you receive or purchase from the public handicappers in the newspapers and the call-in services advertised in the sports sections and the *Daily Racing Form*, especially if they recommend horses sure to go off as heavy favorites in maiden and cheap claiming races.

Most important, on entering the track or a betting facility for the first time, make sure you know where the ATM machines are located. They provide the only guaranteed payoffs in the joint.

BETTING: THE RULES
OF THEIR GAME

As you will learn in the next chapter, any moderately intelligent human being can be taught to read a past-performance chart and how to handicap. All around you at the racetrack you will find yourself surrounded by people studying their *Racing Forms*. Every one of these students believes that he has mastered the art of handicapping a horse race and they all can tell you about those great days when they picked six consecutive winners and went home with wads of cash stuffed into their pockets and purses. One of the highest compliments a track regular can receive from his peers is to hear someone say about him that he's a "good handicapper." That amounts to nothing less than an accolade, because it has come from a competitor.

Serious handicappers are like gladiators in a Roman arena, where only the survivors in a tough game are deemed worthy of applause. For you to win, other people have to lose.

If anyone can be taught to handicap successfully, then how is it possible to win consistently? The house vigorish would eventually pound everyone into poverty. An expert on gambling named John Scarne, whose *Complete Guide to Gambling*, first published in 1961, is considered a definitive textbook on all forms of wagering, devotes a long chapter on horse racing to maintain that no one can beat the races in the long run. Here's what he has to say:

> If you are one of the millions who go to the tracks to bet the horses for fun, remember that you must pay for the privilege. How much you pay is entirely up to you. If you want to keep the price down to what you think the entertainment is worth and what you can afford, here is a good system: Before leaving home, decide how much you want to spend (bet), add the track admission price, the price of a program, an allowance for refreshments and the price of your transportation. The total is your budget. Take this amount with you and no more, so that if you lose you won't be tempted to recoup your losses and lose more than you planned. Then bet the favorite to *show*. Forget about *win* and *place* bets. I don't say this advice will win you any money, but it will cut down your losses.

At the time Scarne wrote his book, this piece of advice could be considered sensible, if all you cared about was the spectacle and didn't mind being bored to extinction. Betting something on the horse of your choice is as intrinsic to the horse-racing experience as any aspect of the sport itself. Much more so than betting on any other game. For this reason, wagering has always been allowed wherever horse racing has flourished. If betting were to be banned, not more than a few hundred people would show up at any race meet and they'd be secretly betting with one another. If the idea is to have fun, as Scarne claims, then why not bet two dollars on long shots? A thirty-to-one shot bouncing in will provide far more entertainment than cashing a $2.10 ticket on Cigar to show. You're going to lose anyway, Scarne says, so at least give yourself a thrill from time to time.

The betting scene has changed dramatically over the past two decades and is still changing. The tracks used to offer only win, place, and show betting (first, second, and third), plus a single daily double on the first two races. Now all tracks offer a huge variety of bets, partly because they have to compete with so many other forms of gambling, legal and otherwise, and partly because the vigorish, or takeout, on the exotic bets is larger. In order to survive, the racetracks have been forced to offer the public more and more inducements to attend, including rock concerts and giveaways—tote bags, glasses, caps, beer steins, cups, umbrellas, T-shirts, and other junk made by sweatshop labor in underdeveloped countries. More important, they now provide, in collaboration with the *Racing Form* and other databases, a lot more information than they ever used to.

In the bad old days for bettors, there were no reliable speed ratings, no equipment or medication information, highly dubious workout statistics, almost no independent investigative reportage on happenings in the industry. The only people who were able to make money at the races were insiders who happened to know something crucial about an animal, some piece of information not available to the general public. This was the golden era of the tout, or tipster, who flourished in the grandstand by being able to convince people that he and he alone had heard something or knew something that, for a small consideration, he would be willing to impart. In other words, without inside information no one could hope to win consistently at the races.

The date that horse racing became a potentially rewarding pastime can be set in 1968, with the publication of Tom Ainslie's *Complete Guide to Thoroughbred Racing*. Ainslie (a nom de plume) had for years been forced to flounder about like the rest of us in search of a winner. When he looked around for sources of information, he was appalled to discover that, apart from the *Daily Racing Form* and its sister sheet, the *Morning Telegraph*, there was almost nothing available to the horseplayer. Singlehandedly, Ainslie set about rectifying this situation and produced a guide that for the first time enabled people to bet with some confidence on the outcome of a race. His book, which has been updated several times since and has never been out of print, is still one of the best handicapping and reference works for anyone who wants to devote a major portion of his life to playing the ponies. And it immediately made John Scarne's pessimistic assessment of horse racing as a gambling proposition outdated, though not entirely invalid. The vigorish is still a heavy burden.

Another reason it's so hard to make a living as a player is that most people don't know how to bet. Here's another statistic I've created, but which I believe to be true: for every hundred expert handicappers, no more than one knows how to manage his money correctly.

The first difficulty to overcome is psychological. "Almost every natural instinct you have as a human being is wrong at the racetrack," says Gerry Okuneff. He's correct. The lower the odds are on a horse, the more most people want to bet on him. When they get behind, the tendency is to bet larger and larger amounts in order to recoup their losses. When they get ahead, caution dictates risking less and less in order not to lose what they've gained. Natural human impulses, but all wrong at the racetrack.

The vast number of exotic bets available is another source of misery. On parlay and combination bets such as the pick-six, the pick-nine, and the trifecta, the potential payoffs are so large that they blind many people to less lucrative but far easier plays. Driven by greed and delusions of grandeur, most horseplayers defeat themselves by spreading their action in too many directions. They pass winner after winner in pursuit of the monster payoff and so all but guarantee themselves a loss.

Again, the name of this game is value. Smart investors in the stock market do not buy overpriced securities; smart horseplayers do not risk serious money on horses going off at unrealistic odds. Smart investors do not buy and sell every day; smart horseplayers do not bet on every race. Not only is it important to know *how*, it is equally crucial to know *when* to bet. One of the best horseplayers I ever met was the late movie director Martin Ritt. A victim of the notorious Hollywood black list in the 1950s, when a number of entertainment personalities were prevented from working because they were suspected of being Communists, Marty managed to support himself for several years by playing the horses at the New York tracks. His survival depended not so much upon his handicapping skills, which were considerable, as on iron self-discipline. Long after he had reestablished himself in show business and no longer needed the money, he would sit through entire cards without once getting up to go to a betting window. Marty wasn't about to allow anybody to play him for a sucker. "The secret of winning," he liked to say, "is to have an iron ass."

The principle is a good one, even though it's not my idea

of having fun at the racetrack. It's a question of priorities. Most people, including me, don't have Marty's self-absorbed dedication. I rarely pass a race entirely, if only because I want to have a rooting interest in it. My way of coping is to bet very little on races I don't like and more on the ones I do favor. Let's call it an adaptation of Marty's rule. Not one I would adopt if I had to make a living at the track, but one that allows me to have some fun without placing myself in harm's way.

A FEW years ago I happened to be at Pimlico in Baltimore with Andrew Beyer, the distinguished racing columnist of the *Washington Post* and the creator of the Beyer Speed Figure in the *Daily Racing Form.* Andy is a formidable player and a man who takes as much pride in his gambling skills as in his literary talent. We had both settled on a horse in the first race as a probable winner and we rose as one to head for a betting window just before post time. The animal, shipped in for the race from Aqueduct in New York, was being ignored by the Maryland fans and was going off at odds of six to one. "Of course you're going to bet him straight," I said as we joined a betting line. Andy looked at me as if I had suggested he bite off the head of a live chicken. "It is beneath my dignity to bet on a horse straight," he answered.

The horse won easily, as did Andy's daily double, enriching both of us. His hilarious rejoinder, however, has stuck in my mind ever since, mainly because few of the big players I know these days do make straight bets anymore. There is such a variety of wagering options available that the tendency among the regulars is always to look for a way to maximize profits by hooking up horses in exotic combinations. I've been as guilty of this practice as most, but that's because it is so tempting to go for the big payoffs. It's still not the best way to bet at the racetrack, at least not unless you are prepared to sustain those long losing streaks. The heavy hitters at the track bring very sizable bankrolls and are willing to take the plunge on the exotic wagers. For a modest player like me, and certainly for anyone who is not prepared to put up with big losses, the method can be disastrous. Even for skillful handicappers, exotic wagering should not dominate their action. Every racetrack press box in the country is populated by professional handicappers who are passing up cashing winning tickets on their horses because they have used them only in the exotic combinations. Most of them are not driving new cars.

Here's a breakdown of the kinds of wagers offered at American racetracks:

STRAIGHT BETS

For those of you who have read this far but still may know nothing about wagering, a straight bet means putting your money on a horse to win, place (run second or better), or show (run third or better). Every other kind of bet is either a so-called combination wager or an exotic.

The straight bet to win is still the safest and the best value anywhere, providing your horse appears to be the best horse in the race and is going off at odds of two to one or better. One of the absolute constants in racing is that the favorites will win one out of every three races. The percentage will vary slightly from meet to meet and from race to race, but year in and year out that figure of one in three will hold up. As you become more sophisticated and astute in your handicapping, you will learn to distinguish easily between the two-to-one shot that represents value and the two-to-one shot that doesn't. But one of the best ways to begin solving the puzzle of how to bet on a race is to find the favorite, figure out whether he is likely to win, and then check the price on him. If he's going off at less than two to one, the chances are that you're betting into a minus expectation. People who bet exclusively on favorites are known as "chalk players." You will find a lot of them at the track and they can often be identified by their wardrobes, which tend to be threadbare and patched.

Since most obvious favorites will go off at odds much lower than two to one, your task is now to find the value in the race: the horse that has a good chance to win but is going off at higher odds because he is being overlooked by the chalk players. If I'm betting intelligently, and haven't succumbed to the constant temptation to go only for the big score, I try never to pass up a win bet on any horse I like going off at odds of four to one or better.

What happens if I like more than one horse in a race? I bet them both, providing a win by either animal will result in a profit. Sometimes I'll have win tickets on as many as three horses, providing at least two of them are long shots. The basic rule is that every bet must guarantee a profit. Never bet merely to break even.

One of the advantages of betting to win is that you'll always know what return you can expect for your money. On your program you'll find the competitors listed in order of post position with assigned odds, the so-called "morning line." These odds are supposedly educated guesses by the track handicapper as to what the actual odds will be, once the money has begun to pour into the betting pool. By post time the public will have established what the true odds will be, after the takeout has been figured in. It's important for you to know what the return will be on your investment. In many exotic wagers, you will be betting blind, which is no way to go through life, let alone the racetrack.

PLACE AND SHOW

Betting on horses to place and show would seem to be a safer tack to take in a game as fraught with unforeseeable risks as this one. Every year horses will find new ways not to win, even though often it's not their fault. They come down the stretch looking like sure winners, but something weird happens and they lose. If that something is serious enough—a breakdown—then it doesn't matter how you've risked your money. Far more often, however, they'll lose but manage to finish at least third. So why not bet them in the place and show holes?

The main reason is that the payoffs are so much lower. This is because they must be calculated on the basis of two or three horses sharing in the same betting pool, again after the track has taken its cut. If there's a heavy favorite in the race and he finishes in the money, the much larger amounts bet on him in the place and show pools greatly reduce the returns on even the longest shots in the contest. Since favorites do finish in the money about eighty percent of the time, the place and show prices on the other competitors will be correspondingly lower. Risking money on a twenty-to-one shot to run third that winds up paying four dollars is equivalent to slapping a dunce cap on your head and proclaiming your incompetence.

If you like a horse well enough to risk any money on him, then *always* bet him to win. It's acceptable to back up a win bet on a horse in the place or show hole, but only if you think the favorite could easily finish up the track and your backup bet will pay enough to guarantee you a profit. To do that, you'll have to master the art of estimating your probable payoff by learning how to calculate it from the figures on the tote board. It's not only time-consuming and boring, but unreliable as well. This is because those grim older men I referred to earlier, who sit around all day waiting for the right moment to plunge into an inviting place or show pool, will usually pick up the overlooked potentially profitable foray and ram their money into the tote at the last minute, thus dramatically lowering the payoffs.

If favorites usually manage to finish among the top three, why not bet only on selected favorites, the "sure things" or "mortal locks" like Cigar, to show? The best way to answer this is now to explain briefly about "breakage," another little scam the tracks have come up with to separate you from your capital. Payoffs at the races are calculated on the basis of a two-dollar bet. What you will be receiving from the track, however, after a successful play is not the actual true payoff, but one calculated back either to the nearest dime or twenty cents. For example, if the true payoff on your show bet is $2.98, the track will pay you either $2.90, as in New York, or $2.80, as in California. This is legalized theft. It's onerous enough on win prices, but horrendously unfair to place and show bettors. The rationale for it is that no one wants to be bothered with pennies and nickels, but those pennies and nickels mount up to provide the tracks and the pols with pyramids of gold. The people who bet only to place and show are bucking an elephant, not a tiger. You'd have to win nine out of ten bets on the average favorite merely to break even. Still, if you wish to join the ranks of the dreary old codgers nursing their pension money and Social Security checks through the parimutuel shredding machines, then be my guest, but kiss the fun times goodbye.

EXOTIC DANCES

All tracks now offer many kinds of combination and exotic wagers. What they offer is unfortunately entirely up to them. Some will provide every sort of play, others may strike absurd poses in defense of what they proclaim to be "the good of the game." For years Santa Anita refused to allow bets of less than five dollars on exacta plays and defended this policy as one designed to protect the fans, by making the wager too expensive and thus preventing them from squandering too much money on a risky form of wagering. I'm surprised they didn't sponsor Gamblers Anonymous meetings in the infield. Eventually, however, competition compelled the racing associations to provide at least a measure of what their customers wanted—a full range of play, with minimum bets in some areas of only a dollar. Most tracks still impose restrictions of one sort or another but are slowly, grudgingly being hauled into the late twentieth century, though not the twenty-first. As a bettor, one of the first things you have to do at a racetrack is discover exactly what options are available and gear your action to the rules of their game.

Every track will schedule at least one daily double, usually on the first and second races, but some will offer more. To hit the double, you have to pick the winners of two consecutive races. The minimum bet is two dollars and it can become costly, if you pick several contestants in each race. I hardly ever play it, unless I can isolate a key horse in one of the two races and that animal has been bet too low in the odds to play straight.

I prefer the pick-three, which requires you to link three winners back to back. Obviously, this would seem to be tougher to accomplish than the double, but it has two advantages. First, because it is a more difficult play, the payoffs are much larger; second, you will probably be allowed to bet in one-dollar increments rather than two, which enables you to spread out a little bit and include a tasty long shot or two. The California tracks have instituted what they call the "rolling triple," which means that you can select whichever race you choose to start your pick-three. My usual style is to use three horses in two of the races and two in the other. At a dollar a horse, my total investment will be eighteen dollars (three by three by two). The investment is modest and the return can be sizable. Even if you fall so in love with this exotic, however, that you want to bet more than one dollar per horse, always make this wager in one-dollar increments. There are tax advantages to doing so that I'm not going to go into detail about. Before you risk your money, ask any knowledgeable horseplayer or wiseguy on the premises what that advantage is and he'll tell you.

Of all the other exotic dances on the card, the only one I'll frequently trip to is the exacta, in which you pick two horses in a race to finish first and second, in the exact order. (At some tracks, this bet is called the perfecta.) Then there is the quinella, or quiniella, a wager in which the horses must also finish first and second, but in no particular order. Most of the time, the exacta is a better bet, because the return is so much larger if the longer of your selections finishes first. I'll consider the quinella only if the two horses I like are favored, in which case I might be better off simply betting one of them straight and/or keying it in a pick-three.

A good many horseplayers favor the trifecta, also known in the East as the triple. You try to pick three horses to come in one-two-three in exact order in a single race. I consider it a possible bet only if you feel strongly about two horses to finish first and second, in which case you can key them on top and use all the other ones to finish third. In a full field of twelve, a one-dollar trifecta will only cost you ten dollars (one by one by ten). Even if your preferred two horses are the favorites in the race, the bet can be rewarding if a big long shot comes in third. There are several other fairly sophisticated ways to make this play, but I usually avoid it. I confess I don't have a good feel for it and I think it's crucial at the races not to ignore your instincts and gut feelings, no matter what the cold logic of a situation may dictate.

One of the oldest and most illusive plays the racetrack offers is the so-called combination or across-the-board wager. You bet equal amounts on your selection to win, place, and show. If your horse finishes first, you collect on all three bets; if he runs second, you lose the win bet but collect on place and show; if he finishes third, you're paid off on show only. It's a tempting prospect, if only because you stand to get something back from coming in at least third. But even if your horse places, you often barely get your money back. If the horse you like is a long shot and a backup bet would show a profit, play him either in the place or show hole, but never in both. In any case, most of your action should be on the animal to win. If he's good enough to finish in the money, he's good enough to come home first. You want to maximize your potential profit, not play to avoid losing.

The sucker traps in the steamy jungle of the exotics are the superfecta, in which you want your selections to finish one-two-three-four in a single contest, and all parlay bets, such as the pick-six, the double-triple, the pick-nine, and variations or extensions on all of the above. Every track provides different betting possibilities and they are constantly changing. With the aid of the new self-service machines, which are gradually replacing the human beings behind the parimutuel windows (racing's own version of downsizing, or people-cleansing), you can design your own exotic plays in the form of various types of parlays. In a parlay, as a cynical definition puts it, you bet until you lose.

The double and the pick-three are the easiest of the parlay wagers, but they are difficult enough. Unaccompanied by straight bets, they may plunge you very quickly into a vast swamp of losing tickets. Consider, therefore, the effrontery inherent in the belief that on any given day you are going to be able to pick six consecutive winners or nine horses in a row to run at least second, as in the pick-nine offered at the Southern California tracks. You will be using more than one horse in most of these races, so that, even at a one-dollar minimum for the pick-nine, your total outlay for a competitive ticket becomes much too expensive. To arrive at that figure, multiply the number of horses you use in each race by the required minimum bet. For example, in a pick-six in which you single three horses but use three animals in each of the other three races, your basic total cost will come to fifty-four dollars (one by one by one by three by three by three times two dollars). Not too costly for you? Then consider this: most pick-six tickets are won by syndicates or groups of bettors, who put in thousands of dollars at a time and rarely hit it. Even when they do, the payoff often doesn't justify the outlay, because at least a couple of genuine long shots are going to have to win to make the ticket worth the play. (The tracks also pay off on five out of six, but the return is pitifully low in relation to the difficulty involved.) If you're prepared to lose, say, two thousand dollars a day on the pick-six, you'd do much better to bet half that much money on a couple of likely-looking selections in single races.

Having said this, I now have to confess that from time to time I do play the pick-six. Why? Because it's fun. Jim Quinn, who rarely plays it, maintains that the only way to approach it is either to buy a piece of a big group ticket or risk no more than eight dollars on your own. I don't entirely share this view, even though I think it's basically a sound approach. Unless you're a skilled handicapper and have put the ticket together yourself, where's the fun? Doing anything as part of a group, including line dancing, doesn't enchant me. I like to bet on horses because I enjoy handicapping and because picking winners is a challenge; solve the puzzle and enjoy the fruits of your victory. Also, playing a small pick-six often keeps you in the game through races you should be passing.

What I suggest is that you devote no more than one tenth of your operating capital to play it. In my case, this means a ticket of no more than thirty or forty dollars. So far I've been lucky and have managed to hit the pick-six two or three times a year ever since it was introduced, usually for modest amounts, but always for at least several thousand dollars. (In the fall of 1995, three of us invested $144 in the national pick-seven offered on Breeders' Cup day and got back about twenty-four thousand before taxes.) I'm well in the black with it and so I persist. On the occasions at the track when no one picks six winners, most of the money in the pool is carried over to the following day. After three or four programs of carry-overs, you can find yourself competing for an ocean of several million dollars. Most of the time the big tickets will split the pool, but not always. You could get lucky.

Some years ago, when the pick-six was first introduced at Del Mar, and before the era of carryovers, I began to play it by cutting a deck of cards. The ace counted for the number one, the jacks and queens for eleven and twelve, respectively.

The king meant I had to play the morning-line favorite. There were also two jokers in the deck. If one of them turned up, I had to use the horse in the race being ridden by a well-known jockey my friends and I used to call the Hillside Strangler, because of his talent for taking up out of the gate on obvious favorites in unimportant races. By choosing only one horse in each of the pick-six races, the price of this ticket was only two dollars. I divided that cost with a friend of mine, who shared a rented condo with me that season. After six or seven days of failure, my friend, a logician of the turf whose faith was rooted firmly in statistics, declined to pick up his half of the expense one morning. I hadn't finished drawing the cards when he announced that he was no longer interested. He was going out to buy himself a tuna salad sandwich and would see me at the races.

That ticket also failed to come up with six winners, or even five. But two of the horses the deck selected were giant long shots that won. I found myself holding a total of four winners, but no one had five or six that day, so the track paid off on four. I pocketed eighteen hundred dollars, which upped the cost of my roomie's tuna salad sandwich to nine hundred bucks. See what I mean? You need dumb luck.

THE MONEY GAME

To sum up, you have to remember whenever you go to the races that it's a game using real money, whether it's at the track itself or a betting emporium somewhere. If you only attend these festivities two or three times a year and don't bring more than twenty or thirty dollars to play with, then it probably won't matter to you if you lose. If you love the sport and also want to play the game more often, then it becomes essential for you to get your betting life in order. You'll discover that it's much easier said than done, but that a losing day can be made more bearable by the knowledge that you haven't made a fool of yourself by betting recklessly in situations in which the percentages are stacked against you.

I don't know of any sure way to stop a losing streak. A friend of mine does it by betting two dollars on every horse in a full field of twelve, in the hope that some long shot will return him a profit. My experience has been that every time I use all the horses in a race, a technique called "wheeling," the favorite is sure to win, thus guaranteeing me a loss. If I'm really desperate, I have been known to bet a likely-looking horse to show or to try to run a small show parlay through four or five races. The risk is minimal and the return can be profitable, but you'll discover that it's not that easy to pull off and that a straight bet to win on those horses would probably have been more rewarding.

Win or lose, though, the game should be fun and full of laughter. One of the pleasures to savor is the cornucopia of good stories horseplayers will tell about their own misadventures. A few years ago, the late Pete Axhelm, a sports writer and commentator, happened to be at the races with Andy Beyer. As they perused the *Racing Form* together, Axhelm asked Andy about a horse he liked. "God put me on this earth to bet horses like this," Andy answered with his customary brio. When the horse ran third, Axhelm turned to Andy and said, "I guess God is a show bettor."

THE *FORM:*
DECIPHERING THE
ROSETTA STONE

There is no way to survive as a bettor at the racetrack without having spent at least an hour or two examining and evaluating the past-performance statistics published either in the *Daily Racing Form* or in the track programs. The figures in the latter are provided by a company called Equibase, headquartered in Lexington, Kentucky, and they are similar in format to those provided by the *Form*, but are not, in my opinion, quite as complete or accurate. Equibase has only been around a few years, whereas the *Form* (also known as the Bible to the regulars) has been on the scene practically from the time Moses was clocked out of the gate beating Pharaoh to the Red Sea. Even though Equibase's figures are provided as part of the cost of the program (currently $1.50 in New York, for instance), you would do better to spend an extra two bucks for the *Form* as well. Unless you're planning to arrive at the track at least a couple of hours early, you aren't going to have enough time to evaluate the statistics, especially if you expect to make any sort of parlay bet.

A couple of hours is not enough for the self-styled pros, most of whom will spend a lot more time than that over the *Form*'s numbers. Gerry Okuneff, for example, will scrutinize those figures with the concentration of a Talmudic scholar poring over the arcane mysteries of the Babylonian Mishnah. He underlines in varicolored inks his more significant discoveries and also jots down trenchant comments on aspects of his observations. By the time he has finished his examination and analysis, the charts in his paper have acquired the intensity of a scientific study. Words, phrases, numbers, underlinings pile up into a dense cobweb out of which, if Gerry feels he has done his work properly, winners will emerge like golden nuggets from a stream bed. Gerry is convinced that survival at the racetrack depends on this sort of total commitment.

I don't entirely subscribe to this view of the game. The pros' approach is entirely dedicated to mastering facts, whereas real life has a way of circumventing mere facts. The accumulation of statistical knowledge is a powerful tool, but it has to be supplemented by inspiration and inventiveness. And luck. By any statistics available to us, we should have won the Vietnam War. Sometimes all the numbers will add up splendidly on a particular horse, but he will lose to some untried competitor who has suddenly found himself and made mockery of the numbers.

The pros will contend that in the long run the only way to bet is their way. Maybe so, but with reservations. Occasionally, but often enough to make a difference, it is wiser to trust your instincts and to heed the small but insistent voice that whispers to you from the depths, as Vincent Van Gogh must have trusted his when he painted *Starry Night*, a picture no one could have created by the numbers. There is such a thing as too much factual knowledge, especially in the creative arts. And betting on horses is nothing if not a creative art.

The first time I ever took a good look at the *Daily Racing Form*, I couldn't believe my eyes. Most of the paper seemed to be merely a mass of charts containing numbers and arcane commentary on racing events. What did such remarks as "4 wide stretch" and "boxed 5/16 to 1/8" mean? I found myself confronted by something as undecipherable as a stone tablet covered with runic inscriptions.

The first section of the publication was understandable enough. It consisted of articles about various goings-on in the sport. Profiles of horses, trainers, owners, and jockeys; reports on the activities of racing stables; developments in wagering options; assignments of racing dates; news tidbits on happenings in racing all over the globe. There was even a single miserable column devoted to world events. A recent one was made up of two very short paragraphs under the headlines, "Arafat Says He's Ready . . ." and "Madonna Gives Birth . . ."

What you realize immediately from even the most cursory examination of the *Form* is that its readers are single-minded in pursuit of a winner. Wars, pestilence, famine, revolutions, natural cataclysms do not impinge upon their daily lives, not unless they are grave enough to result in the cancellation of that day's card. A perfect example of this attitude is the classic story of the two friends who for years had spent every Sunday afternoon together at the races in Tijuana, at the Agua Caliente track, then the only one open on Sundays. On

December 7, 1941, one of the men arrived late, only a few minutes before the first race. His friend had become worried about him. "Where have you been?" he asked. "Didn't you hear?" his buddy answered. "The Japanese just bombed Pearl Harbor." "Yeah? No kidding?" his friend replied. "So who do you like in the double?"

Now that you understand about priorities, here's what a past-performance chart, as published in the *Daily Racing Form*, looks like, with appropriate explanations. Don't panic; it's not as complicated as it looks, nor is most of this information absolutely essential to your having a winning day. Take a minute now to flip to pages 90–91.

A close study of this chart, with all its abbreviations and symbols, will provide you with the basic education you need to become at least a part-time horseplayer. You would still not know, however, what some of this information means or— more important—how significant it might turn out to be. Let's take a closer look and try to isolate the crucial items, reading line by line from left to right.

Pay attention, first of all, to the age and sex of the horse. Tobin Ruler is a five-year-old gelding. Male horses compete against all comers, whereas fillies and mares run mainly in their own category. When they do test the boys, they rarely win, at least in this country. Only the very best females can compete on equal terms with males, which is why only a handful of them have ever won the Kentucky Derby. Even the great ones would do better not to try, except in long-distance turf races, where stamina and class count for more than pure speed. Some top fillies can also sprint with the colts, but they are the exceptions to the rule.

As for age, two-year-olds and three-year-olds compete early in the year exclusively against one another. Young horses these days almost never challenge older ones until well into their third year. In maiden contests (for horses that have never won a race), four-year-olds, especially in the cheaper events, will have a distinct advantage early in the year over three-year-olds and provide useful betting opportunities.

One of the most important statistics to observe is the claiming price, in this case "$10,000." When a horse runs for a so-called claiming tag, it means that the animal is for sale at that price. Up to twenty minutes before post time, anyone wishing to buy him can drop a claiming tag into a box near the winner's circle, in front of the stands. The horse becomes his property immediately *after* the race, whereas the present owner retains ownership until that race is concluded and keeps whatever purse money the horse may have earned. (In case two or more people claim the same contestant, the new owner is determined by lot.) If the horse breaks down during the race or dies, however, the new owner is saddled with the loss, which can be considerable. (Some horses can be claimed for as much as a hundred thousand dollars or more.) You can take out insurance against such an eventuality, but it's costly and few people do so.

The purpose of the claiming price is to ensure that all the horses in a particular race will be evenly matched so that even the less talented competitors will be able to win some purses. Otherwise all of the races would be won only by the best horses on the grounds. Obviously, no one is going to enter a stakes winner in a cheap claiming race, where he will almost certainly be taken. Claiming races, the most common contests on every American racing program, even out the competition. You will note in the claiming price column of his past races that Tobin Ruler was claimed out of his previous race (the small *c* mark), also for ten thousand dollars. Keep going down this column and you'll notice that only once before in his career had he ever run as cheaply, so the claim represents a risky

PAST PERFORMANCE EXPLANATION

Claimed from line, Layoff line (double line indicates year or more)

Horse, Country of origin (if foreign), Owner, Jockey with record at meet

Jockey record year to date

Claiming price

Color, Sex, Age, Month of foaling, (2/3 year olds) Sire (sire's sire), Dam (dam's sire)

Breeder, State or country of foaling, Trainer with record at meet

Trainer record year to date

Medication, Weight to be carried today

Record for current and prior year, Record at today's track (separate for turf & dirt)

Lifetime record in all races

Lifetime record in turf races, Lifetime record on wet tracks, Record at today's distance

Tobin Ruler

Own: Anson Ronald & Susie

HUNTER M T (55 6 4 6 .11) 1996:(253 32 .13)

Dk b or br g. 3 (MAR)
Sire: J. O. Tobin (Never Bend)
Dam: Leaping Princess (Cornish Prince)
Br: Randal Mr & Mrs Robert D (Cal)
Tr: Peterson Douglas R (13 4 1 4 .31) 1996:(53 9 .17)

$10,000

L 117

Lifetime Record: 14 2 1 4 $46,165

					Turf	1 0 0 0	$4,450
1996	2 1 0 0				Wet	2 0 0 0	$750
1995	2 0 0 0				Dist	2 1 0 1	$13,740
Dmr	2 1 0 0						

Weakened 11

Claiming price

Age, Sex, Restrictions, Class of race

Fractional times for horse in lead, Final time of winner

Beyer Speed Figure

Post position, Fractional calls with margins, Finish with margin

Jockey, Medication, Weight, Equipment

First three finishers, Weights, Margins

Odds to $1, (* indicates favorite) Speed rating, Track variant

Comment line, Number of starters

WORKOUTS: Workouts: date, track, distance, track condition, final time, comment, ranking

Date, Race number, Track, Track condition, Distance, Surface

Previous trainer line

Previously trained by Sahadi Jenine

Claimed from Evergreen Farm, Bonde Jeff Trainer

Lugged in early, clear on turn, weakened

SYMBOLS

◉ ◘	=	Inner dirt track	♦	=	Dead-Heat (symbol used next to finish position)	Ⓕ = Race for fillies, or fillies and mares
		Disqualified (symbol located next to odds and company line)	3+	=	Race for 3-year-olds and up	Ⓜ = Main turf course
DH	=	Dead-Heat (symbol located in company line if horses are among first three finishers)	♦	=	Foreign race (outside of North America)	Ⓘ = Inner turf course
			⊗Ⓡ	=	Restricted race for state-breds only	⊗ = Race taken off turf
			●	=	Restricted race for horses who meet certain conditions	• = About distance
						+ = Start from turf chute

HOW SPEED RATING & VARIANT ARE COMPUTED

The Speed Rating is a comparison of a horse's final time with the best time at the distance at that track in the last three years. The best time is given a rating of 100. One point is deducted for each fifth of a second by which a horse fails to equal that time. Thus, in a race where the winner equals the best time (a Speed Rating of 100), another horse who is beaten 12 lengths gets a Speed Rating of 88 (100 minus 12).

Daily Racing Form's Track Variant takes into consideration all races run on a particular day under the same conditions of distance and track surface. The Speed Ratings of all winners in each type of race are added together and an average is computed. This average is deducted from the par of 100 and the difference is the Track Variant. (Example: if the average Speed Rating of winners sprinting on the main track is 86, the Track Variant is 14 (par of 100 minus 86). The lower the track variant, the faster the track, or the better the overall quality of the competition.

POINTS OF CALL & FRACTIONAL TIMES

Distance	1st call	2nd	3rd	4th	5th	Fractional Times		
3½f	start	1/4	—	str	finish		1/4	3/8 finish
4f	start	1/4	—	str	finish		1/4	3/8 finish
4½f	start	3/16	3/8	str	finish	1/4	1/2	finish
5f	start	1/4	3/8	str	finish	1/4	1/2	finish
5½f	start	1/4	3/8	str	finish	1/2	5/8	finish
6f	start	1/4	1/2	str	finish	1/4	3/4	finish
6½f	start	1/4	1/2	str	finish	1/4	3/4	finish
7f	start	1/4	1/2	str	finish	1/4	3/4	finish
7½f	1/4	1/2	3/4	str	finish	1/4	3/4	finish
1 mile	1/4	1/2	3/4	str	finish	1/2	3/4	finish
1 m70 yds	1/4	1/2	3/4	str	finish	1/2	3/4	finish
1 1/16	1/4	1/2	3/4	str	finish	1/2	3/4	finish
1 1/8	1/4	1/2	3/4	str	finish	1/2	3/4	finish
1 3/16	1/4	1/2	mile	str	finish	1/2	mile	finish
1 1/4	1/4	1/2	1 1/4	str	finish	1/2	mile	finish
1 5/16	1/4	1/2	1 3/16	str	finish	1/2	mile	finish
1 3/8	1/2	mile	1 1/4	str	finish	1/2	mile	finish
1 3/4	1/2	mile	1 5/8	str	finish	1/2	1 1/4	finish
1 7/8	1/2	mile	1 3/4	str	finish	1/2	1 1/4	finish
2 miles	1/2	mile	1 3/4	str	finish	1/2	1 1/2	finish
2 1/8	1/2	mile	1 7/8	str	finish	1/2	1 1/2	finish

ABBREVIATIONS FOR TYPES OF RACES

Alw 15000n1x	Non-winners of one race (or more, depending on the number after N) other than maiden, claiming or starter. Used for non-winners of up to 5 races "other than"
Alw 15000n1y	Non-winners of one race (or more, depending on the number after N) in, or since, a specified time period.
Alw 15000n2L	Non-winners of two (or more) races lifetime
Alw 15000nSy	Non-winners of a specific amount of money in a specified time period
Alw 15000n1m	Non-winners of one (or more) races at a mile or over in a specified time period
Alw 15000n$mY	Non-winners of a specific amount of money OR races at a mile or over in, or since, a specified time period
Alw 15000s	Non-winners of one (or more) stakes lifetime
Alw 15000n1t	Non-winners of one (or more) turf races
Alw 15000nmmt	Non-winners of one or more turf races at a mile or more
Alw 150000nc	Allowance race with no conditions
Alw 15000c	Allowance race with multiple conditions or restrictions
Alw 15000s	Starter allowance (number indicates minimum claiming price horse must have started for) to be eligible

CLM 10000	Claiming race (entered to be claimed for $10,000)
Clm 10000n2L	Non-winners of two races (or more, depending on the number after N) lifetime
Clm 10000n2x	Non-winners of two races (or more, depending on the number after N) other than those described in the conditions of a race.
Clm 10000n1y	Non-winners of one race (or more) in, or since, a specified time period.
Clm 10000n1mY	Non-winners of one race (or more) at a mile or over in, or since, a specified time period
Clm 10000n$Y	Non-winners of a specific amount of money in, or since, a specified time period
Clm 10000n$mY	Non-winners of a specific amount of money OR races at a mile or over in, or since, a specified time period
Clm 10000a	Beaten claimers
Clm Stk 10000	Claiming stakes (number indicates claiming price)
OClm 10000	Optional claiming race. Entered to be claimed
OClm 10000N	Optional claiming race. Entered NOT to be claimed
Hcp 10000s	Starter handicap race. Number indicates minimum claiming price horse must have started for to be eligible

OTHER CONDITIONS

Md Sp Wt	Maiden Special Weight race (for horses that have never won)
Md 32000	Maiden Claiming race (entered to be claimed for $32,000)
Handicap 40k	**OVERNIGHT HANDICAP RACE (Purse of $40,000)**
Ky Derby–G1	Graded Stakes race, with name of race (North American races are graded in order of status, with G1 being the best)
PrincetonH 40k	Ungraded, but named Stakes race (H indicates handicap) Purse value is $40,000

TRACK CONDITION

DIRT TRACKS

fst	=	Fast
wf	=	Wet-Fast
gd	=	Good
sy	=	Sloppy
my	=	Muddy
sl	=	Slow
hy	=	Heavy
fr	=	Frozen

TURF & STEEPLECHASE

hd	=	Hard
fm	=	Firm
gd	=	Good
yl	=	Yielding
sf	=	Soft
hy	=	Heavy

WORKOUT LINE

●	=	Best of day/distance
B	=	Breezing
D	=	Driving
(d)	=	Worked around dogs
E	=	Easily
g	=	Worked from gate
H	=	Handily
tr.t	=	Training track
TR	=	Training race
3/25	=	Workout ranking
(W)	=	Wood Chips

EQUIPMENT & MEDICATION

b	=	Blinkers
f	=	Front bandages
B	=	Butazolidin
L	=	Lasix (furosemide)

investment, since, if the horse were sound, why would his previous owners have dropped him down in class to run against animals he'd have horrified earlier in his career?

This is the danger in claiming races; you risk purchasing an unsound or injured animal that may never be able to run again, assuming he doesn't break down in this particular race. Some trainers make a specialty of this kind of racing and are very good at it. They can take an unsound horse, or one that may need a change of equipment (a different kind of shoe or bit, a shadow roll, blinkers), or different racing tactic, or a switch in racing surface (dirt to turf or vice versa), and turn him around, make him into a winner. A few claiming horses can not only be transformed into winners, but moved up in class to challenge the best. For the top horsemen in the game, however, claiming animals, in the immortal words of a veteran conditioner named Lefty Nickerson, "is like trying to make a living by going through garbage cans." Nevertheless, for the bettor the claiming race often offers the best opportunities for making a score.

The next important statistic to pay attention to is the one regarding medication, which is listed next to the assigned weight in the race, in this case 117 pounds. Tobin Ruler has been running on Lasix and Butazolidin and will be on those medications again in his next race, even though, for some reason, the B is always missing from this part of the chart. Lasix is a trade name for the drug furosemide, a diuretic that drains fluid out of the body. Horses can only breathe through their nostrils and the stress of running hard can rupture tiny capillaries in their lungs. This causes bleeding and, though it does not endanger the animal's life, it can compel him to fight for air and thus be unable to exert himself fully. Butazolidin is a drug that eases swelling and pain in joints. Dozens of other medications are administered regularly to racehorses, but these are the only two listed at the moment, probably because they are the most common. A wise bettor will take note of changes in a horse's medication, especially since many animals will show dramatic improvement when running for the first or second time on either Lasix or "Bute," or "the cocktail," as some cynical regulars refer to the combination of the two. In Tobin Ruler's case, he's been medicated in every race over the past two years.

You should pay some attention to the numbers in parentheses after the names of the jockey and the trainer. The first set indicates the number of races they have competed in at the current meet, followed by their wins, seconds, and thirds. The second set tells you their records for the year to date at all tracks.

To the right of the class-of-race descriptions, you will note a column of numbers described only as the "Beyer Speed Figure." Pay close attention to these numbers, because they represent the single most important development in handicapping during the past decade. Created by Andy Beyer, the figs, as they are sometimes referred to, provide a pretty accurate estimate of the horse's performance in every race, with the higher numbers representing superior efforts. For most knowledgeable bettors, the Beyer figs have replaced the old-fashioned speed ratings and so-called track variants, which are listed directly under the weight being carried by the horse that day. It's not important for you to know by what exquisitely time-consuming method these figures have been arrived at, though explanations are readily available; for your purposes as a bettor, all you need to be sure of is that the Beyer figs are crucial to your financial well-being, whereas the other ratings are not.

Immediately to the right of the assigned weight, you'll notice the small letter *b* (although, like Butazolidin, it's missing from the top of the chart). This indicates that Tobin Ruler runs wearing blinkers, an important piece of equipment. Blinkers, also known as shades, tend to concentrate the animal's attention on the task at hand by eliminating his peripheral vision. Horses have a herding instinct, whereas what you are asking them to do is break away from the herd. The addition of blinkers to an animal's equipment will keep him from socializing with his peers, or "hanging." (The removal of blinkers is not as significant and can safely be pretty much ignored as a wagering concern.)

If you note an *f* next to the weight in the previous race column, pay attention. This means that the horse is wearing front bandages, or "front wraps," as they are frequently called. Unless the animal has run in them before, the addition of bandages, especially on cheap claiming horses, can indicate tendon or ankle problems. Occasionally, in these kinds of races, sometimes referred to as Hospital Handicaps, most of the contestants will appear on the track looking like mummies. Somebody has to win these contests, but you'd often do better to pass them.

The comment line, all the way over on the right, can be helpful. "Weakened," the observation made regarding Tobin Ruler's last race, indicates the observer's opinion that the horse showed early speed but tired. "Steady drive" tells us that the gelding ran very well off a fifteen-month layoff to beat a field of nine at Pleasanton, a track in Northern California. When you look at charts for entries in various races, you'll note comments that can be useful to you, especially ones concerning difficulties the horse may have encountered in the race, such as "boxed 5/16 to 1/8" (meaning he was behind and between horses, unable to find running room), or "forced to check" (he was making a move but had to slow down abruptly for some reason), or "fanned wide on turn." Horses can get into all kinds of trouble in a race and are unable to give their best. Most American racetracks are a mile in circumference, much narrower than tracks overseas. And in this country the turf courses are laid out inside the dirt ovals, causing traffic problems, especially on the turns. This is another reason why most savvy American horseplayers look to bet on horses with speed, since your champion is not going to get shut off, fanned on turns, or otherwise interfered with, if he's fast enough to open up a lead in the first few hundred feet out of the starting gate.

This question of speed is the crucial factor that every bettor must pay attention to. The Beyer fig is very reliable, as I've already indicated, but you can acquire some idea on your own of its significance; not by looking at the finishing time of a race, but by checking the so-called interior fractions. Look at the box on the lower right entitled "Points of Call & Fractional Times." You'll note that every race is broken down to give you a picture of how fast the race was run at every point in it and where your particular animal was at the time. Since horses can only run at top speed for at most half a mile, the fractional breakdowns will tell you fairly accurately where your horse did his best work. For example, an animal that wins a long race on the lead by loping along at slow fractions is not a likely candidate to win the same sort of race in which he will be pressed to run much faster earlier. This is why horseplayers can spot future winners by finding animals that may have used themselves up too soon but who are now entered in a race in which they will not be pressed hard early and will have plenty left for the drive. A good fractional time will excite a bettor because it can lead to at least temporary wealth. What higher praise from a horseplayer could there be than the encomium I once overheard from a man in the Del Mar grandstand, who had just spotted a beautiful woman walking down the aisle past his box? "Great interior fractions," he said as she sailed past, an obvious winner.

The margins of victory and defeat, by the way, are indicated by the smaller numbers next to the ones depicting where the horse was at every recorded point in the race. Thus, on July 5, Tobin Ruler, breaking from post position four, was second out of the gate, had the lead at the quarter mile by two lengths, held it through the half mile, opened it up to four lengths by the head of the stretch, and won by two. In his next race, on July 28, he was 2¾ lengths *behind* at the quarter and fell farther behind as the race progressed. On the lead, the numbers indicate lengths ahead of the other horses; when not on the lead, the numbers indicate lengths behind the leader. I allow about one fifth of a second for every length, which will give you also a rough idea of how fast the horse can run when he doesn't have the lead. Still, you'd do better to rely on the Beyer numbers, which are far more sophisticated and take into account such factors as the condition of the track.

The distance, surface, and conditions of the race are very important to your handicapping health. According to his chart, Tobin Ruler has competed at distances ranging from five and a half furlongs, which is just under three quarters of a mile, to a mile and a sixteenth, mostly on dirt surfaces. (A furlong is one eighth of a mile.) Outside of the United States, Thoroughbreds compete mainly on grass, the animal's natural terrain, but in this country most races are run on dirt. The turf courses, which require more maintenance and can't be run on too often, are usually reserved for the better animals on the grounds. Tobin Ruler's lone effort on turf, indicated by the symbol ⓣ, was unsuccessful, though, as usual, he showed early speed.

If it's been raining, you'd want to check the condition of the track on the days he's run, as some horses can't handle anything but a fast surface, while others may have proven to be "mudlarks," horses that love the goo, the sloppier the better. Tobin Ruler clearly doesn't like an "off-track," having finished out of the money on two wet surfaces, January 28 and March 11. I'll have more to say about this kind of racing later.

A final word now about "Workouts," the line at the bottom of the chart. These statistics provide information regarding the process of conditioning to which the animal has been subjected. More important than the time of the workout is how fast the horse ran in relation to all of the other horses working at the same distance that morning. This is the last figure for each date. For example, Tobin Ruler last worked on August 26, finishing eighth out of the fourteen animals that trained at the distance, three furlongs (three eighths of a mile). This is the only workout you need to pay some attention to here, because it's the only one showing for Tobin Ruler since his last race.

Workout figures can be useful to you, but they're approximate and may not reflect the animal's real ability or lack of it. We aren't told who was on the horse at the time, whether it was a jockey or an exercise rider, some of whom can weigh up to a hundred and thirty pounds. This is the sort of weight that can trim a second or two off the final time. Some trainers like to work their horses fast, others don't. Every conditioner has his own set of criteria and methods for bringing his charge up to a race. If you aren't familiar with a trainer's style, you had best consider the workout line with a highly skeptical eye, especially outside of California. Only in the West are the numbers at all reliable; in the East you'd do better to ignore them entirely.

Now that you know how to read a past-performance

chart, you'll be able easily to decipher the other kind of chart published by the *Racing Form*. This is the chart of what happened in the race itself that the *Form* publishes in subsequent editions, usually two or three days after the event. It looks like this:

FIFTH RACE				
Del Mar				
AUGUST 30, 1996				

FIFTH RACE — 1¹⁄₁₆ MILES. (1.40) CLAIMING. Purse $12,000. 3–year–olds and upward. Weights: 3–year–olds, 118 lbs. Older, 122 lbs. Non–winners of two races at one mile or over since July 15, allowed 3 lbs. Of such a race since August 1, 5 lbs. Claiming price $10,000. (Maiden or races when entered for $8,500 or less not considered.)

Value of Race: $12,000 Winner $6,600; second $2,400; third $1,800; fourth $900; fifth $300. Mutuel Pool $349,807.90 Exacta Pool $258,021.00 Trifecta Pool $300,599.00 Quinella Pool $48,317.00

Last Raced	Horse	M/Eqt A.Wt	PP	St	¼	½	¾	Str	Fin	Jockey	Cl'g Pr	Odds $1
28Jly96 2Dmr10	Tobin Ruler	LBb 5.117	1	2	1¹	11½	1²	13½	1⁴	Hunter M T	10000	9.90
29Jly96 9Dmr7	Win The Case	LBb 5 117	4	9	8¹	92½	6⁴	5hd	2½	Desormeaux K J	10000	4.40
17Aug96 10Dmr6	Cutlass Pro	LBb 4 117	6	1	3½	3¹	32½	2hd	3½	Douglas R R	10000	5.50
3Aug96 1Dmr8	Hidden Resource	LBb 4 117	5	11	1²	11hd	9⁴	7²	4²	Gonzalez S Jr	10000	70.40
16Aug96 8Dmr5	Steps In Time	LBb 4 117	2	5	4²	2hd	2½	31½	5¹	Espinoza V	10000	6.50
28Jly96 2Dmr11	Vasarelli–IR	LB 7 117	9	12	10⁵	8hd	5¹	6¹	6²	Almeida G F	10000	27.90
3Aug96 1Dmr5	Ninth Fleet	LBb 5 117	10	8	51½	5³	4¹	4¹	7³	Valenzuela P A	10000	3.90
17Aug96 10Dmr7	Aspen Run	LB 8 117	7	6	7½	7½	7½	9⁶	8½	Black C A	10000	8.90
7Jan95 4SA9	Lanky Lord	LBf 7 117	3	4	61½	6¹	8¹	8²	910	Pedroza M A	10000	26.70
17Aug96 10Dmr5	Clever Talk	LBb 4 117	8	3	9¹	10³	12	118	10²	Antley C W	10000	*3.90
11Jly96 2Hol6	Desert Bronze	LBbf 5 117	12	10	11²	12	101½	10hd1123		Berrio O A	10000	a–26.50
7Aug96 2Dmr6	Gas Man	LBbf 8 117	11	7	2hd	4²	111	12	12	Atherton J E	10000	a–26.50

*—Actual Betting Favorite.
a–Coupled: Desert Bronze and Gas Man.

OFF AT 4:06 Start Good. Won driving. Time, :22³, :45⁴, 1:10², 1:36⁴, 1:44 Track fast.

$2 Mutuel Prices:	2–TOBIN RULER	21.80	11.00	7.20
	5–WIN THE CASE		5.80	3.60
	7–CUTLASS PRO			4.40

$2 EXACTA 2–5 PAID $131.00 $2 TRIFECTA 2–5–7 PAID $740.40 $2 QUINELLA 2–5 PAID $63.60

Dk. b. or br. g, by J. O. Tobin–Leaping Princess, by Cornish Prince. Trainer Peterson Douglas R. Bred by Randal Mr & Mrs Robert D (Cal).

TOBIN RULER came out a bit while being sent to the early lead, set the pace along the inside and won clear under steady handling. WIN THE CASE was inside ASPEN RUN early, came off the rail leaving the second turn, angled out into the stretch and just got the place. CUTLASS PRO was under a tight hold between rivals on the first turn, attended the pace outside STEPS IN TIME to the stretch and just lost second. HIDDEN RESOURCE was off a bit slowly, saved ground off the pace to the second turn, came out for the stretch with a late bid. STEPS IN TIME steadied slightly early, saved ground just behind the pace to the stretch and weakened. A claim of foul by the rider of STEPS IN TIME against the winner for alleged interference after the start was not allowed by the stewards, who ruled the video tape did not substantiate the claim. VASARELLI broke awkwardly, settled off the rail, came outside NINTH FLEET on the second turn and lacked a further response. NINTH FLEET five wide into the first turn, angled to the rail leaving the backstretch, remained inside, steadied in deep stretch and weakened. A claim of foul by the rider of NINTH FLEET against STEPS IN TIME for alleged interference late also was not allowed for the same reason. ASPEN RUN outside WIN THE CASE early, failed to menace. LANKY LORD raced toward the inside and gave way. CLEVER TALK lugged out into the first turn and raced wide. DESERT BRONZE was never close. GAS MAN forced the pace three deep after being four wide into the first turn and gave way badly after a half mile.

Owners— 1, Anson Ronald & Susie; 2, Salter Brett; 3, Fink Charles G; 4, Wira Richard; 5, Keh & Knudson; 6, Baker & Duffield; 7, Belzberg Linda; 8, Mascari James E; 9, Neyman Brady; 10, Rockin A Ranch; 11, Aldabbagh Sam H; 12, Aldabbagh Sam H

Trainers— 1, Peterson Douglas R; 2, Olivares Frank; 3, Van Berg Jack C; 4, Marini James V Jr; 5, Marshall Robert W; 6, Baker James R; 7, Lloyd Kim; 8, Mascari James E; 9, Koriner Brian; 10, Kruljac J Eric; 11, Aldabbagh Sam H; 12, Aldabbagh Sam H

Win The Case was claimed by Kelley Cyndi; trainer, Kelley Cyndi.
Clever Talk was claimed by Stein Roger M; trainer, Stein Roger M.
Scratched— Major Funding (10Aug96 2DMR5), Trophy Time (17Aug96 10DMR10)

$3 Pick Three (6–8–2) Paid $1,642.20; Pick Three Pool $129,636.

As you can see, Tobin Ruler proceeded to win the next race of his career, at the delicious odds of nearly ten to one. Could he have been played? Absolutely. I was there that day and had ten dollars on him to win, even though my pick-three attempt failed to complete. The reason I liked him was his speed. Every race on his past-performance chart revealed that he was an animal who needed to get to the front early in order to be competitive. On July 5, after a two-month break, he had returned to the racing wars against much cheaper horses than he had ever faced before and won easily, posting an excellent Beyer fig of 86. In his next race, on July 28, he had failed to get the lead, then dropped back to next to last. But the horses he had gone up against that day had been too tough for him. Both Wolf Creek and Auriga were classy competitors fallen on hard times, but who figured to beat Tobin Ruler, especially since Wolf Creek, another horse coming back off a long layoff, had shown superior speed in the past.

For the contest on August 30, I expected Tobin Ruler to be all alone on the lead, since he had the speed of a sprinter and the race was being run at a longer distance. Speed horses can get courageous when they bounce out there on the lead all by themselves and are not being pushed too hard early by their riders. This is exactly what happened and the reason Tobin Ruler was overlooked by the bettors is that, having failed to win going short, how could he be expected not to tire going long? A natural human reasoning process and, of course, all wrong at the racetrack. Some of the best bets you'll ever make are on horses stretching out to a mile or more after showing speed but tiring in sprints.

From looking at the chart of this race, you should have a pretty good picture of how it was run. Of particular importance in these accounts are the placings of the horses in relation to the fractional times set by the animal in front at various points in the race. (The margins here indicate how far each animal is *ahead* of the one behind him.) Also useful are the comments written by the chart caller on how each horse performed, especially if one or more of the competitors experienced trouble during the running of the race.

There are handicappers who base their betting action entirely on what is known as the trip factor. What sort of trip did the horse have in his last race? they ask themselves. Did he stumble or take up out of the gate? Was he pinched back between horses on the turn? Was he blocked on the inside when he tried to make a move? Was he forced wide around both turns? Was he bumped off stride and forced to steady, which is what happened to Steps in Time?

All these considerations and many others are essential knowledge to the trip handicapper, who will routinely collect and save all of his race charts and base his action on what he learns from them. If you decide to become a full-time horse-player, you will discover that the racetrack has made a magpie of you. No detail, no tiny item of information, will seem too minute or unimportant to be preserved, weighed, and computed into your final betting calculations. Welcome to the wonderful wacky world of statistics, endlessly preserved in the many hundreds of charts going back at least several years that you will pile up in corners or paste into notebooks or load into your computer.

Someone once estimated that there are at least several hundred factors that have to be considered whenever you sit down to handicap a race. Maybe so, but is it worth such an effort? Not unless the rest of your life means nothing to you. There are people who derive exquisite pleasure from staring endlessly at numbers, but I'm not one of them. Unraveling the puzzle that each race represents is part of the fun of going to the races, but it shouldn't take up all of your time nor does it need to. What I suggest you now develop is a basic handicapping method and betting strategy that will yield sizable profits on good days and will not impoverish you on bad ones. The whole trick at the track, as every dedicated horseplayer knows, is to stay alive.

Andy Beyer tells a great story about when Harry S Truman died during the course of a racing day at one of the Maryland tracks. The announcer informed the public of this unhappy event. Our beloved ex-President had expired that afternoon at his home in Independence, Missouri, the announcer intoned, where he was to be buried the following day. The announcer then asked the crowd to rise and to observe a moment of silence in honor of our fallen hero. As the throng stood quietly in place, a plaintive cry rang out from some despairing railbird below. "Fuck Harry S Truman," the voice proclaimed, "I'm getting buried right here!"

Getting buried is what happens to too many horseplayers every day at the track. Your concern is to remain above ground.

A Fun Day: Winning
at Santa Anita

The best day at any racetrack is the one during which you've cashed the most tickets. It's all very well to maintain, as I have, that a losing day can also be fun, but on those occasions you're likely to leave the premises with at least a slightly sour taste in your mouth. You look back over the races you should have passed, the bets you shouldn't have made, the winners that shouldn't have eluded you, and, worst of all, the mistakes in betting strategies that have cost you dearly. I vividly still remember a day back in the 1950s when I chose to pay a visit with a couple of friends to Monmouth Park, on the New Jersey shore, by taking a boat from lower Manhattan. It was a glorious day and the two-hour ride passed quickly, a laugher all the way. Then came the races, at which we failed to cash a single ticket. The boat trip back seemed interminable, a grim voyage down the river Styx with Charon at the oars. Even the splendid sunset we witnessed seemed an insult. We hardly exchanged a word as we rode glumly back uptown on the subway, our wallets as empty as our hearts.

Because this is a book about having fun, I've chosen to take you through a winning day. Not a spectacular one and free of errors, but one I like to think of as ordinary. The place is Santa Anita Park and the date is October 10, 1996, the seventh day of the Oak Tree Association's fall meet. It's one of my favorite times of the year to go racing, because it hardly ever rains in Southern California in the fall and the track surfaces are fairly constant, mostly favoring speed on both dirt and grass. The card consists of nine races, ranging in quality from cheap to fairly decent and in distance from six furlongs to a mile and a sixteenth, with the best race contested on the turf course. It's a typical card on a typical day at one of the most beautiful hippodromes in the country. What better way to break your maiden at the races? It's nearly post time, so let's have a look at the first race. Flip to pages 106–109, and take a quick glance at the chart.

■   RACE 1: One of the best ways to handicap any race is to eliminate the horses that have little or no chance to win. Unfortunately, in this particular race it's not so easy to do. Cee's Maryanne, a logical contender, has been scratched prior to post time, meaning either that her connections have decided to take her out of the race, perhaps because they think the contest is too tough and they want to find an easier spot for her, or that she's been removed from it for some physical reason. This helps a little, but it reduces the field to six horses, only one of whom I can throw out.

This is Check Request, the only three-year-old in the

race, who has been running poorly of late and showing no speed. Take note of the comment next to her chart by Randy Franklin, one of the *Form*'s staff handicappers, who also thinks little of her chances. Apropos of his assessment, we'll come back to these comments later, as to whether we should pay much attention to them in our calculations.

The only other horse we can think about eliminating here is Sidepocketsue, who also has no speed and whose Beyer figs are relatively low. I decided not to, mainly because her jockey, Kent Desormeaux, is riding for his brother Keith, the animal's trainer, a guarantee he'll be trying hard to win. More important is the fact that, of this mare's seven lifetime wins, five have been at this distance and two of them at Santa Anita. She has no speed and I don't like to bet on so-called closing sprinters, but I can't throw her out.

In fact, the longer we look at the race, the more difficult it becomes to find a bet. Persistant Sal picks up a good jockey, has speed, likes Santa Anita, has a good lifetime record, and has been lightly raced since January. But she's mired on the rail, where she could be shuffled back by the three speed horses outside her or forced by them to run too fast early. Most horses can only run at top speed about three eighths of a mile. Where they use that speed is one of the keys to winning. Persistant Sal doesn't have enough of it to guarantee she'll clear her competitors and she doesn't really want to run from too far off the pace.

As for the other contenders, Lite 'n Comfy has a ton of speed but has been competing against much cheaper horses and her highest Beyer is an 87. Dangerous and game, but no thanks. Garden Of Roses is the class of the race, but she hasn't run since August, her last was very poor, and the drop in class is suspicious. Also, most of those races have been up north,

1 Santa Anita Park

6 Furlongs (1:071) **CLAIMING.** Purse $30,000. Fillies and mares, 3-year-olds and upward. Weights: 3-year-olds, 120 lbs. Older, 122 lbs. Non-winners of two races since August 1, allowed 3 lbs. Of a race since September 1, 5 lbs. Claiming price $40,000; if for $35,000, allowed 2 lbs. (Maiden or races when entered for $32,000 or less not considered.)

START
6 FURLONGS
FINISH

Coupled - Lite 'n Comfy and Cee's Maryanne

Persistant Sal

Own: Alsdorf & Coelho & Valenti
$40,000
ANTLEY C W (2 0 0 0 .00) 1996:(699 106 .15)

B. m. 5
Sire: The Irish Lord (Bold Ruler)
Dam: Borntobecourageous (Native Prospector)
Br: Coelho John & Valenti Peter (Cal)
Tr: Sadler John W (7 0 1 0 .00) 1996:(211 26 .12)

L 117

Lifetime Record :	12 4 3 2	$127,937			
1996	3 0 3 0	$21,410	Turf	0 0 0 0	
1995	6 2 0 2	$61,075	Wet	1 0 1 0	$7,400
SA	3 1 1 0	$31,825	Dist	6 1 2 1	$48,185

29Sep96- 8Fpx fst 6f :214 :451 :582 1:12 3↑ⒻClm 40000 77 4 6 22½ 44 22 31 Sorenson D LB 116 *1.50 88-09 [D]Monterey Gold1161 Promo Tape116hd Persistant Sal116nk 9
In tight 1/4; steadied 1/16 Placed second through disqualification.
26Aug96- 7Dmr fst 6f :214 :444 :572 1:101 3↑ⒻClm 45000 83 2 4 1½ 11½ 11 22½ McCarron C J LB 115 2.40 85-17 Dezibelle's Star1172½ PersistantSal1153¾ ChattaCode117½ Inside, 2nd best 7
31Jan96- 1SA sly 5½f :211 :433 :554 1:021 4↑ⒻClm 40000 89 1 6 31½ 21½ 32½ 25 McCarron C J LB 117 2.30 94-12 Chief Charley1175 Persistant Sal1171½ Silent Lord1192¼ Inside trip 6
30Dec95- 3SA fst 6f :211 :441 :563 1:094 3↑ⒻClm 57500 79 4 1 31½ 32½ 31½ 43 McCarron C J LB 117 *2.20 85-08 Eureka Lass117¾ Valid Symmetry113hd Gorky Square1162 No late bid 6
2Dec95- 3Hol fst 6f :222 :453 :571 1:093 3↑ⒻClm 50000 89 4 2 21 21 21½ 32¼ Stevens G L LB 119 *.90 90-09 Silent Lord1181¾ Chemainus112½ Persistant Sal1191¼ 5
Broke thru gate, rail bid
5Nov95- 3SA fst 5½f :22 :45 :564 1:031 3↑ⒻClm 62500 97 2 4 22 21½ 1½ 1no Stevens G L LB 117 *1.00 94-13 Persistant Sal117no Cee's Maryanne1172½ Ballasecret1163 Game inside 5
18Sep95-11Fpx fst 6½f :222 :454 1:10 1:162 3↑Ⓕ[R]Pio Pico49k 87 6 2 2½ 2hd 22 34¼ Castro J M LB 122 3.60 92-10 Salta's Pride1222½ Dezibelle's Star1152 Persistant Sal122hd Weakened 7
2Sep95- 7Dmr fst 6f :214 :441 :562 1:084 3↑Ⓕ[R]June Darling H76k 77 9 4 2hd 2hd 21 99 Stevens G L LB 115 *1.70 88-07 Miss L Attack115no Airistar116½ Sophisticatedcielo1161¼ 9
Hopped, veered out start
9Aug95- 3Dmr fst 6f :212 :444 :564 1:092 3↑ⒻAlw 47000N2x 89 6 1 21½ 21 12½ 12¾ Stevens G L LB 117 *1.10 94-07 Persistant Sal1172¾ Snowy's Mark1171¾ That'll Be Fine117½ Ridden out 6
16Sep94-12Fpx fst 6½f :211 :444 1:11 1:173 Ⓕ[R]Las Ninas48k 77 4 3 2½ 2hd 21 43 Flores D R LB 117 *.80 86-13 MlibuLight1171½ GmblingMistrss1171 KlssyKim120½ Drifted out bit 4 1/2 5

WORKOUTS: Sep26 SA 3f fst :372 H 6/8 Sep20 SA 6f fst 1:132 H 4/19 Sep14 SA 5f fst 1:021 H 25/37 Sep6 Dmr 4f fst :492 H 28/48 Aug18 Dmr 4f fst :47 H 3/58 Aug11 Dmr 5f fst 1:001 H 9/55

Sidepocketsue

Own: Lagniappe Stables Inc
$40,000
DESORMEAUX K J (21 2 2 3 .10) 1996:(818 147 .18)

Dk. b or br m. 6
Sire: Mike Fogarty*Ire (Royal and Regal)
Dam: Carols Dewan (Dewan)
Br: Sardo Tony (Cal)
Tr: Desormeaux J Keith (1 0 0 1 .00) 1996:(50 9 .18)

L 117

Lifetime Record :	48 7 10 6	$216,280			
1996	11 2 1 2	$55,473	Turf	4 0 0 1	$8,850
1995	10 0 1 1	$22,150	Wet	4 1 1 1	$28,450
SA	14 2 2 3	$68,025	Dist	23 5 6 5	$135,430

29Sep96- 8Fpx fst 6f :214 :451 :582 1:12 3↑ⒻClm 40000 77 6 8 910 78 77½ 41½ Atkinson P LB 116 b 9.80 88-09 [D]Monterey Gold1161 Promo Tape116hd Persistant Sal116nk Wide rally 9
14Sep96-10Fpx fst 6f :22 :454 :584 1:113 3↑ⒻClm 32000 79 6 6 69½ 55½ 32½ 11 Black C A LB 116 b 4.50 91-12 Sidepocketsue1161 PromoTpe1162 Cee'sMrynne1166 Strong wide rally 6
30Aug96- 1Dmr fst 1 :224 :462 1:111 1:371 3↑ⒻClm 32000 69 1 5 44 43 53½ 58 Desormeaux K J LB 117 b 4.90 76-21 Saucy Lady B1172 HighDecision116½ CracklingSike1175 4 wide into lane 6
4Aug96- 1Dmr fst 6½f :214 :443 1:101 1:163 3↑ⒻClm c-25000 80 6 9 99½ 87¼ 53¼ 23 Pincay L Jr LB 117 fb 8.50 85-11 Sarita Sarita1173 Sidepocketsue117hd Queen Gen1174 Wide into lane 9
Claimed from Sardo Tony, Dolan John K Trainer
5Jun96- 1Hol fst 6f :222 :45 :564 1:091 4↑ⒻClm 32000 72 1 6 69¼ 610 67½ 48¾ Douglas R R LB 118 b 9.70 84-11 Hemet Eagle1166 Missoula Lula1171½ Binthar Dundat1161½ Off step slow 6
15May96- 6Hol fst 6f :214 :451 :573 1:102 4↑ⒻClm 32000 81 7 8 912 89½ 56½ 1no Douglas R R LB 116 b 15.60 87-13 Sidepocketsue116no Binthar Dundat116no Tiny Boots111½ 9
Lost whip into lane; goggle urging, wide rally
18Apr96- 7SA fm *6½f Ⓣ :221 :45 1:092 1:154 4↑ⒻClm 45000 80 3 6 612 513 56¼ 42 Douglas R R LB 114 b 8.70 79-19 ExpensiveStar109½ HllelujhAngel116nk BinthrDundt1141½ Drifted out lane 6
27Mar96- 5SA fst 6f :214 :444 :571 1:102 4↑ⒻClm 20000 77 5 7 710 79 66½ 62½ Douglas R R LB 116 b 6.80 83-16 Really Talented116no It's Ben Freezing113½ Icy Luck1161½ Mild bid 7
7Mar96- 3BM fst 6f :222 :444 :563 1:091 4↑ⒻClm 25000 79 1 4 58½ 57½ 55½ 32¼ Valdivia J5 LB 113 b 4.30 93-09 Lika Pirate1162 Slyce116nk Sidepocketsue1131 Rallied wide drive 5
28Jan96- 7SA fst 6f :213 :442 :564 1:102 4↑ⒻClm 20000 78 6 8 911 910 88¾ 31½ Douglas R R LB 117 b 9.00 84-15 'Tiz Free116½ Star Sign1171 Sidepocketsue1171 Late bid 9

WORKOUTS: Aug13 Dmr 4f fst :48 H 20/49 Jly20 SA 4f fst :482 H 5/16

A CLOSER LOOK

1st Santa Anita

Persistant Sal

Inclined to pretty much toss the Fair affair as mare had mega trouble; she's capable this level, capable from on or off the pace; Beyerwise a strong fit as well; quick return means she's okay fitness-wise; tripwise can't help but be in a good spot as she's speed without any speed in the stalls to her right; consider.

Sidepocketsue

Didn't have any trouble when last seen in actually a slowish race for the level at the Fair; mare can overrun foes on her best day, even proven capable winwise at this track; but her off-pace style just doesn't enthuse, and the pace here might not be all that hot; minor award could be the ceiling.

Check Request
Own: Glen Hill Farm
$40,000
VALENZUELA P A (33 2 5 4 .06) 1996:(491 60 .12)

Dk. b or br f. 3 (Apr)
Sire: Sovereign Dancer (Northern Dancer)
Dam: Segovie (Targowice*Fr)
Br: Glen Hill Farm (Fla)
Tr: Proctor Willard L (2 1 0 0 .50) 1996:(41 2 .05)
L 115

Lifetime Record:	8 1 0 1	$25,975			
1996	8 1 0 1	$25,975	Turf	3 0 0 1	$5,925
1995	0 M 0 0		Wet	0 0 0 0	
SA	3 1 0 0	$16,900	Dist	2 1 0 0	$16,900

1Sep96-4Dmr fst 6½f :214 :444 1:094 1:163 ⒻClm 50000 69 9 11 1010 97¾ 119¼ 98¼ Valenzuela P A L 116 b 23.00 79-13 AvenueShopper116½ Lurinburg1161¼ HonyBGood1184 Reared start, wide 11
5Aug96-7Dmr fst 6½f :22 :442 1:091 1:153 ⒻClm 50000 74 1 12 1210 109¼ 79 49 Delahoussaye E LB 116 b 28.00 84-09 Himiko1161¼ Imllzeledup1166¾ OurGoldnPromis1161 Slow, awkward start 12
11Jly96-7Hol fm 1 Ⓣ :232 :47 1:104 1:353 ⒻAlw 39500N1X 63 11 5 51¾ 63¾ 1212 1212 Flores D R L 117 b 37.60 73-15 Closed Escrow119hd Hilary1193¾ Slide By119no Gave way 12
8Jun96-4Hol fm 1 Ⓣ :232 :464 1:11 1:351 3↑ ⒻAlw 39500N1X 82 1 2 23 21½ 32 33¾ Nakatani C S L 113 b 11.00 83-15 MissExcitement1182¾ OklahomMorn1201¼ CheckRequest113no Inside trip 7
12May96-6Hol fm 1⅙ Ⓣ :234 :471 1:111 1:413 ⒻAlw 43000N1X 68 1 5 89¾ 97¼ 86¼ 89¼ Stevens G L L 117 10.80 78-08 Rumpipumpy1211¼ Slide By1192¼ Little Gumpher119¾ 10
Rank early, lugged out badly 1st turn
19Apr96-7SA fst 6f :213 :442 :564 1:094 ⒻAlw 42000N1X 76 3 7 77¼ 68¼ 56¼ 45¾ Douglas R R L 115 30.30 83-13 Tiffany Diamond117¾ Citi Nites1173 Ghibelline1152 Mild bid 7
20Mar96-2SA fst 6f :223 :46 :581 1:103 ⒻMd 45000 75 4 2 1½ 2hd 1½ 12½ Stevens G L L 115 3.40 85-15 Check Request1152½ Ahtena1171 Rose Cafe1101½ Ridden out 6
14Feb96-6SA fst 6½f :221 :452 1:11 1:172 ⒻMd 50000 57 6 4 11½ 11½ 32 68¾ Valenzuela F H B 117 b 22.10 74-18 Toot Sweet1174 B J Ballet115hd Main Attraction117no Lost footing 8
WORKOUTS: Sep30 SA 4f fst :494 H 27/35 Sep22 SA 5f fst 1:013 H 26/46 Sep13 SA tr.t 3f fst :364 H 4/5 Aug26 Dmr 4f fst :491 H 51/74 Aug17 Dmr 4f fst :502 H 47/55 Jly24 Dmr 4f fst :49 H 21/49

Check Request

Trainer has had a very poor year; starts filly against her elders while trying to find her proper class level; Beyerwise this one just doesn't seem to fit with these but her form could be clouded via the poor starts the last pair; price possibility?; she just doesn't look all that appealing.

Lite 'n Comfy
Own: Three Point Stable Inc
$40,000
STEVENS G L (9 3 1 1 .33) 1996:(553 115 .21)

B. m. 5
Sire: Kennedy Road (Victoria Park)
Dam: Finest Feathers (Silveyville)
Br: Headley & Old English Rancho & Pagliuso (Cal)
Tr: Marshall Robert W (3 1 1 0 .33) 1996:(139 25 .18)
L 119

Lifetime Record:	21 8 4 0	$132,750			
1996	12 6 2 0	$78,950	Turf	1 0 0 0	
1995	9 2 2 0	$53,800	Wet	0 0 0 0	
SA	2 0 1 0	$6,775	Dist	10 5 3 0	$73,925

27Sep96-12Fpx fst 6f :214 :452 :581 1:111 3↑ ⒻAlw 10000s 82 6 3 53 1hd 11½ 11 Flores D R LB 121 *1.00 93-08 Lite 'n Comfy1211 Sham Pain1151 Erinova1152 Gamely held 7
16Sep96-10Fpx fst 6f :213 :451 :583 1:113 3↑ ⒻAlw 36000N2X 82 4 6 55¼ 31½ 11½ 1no Flores D R LB 121 7.70 91-10 Lite 'n Comfy121no Hemet Eagle1211¼ Choice Blend118¾ 10
Drifted out, bumped at wire
31Aug96-3Dmr fst 6½f :22 :45 1:094 1:162 3↑ ⒻClm c-25000 87 3 1 31½ 41¾ 31 1½ Desormeaux K J LB 117 *.80 89-13 Lite'nComfy117½ QueenGen1171 CarolsWorld1171½ Bobbled strt,4-wd 1/4 7
Claimed from Hutton William, Lewis Craig A Trainer
17Aug96-1Dmr fst 6f :221 :451 :573 1:101 3↑ ⒻClm c-20000 84 8 2 41½ 31 2hd 2½ Antley C W LB 117 *1.00 87-12 Smiling Lass117½ Lite 'n Comfy1172 Slyce117½ 4 wide,led late,caught 8
Claimed from Pacifica West Stables, Spawr Bill Trainer
3Aug96-2Dmr fst 7f :223 :451 1:093 1:224 3↑ ⒻClm c-16000 87 8 1 11 12½ 14½ 11¾ Antley C W LB 117 *2.40 86-08 Lite 'n Comfy1171¾ Aerosal1173¼ Facultative Lady1172 Clearly best 8
Claimed from Henderson & Huston & Wolkoff, Abrams Barry Trainer
19Jly96-7Hol fst 6f :222 :451 :573 1:101 4↑ ⒻClm 18000 83 6 1 32 31½ 2hd 2nk Antley C W LB 115 2.60 88-13 DnsLingo116nk Lite'nComfy1152¼ EnjoyTheView1162 Led, caught on wire 6
10Jly96-3Hol fst 6f :22 :452 :574 1:104 4↑ Ⓕ[S]Clm c-10000 81 3 2 23½ 23 2½ 14½ Delahoussaye E LB 116 *1.50 85-16 Lite 'n Comfy1164½ Damsela1162½ Leggy Lisa11610 Ridden out 5
Claimed from Becker & Owens & Smith, Robbins Jay M Trainer
15Jun96-9GG fm 1⅙ Ⓣ :234 :48 1:121 1:451 + 4↑ ⒻClm 16000 57 6 2 21½ 33 67 810½ Warren R J Jr LB 116 8.00 70-17 Lotta Zoom1161 Double Jewel116½ Country Lass1183 Stopped 8
29May96-7Hol fst 7½f :22 :45 1:10 1:294 4↑ ⒻClm 25000 59 1 2 33 31½ 55 610½ Flores D R LB 117 24.30 74-13 Falstaff's Issue1161 Binthar Dundat1161½ Sarita Sarita1162½ Gave way 7
13May96-4Hol fst 1⅙ :222 :461 1:104 1:44 4↑ ⒻAlw 16000s 62 4 2 32½ 55½ 56½ 59¾ Black C A LB 116 9.00 71-15 Made Of Jade1151½ My Miss Ilse119¾ Response1102 Gave way 8
WORKOUTS: Sep23 Hol 5f fst 1:022 H 21/36 ●Aug25 Dmr 4f fst :46 H 1/60

Lite 'n Comfy

On a roll these days; mare is a gamer, can race from on or off the pace; classwise seems a fit with these and this isn't the strongest field in the world for the level; pacewise figures to get a good trip from just off; obviously the stronger part of the entry and tough to take a stand against.

continued

Garden Of Roses

Own: Golden Eagle Farm
$40,000
SOLIS A (30 5 5 6 .17) 1996:(1087 198 .18)

Ch. m. 5
Sire: Half a Year (Riverman)
Dam: Laura's Bouquet (Beau's Eagle)
Br: Mabee Mr & Mrs John C (Cal)
Tr: Carava Jack (3 0 0 2 .00) 1996:(333 53 .16)

L 117

Lifetime Record : 21 8 3 3 $167,285

1996	3	1	1	0	$23,000	Turf	0	0	0	0	
1995	10	3	2	2	$84,175	Wet	3	2	0	1	$27,800
SA	2	1	0	0	$9,900	Dist	17	5	3	2	$124,125

1Aug96-9SR fst 6f :22 :442 :572 1:093 3↑ⒻE Destruel H31k 52 8 1 2½ 21½ 49 814 Chapman T M LB 116 fb 4.40 79-07 O'hacco1162 Salta's Pride1192½ Truce In Balance1171 Speed, stopped 8
29Jun96-10Pln fst 6f :212 :44 :56 1:091 3↑ⒻAlw 30450NC 88 4 2 1½ 12 12 11 Chapman T M LB 115 b 4.70 95-08 Garden Of Roses1151 Baby Shea1162¼ Just Plain Fancy117¾ Held gamely 9
24May96-6GG fst 6f :214 :443 :571 1:102 3↑ⒻClm 65000 88 1 3 11 12 11 1hd Chapman T M LB 116 b 3.40 87-16 ⒹGarden Of Roses116hd Left The Latch121¾ Baby Shea1166 Drifted out 6
Disqualified and placed second
19Nov95-8GG fst 6f :213 :441 :563 1:091 3↑ⒻArchesOGoldH35k 77 4 2 3½ 3½ 22 47 Chapman T M LB 114 b 9.60 86-11 Airistar1172 Truce In Balance1162 Lethal Leta1173 Wide, gave way 5
25Aug95-8BM fst 6f :214 :442 :57 1:102 3↑ⒻⓇFlagIsUpFrmH35k 55 8 1 31½ 41¾ 87½ 1014½ Chapman T M LB 117 b 7.50e 74-13 Sportful Snob119¾ Monterey Gold1151½ Tiny Boots1151½ Wide, stopped 11
2Aug95-11SR fst 6f :214 :442 :563 1:093 3↑ⒻE Destruel H32k 86 2 2 1½ 1½ 1hd 32 Warren R J Jr LB 120 b 2.40 94-04 Shu Biz Annie1131 Isleo Bebe1161 Garden Of Roses120hd Weakened late 7
2Jly95-7Pln fst 6f :221 :444 :564 1:093 3↑ⒻAlw 29400C 93 1 1 11 11 1½ 1hd Chapman T M LB 118 b 1.80e 90-10 Garden Of Roses118hd Beautiful Gem114¾ Tina Fleet1163 Held gamely 6
13May95-8GG sly 6f :214 :444 :57 1:093 3↑ⒻLuisant H35k 88 4 2 11½ 1hd 31½ 34¼ Chapman T M LB 115 fb *1.10e 87-14 Run AwayStevie1163½ BeautifulGem114¾ GardenOfRoses11510 Weakened 5
28Apr95-7GG fst 6f :212 :441 :57 1:094 4↑ⒻArchesOfGldH35k 61 1 1 1hd 2hd 54 612¼ Chapman T M LB 116 b *1.70 78-14 Jessie Janey1172¼ BabyShea116hd BonneNuite1162½ Angled out midstretch 6
9Apr95-8BM fst 6f :222 :452 :574 1:102 3↑ⒻⓈB M Matron H54k 94 6 1 11 12 11 2½ Chapman T M LB 115 b 3.60 88-16 Flying In The Lane119½ Garden Of Roses1155 Baby Shea116½ Held well 7

WORKOUTS: Oct2 Hol 5f fst 1:002 H 3/33 Sep25 Hol 5f fst 1:011 H 10/30 Sep18 Hol 5f fst :591 H 3/33 ●Sep10 SLR tr.t 5f fst 1:00 H 1/10 Sep2 Dmr 4f fst :493 H 39/66 Aug26 SLR tr.t 5f fst 1:00 H 3/15

Cee's Maryanne

Own: Three Point Stable Inc
$40,000
DELAHOUSSAYE E (17 4 2 6 .24) 1996:(800 134 .17)

Ch. m. 5
Sire: Naevus (Mr. Prospector)
Dam: Marraine (Paderoso)
Br: Straub-Rubens Cecilia (Ky)
Tr: Marshall Robert W (3 1 1 0 .33) 1996:(139 25 .18)

L 117

Lifetime Record : 28 5 8 7 $221,925

1996	10	1	3	2	$72,970	Turf	5	0	0	2	$21,150
1995	12	3	3	3	$105,925	Wet	2	0	1	1	$14,700
SA	7	2	3	1	$76,300	Dist	14	3	3	4	$112,925

14Sep96-10Fpx fst 6f :22 :454 :584 1:113 3↑ⒻClm 32000 71 3 4 43½ 31 22 33 Espinoza V LB 116 b 3.30 88-12 Sidepocketsue1161 PromoTpe1162 Cee'sMrynn1166 Drifted out 1st turn 6
26Aug96-7Dmr fst 6f :214 :444 :572 1:101 3↑ⒻClm 50000 54 5 2 3½ 42 54½ 613¾ Nakatani C S LB 117 b 4.20 74-17 Dezibelle's Star1172½ Persistant Sal1153¾ Chatta Code117½ Wide into lane 7
2Aug96-3Dmr fst 6½f :221 :45 1:092 1:154 3↑ⒻClm c-40000 83 7 2 2hd 22 22½ 24 Delahoussaye E LB 117 b *1.20 88-08 BothWays1174 Cee'sMaryanne1171¼ JustPlainFncy1174½ Dueled, 2nd best 7
Claimed from Straub-rubens Cecilia P, Robbins Jay M Trainer
26Jun96-7Hol fst 7f :223 :451 1:091 1:212 3↑ⒻAlw 47000N3X 57 2 4 2½ 1hd 66½ 819 Nakatani C S LB 116 b 4.10 76-16 Dixie Pearl116¾ Texinadress1185½ Two NinetyJones116½ Inside, gave way 8
26May96-7Hol fst 7f :214 :442 1:091 1:221 4↑ⒻClm 80000 84 3 3 1hd 1hd 1hd 23 Nakatani C S LB 116 b *2.60 88-11 Above The Table1183 Cee'sMaryanne1161½ LagunaQueen116no Inside duel 8
3May96-8Hol fm 5½f Ⓣ :21 :43 :551 1:014 4↑ⒻClm 80000 85 1 4 24½ 28 36 43 Delahoussaye E LB 116 b 2.20 90-07 ChiefCharley1162¾ Ballasecret109nk MarfaSmerld117no Between foes lane 7
21Mar96-3SA fst 6½f :214 :444 1:093 1:16 4↑ⒻAlw 53000N3X 95 5 1 11 1½ 1hd 2hd Delahoussaye E LB 117 b 3.60 90-13 La Malpensada117hd Cee's Maryanne1173 Call Now1174 Caught on wire 6
29Feb96-3SA fst 6f :22 :444 :57 1:094 4↑ⒻClm 62500 98 5 1 2hd 2hd 11½ 1nk Delahoussaye E LB 117 b 3.70 89-18 Cee'sMaryanne117nk Wesley'sDelight1173 LagunQueen117nk Held gamely 8
9Feb96-6SA fm *6½f Ⓣ :213 :441 1:083 1:151 4↑ⒻClm 75000 87 10 2 2hd 2½ 3½ 3¾ Delahoussaye E LB 116 b 8.00 83-16 Ka Lae117nk Sunsamia116½ Cee's Maryanne116½ Willingly 10
11Jan96-6SA fm *6½f Ⓣ :222 :444 1:092 1:16 4↑ⒻClm 80000 89 3 2 1½ 21½ 33 42¼ Delahoussaye E LB 119 b 4.20 78-20 Bet Birdie1171¼ Phoenician Miss117½ Dezibelle's Star117½ Willingly 9

WORKOUTS: Oct4 Hol 5f fst 1:012 H 5/18 Sep28 Hol 4f fst :484 H 13/23 Sep8 Dmr 4f fst :492 H 25/40 Aug20 Dmr 5f fst 1:041 H 29/34 Aug14 Dmr 4f fst :511 H 43/46 Jly30 Dmr 4f fst :462 H 2/27

Garden Of Roses

A couple big Beyers on her card for this year and runner has proven capable fresh as well; perhaps the effort at Santa Rosa should be tossed as a vacation ensued?; maybe; the again, the 'for sale' sign is now out which could mean there's a leak in the boat; claim-bait?; possibly, and maybe those front wraps from last time should be taken into consideration.

Cee's Maryanne

Class drop looked like a giveaway a month ago and runner really wasn't all that good in a slowish heat; certainly isn't up to her old snuff from a Beyer standpoint, even lacked oomph since March; gets involved in the pace as a helpmate for Lite 'n Comfy?; maybe, but then again that one might not need any help at all.

Promo Tape

Own: Belmonte & Moll

$40,000

B. f. 4
Sire: Relaunch a Tune (Relaunch)
Dam: Atomic Eyes (Blue Eyed Davy)
Br: Sledge Stable (Cal)
Tr: Mitchell Mike (7 2 2 0 .29) 1996:(306 69 .23)

NAKATANI C S (20 5 5 0 .25) 1996:(866 191 .22)

L 119

Lifetime Record :	19	6	4	2	$145,197						
1996	7	2	1	1	$52,977	Turf	1	0	0	0	
1995	12	4	3	1	$92,220	Wet	0	0	0	0	
SA	3	1	1	0	$17,000	Dist	11	5	1	2	$104,777

29Sep96- 8Fpx fst 6f :214 :451 :582 1:12 3↑ Ⓕ Clm 40000 77 9 4 3½ 23 3½ 21 Toscano P R LB 116 b 5.10 88-09 [D] MontereyGold1161 PromoTpe116hd PersistntSl116nk Drifted in,out lane 9
Placed first through disqualification.
14Sep96-10Fpx fst 6f :22 :454 :584 1:113 3↑ Ⓕ Clm c-32000 76 4 2 21 11 12 21 Almeida G F LB 116 fb 2.90 90-12 Sidepocketsue1161 Promo Tape1162 Cee'sMaryanne1166 Bumped break 6
Claimed from Massengale & Massengale & Sledge St, Perdomo A Pico Trainer
16Aug96- 8Bmf fst 5½f :212 :443 :572 1:04 3↑ Ⓕ Alw 30920NC 82 3 4 1hd 2½ 32 43 Gonzalez R M LB 115 b 1.40 85-10 CarrieCan1161 MadeToPerfection115½ DncinAtTheWire1161½ Weakened 4
19Jly96- 8Hol fst 6f :214 :443 :57 1:094 3↑ Ⓕ [S] Alw 41500N2X 67 5 1 3½ 42 5½ 5¾ Flores D R LB 116 b 3.30 81-13 Seattle Carla1161¼ Hemet Eagle116½ Rapidlaunch1173 4 wide into lane 6
30Jun96- 6Hol fm 5½f Ⓣ :214 :441 :553 1:014 4↑ Ⓕ Clm 62500 84 2 1 1½ 1½ 2hd 64 Flores D R LB 116 b 10.30 89-07 Seattle Carla1161¾ Dezibelle's Star118hd Miss Kyama116no Inside duel 10
9Jun96- 4Hol fst 6f :22 :442 :561 1:084 4↑ Ⓕ Clm 50000 95 1 3 11 11 11 1no Flores D R LB 117 b 2.60 95-07 Promo Tape117no Seattle Carla1142 Lady Evening Belle1165 Game inside 6
16May96- 8Hol fst 6f :213 :45 :564 1:091 3↑ Ⓕ [S] Alw 45000N2X 83 2 4 1½ 1½ 1hd 35 Flores D R LB 117 b 10.30 88-14 DstngushForm1163 LdyEvnngBll1162 PromoTp1171¾ Dueled, outfinished 6
14Dec95- 8Hol gd 5½f ⊗ :214 :452 :573 1:043 3↑ Ⓕ Clm 62500 78 4 1 2hd 2hd 21 43 Douglas R R LB 117 b 6.80 85-17 BrendsWildindin1172 HllelujhAngel117hd Bllscrt119¾ Dueled, outfinished 7
22Nov95- 7Hol fst 6f :22 :45 :57 1:093 3↑ Ⓕ [S] Alw 34000N1X 89 3 2 12½ 12½ 11½ 1½ Flores D R LB 118 b 8.20 92-11 Promo Tape118½ Ole' Sis1183½ Nicolletta1183 Held on gamely 6
22Oct95- 1SA fst 6½f :214 :451 1:101 1:162 Ⓕ Clm 40000 78 6 1 21 2hd 11 24 Douglas R R LB 115 b 3.70 86-10 Venetian Peach1154 Promo Tape1154½ Dell Rapids1171½ Led, 2nd best 6

WORKOUTS: Sep23 Hol 3f fst :373 H 6/7 Sep7 Hol 5f fst 1:004 H 4/14 Sep2 Hol 4f fst :474 H 3/16 Aug10 Hol 5f fst 1:001 H 3/24 Aug4 Hol 4f fst :501 H 11/20 Jly28 Hol 5f fst 1:02 H 6/8

Promo Tape

Neither Fair affair was particularly fast for the level; had a poor post for an excuse last time, could move forward this time for heavy duty Mitchell-Nakatani team; but a couple others in here are on their game, are tough customers with better recent Beyers; thus, we'll try to beat this one for the 1-2 slots.

—Randy Franklin

where the competition is easier. And why did she run in front bandages last time? Promo Tape has the second best Beyer in the bunch and was claimed two races back by Mike Mitchell, a trainer who has made a specialty of winning with claimers recently taken from other people. But Promo Tape's recent Beyers have been unimpressive and she was beaten on September 14 by Sidepocketsue, even though she had an excuse that day: "Bumped break." It could have cost her a length or two at the start. Then please note Randy Franklin's negative comment on her chances.

What to do, what to do? Here's what happened:

FIRST RACE	6 FURLONGS. (1.07¹) CLAIMING. Purse $30,000. Fillies and mares, 3-year-olds and upward. Weights:

Santa Anita

OCTOBER 10, 1996

6 FURLONGS. (1.07¹) CLAIMING. Purse $30,000. Fillies and mares, 3-year-olds and upward. Weights: 3-year-olds, 120 lbs. Older, 122 lbs. Non-winners of two races since August 1, allowed 3 lbs. Of a race since September 1, 5 lbs. Claiming price $40,000; if for $35,000, allowed 2 lbs. (Maiden or races when entered for $32,000 or less not considered.)(Day 7 of a 27 Day Meet. Clear. 86.)

Value of Race: $30,000 Winner $16,500; second $6,000; third $4,500; fourth $2,250; fifth $750. Mutuel Pool $172,748.00 Exacta Pool $132,335.00 Quinella Pool $24,272.00

Last Raced	Horse	M/Eqt. A.Wt	PP	St	¼	½	Str	Fin	Jockey	Cl'g Pr	Odds $1
29Sep96 8Fpx²	Promo Tape	LBb 4 119	6	2	2½	2²	1¹½	1¹½	Nakatani C S	40000	4.00
29Sep96 8Fpx⁴	Sidepocketsue	LBb 6 117	2	6	6	6	4½	2¹½	Desormeaux K J	40000	7.80
27Sep96 12Fpx¹	Lite 'n Comfy	LB 5 119	4	3	4½	3ʰᵈ	3¹½	3³	Stevens G L	40000	3.90
29Sep96 8Fpx³	Persistant Sal	LB 5 117	1	4	3²	4²	5²	4ⁿᵏ	Antley C W	40000	2.10
1Aug96 9SR⁸	Garden Of Roses	LBb 5 117	5	1	1¹	1½	2¹	5²½	Solis A	40000	2.30
1Sep96 4Dmr⁹	Check Request	Lb 3 115	3	5	5⁵	5½	6	6	Valenzuela P A	40000	20.80

OFF AT 1:00 Start Good. Won driving. Time, :21², :44³, :57, 1:10 Track fast.

$2 Mutuel Prices:	6-PROMO TAPE	10.00	5.60	3.40
	2-SIDEPOCKETSUE		7.00	3.80
	4-LITE 'N COMFY			3.20

$2 EXACTA 6-2 PAID $55.60 $2 QUINELLA 2-6 PAID $29.20

B. f, by Relaunch a Tune-Atomic Eyes, by Blue Eyed Davy. Trainer Mitchell Mike. Bred by Sledge Stable (Cal).

PROMO TAPE prompted the pace outside PERSISTANT SAL on the backstretch and off the rail on the turn, took a short lead outside GARDEN OF ROSES leaving the turn and pulled clear under urging. SIDEPOCKETSUE was unhurried a bit off the rail on the backstretch, ranged up outside CHECK REQUEST leaving the turn, swung out for the stretch and finished well. LITE 'N COMFY raced outside CHECK REQUEST on the backstretch and outside PERSISTANT SAL leaving the turn and could not match the top pair. PERSISTANT SAL saved ground prompting the pace on the backstretch, remained inside on the turn, came out in upper stretch and weakened. GARDEN OF ROSES sprinted to the early lead, found the rail on the turn and weakened in the stretch. CHECK REQUEST was a bit crowded in the early stages, saved ground to the stretch, came out and also weakened.

Owners— 1, Belmonte & Moll; 2, Lagniappe Stables Inc; 3, Three Point Stable Inc; 4, Alsdorf & Coelho & Valenti; 5, Golden Eagle Farm; 6, Glen Hill Farm

Trainers— 1, Mitchell Mike; 2, Desormeaux J Keith; 3, Marshall Robert W; 4, Sadler John W; 5, Carava Jack; 6, Proctor Willard L

Scratched— Cee's Maryanne (14Sep96 10FPX3)

Promo Tape won the race very impressively and paid ten dollars, a notch above her morning line of three to one. She had been my second choice, but I had been put off by Franklin's negative comment on her. A mistake on my part, but luckily a minor one. My basic rule on professional handicappers, whether in the *Form* or anywhere else, is to pay very little attention to them. It's only their opinion against yours and you have to bear in mind that they have to handicap a lot of races every day, while having to do so a day in advance of you. Their judgments can't take into consideration late scratches or the condition of the racing surfaces, which can vary enormously from day to day. The best thing to do about all such comments is to read them for the nuggets of information they contain about such factors as breeding, medication, equipment changes, and ignore all expressions of opinion. Don't be intimidated by supposedly superior expertise. It was superior expertise that got us into Vietnam and Somalia.

The reason I wasn't annoyed about having allowed myself to be dissuaded from betting on Promo Tape is that I passed the race. I had liked Persistant Sal at least as much as the winner and I had been unable to eliminate all but one of the other entries. You'll hear a lot of people at the track say they lost this or that by having failed to make it, but passing a race can never be counted as a loss, especially early in the day, with eight other puzzles to solve. Let's have a look at the next race, on pages 112–114:

RACE 2: These are bad horses that have already established their mediocrity by having run, in all but two cases, at least several times without revealing even a smidgin of ability. Because they are still maidens it's conceivable they could improve a bit in time, but enough in this race to make us want to risk money on them? Doubtful. It's a Screecher looks like

2 Santa Anita Park

1 MILE. (1:332) MAIDEN CLAIMING. Purse $18,000. 3-year-olds and upward, bred in California. Weights: 3-year-olds, 120 lbs. Older, 122 lbs. Claiming price $32,000; if for $28,000, allowed 2 lbs.

1 MILE
START & FINISH

Nino Gatico

Own: Granja Vista Del Rio Stable — $28,000
GARCIA M S (10 0 1 0 .00) 1996:(464 37 .08)

Ch. g. 3 (Jan)
Sire: Afleet (Mr. Prospector)
Dam: Pleasure Bought (Marfa)
Br: Granja Vista Del Rio (Cal)
Tr: Tinsley J E Jr (1 0 0 0 .00) 1996:(84 7 .08)

L 118

Lifetime Record:	6 M 0 2	$8,138			
1996	5 M 0 2	$8,138	Turf	0 0 0 0	
1995	1 M 0 0		Wet	0 0 0 0	
SA	0 0 0 0		Dist	1 0 0 0	$1,238

4Sep96-9Dmr fst 1 1/16	:224 :47 1:114 1:433 3↑	Ⓢ Md 28000	53	2	5	42½	33½	48½	418¾	Toscano P R	LB 116 b	3.50	66-14	Prized Fighter11811 It's A Screecher1185½ Tell The Monk1181¾	Rail trip	9
7Aug96-9Dmr fst 1 1/16	:23 :464 1:114 1:443 3↑	Ⓢ Md 28000	64	11	5	42½	52½	34½	34	Toscano P R	LB 116	4.70	75-20	HonestDelight1163½ BlackPheasnt122½ NinoGtico1162¾	4 wide to 2nd turn	12
12Jly96-4Hol fst 1 1/16	:232 :463 1:12 1:461 3↑	Ⓢ Md 32000	51	2	4	45½	26	26	36½	Toscano P R	LB 116	12.20	63-30	Work 'n' Man1146 Acivdarb120½ Nino Gatico1161	Just lost 2nd	11
19Jun96-9Hol fst 7½f	:222 :453 1:102 1:293 3↑	Ⓢ Md 32000	47	4	6	52½	53¼	57	416	Pfau R K	LB 116	18.80	70-12	Ogata Be Good122½ Liberty Town11511 Fantasy AndMagic120½	Gave way	8
8May96-9Hol fst 7f	:22 :444 1:10 1:224 3↑	Ⓢ Md 32000	49	4	11	95¼	89	88¾	813	Pfau R K	LB 115	49.80	75-13	Cndelotto110hd TouchdownMimi1151 NrlyPrfct1172¾	Off slow;4 wide turn	11
29Jun95-4Hol fst 5½f	:222 :451 :581 1:043	Ⓢ Md Sp Wt	27	4	6	77½	77	78	616	Valenzuela P A	B 118	32.80	72-11	Riva Ranger1181¼ Te Atua1182 Prototype1183½	Steadied 5/8	8

WORKOUTS: Oct2 SA 6f fst 1:143 H *11/19* Aug31 Dmr 4f fst :503 H *47/51* Aug23 Dmr 5f fst 1:004 H *11/57* Aug1 Dmr 5f fst 1:014 H *50/71* Jly23 Dmr 4f fst :472 H *2/34*

It's a Screecher

Own: Dye & J B T T Inc & Wernicke — $28,000
PEDROZA M A (23 4 3 1 .17) 1996:(1021 125 .12)

B. c. 3 (Feb)
Sire: Pirate's Bounty (Hoist the Flag)
Dam: Shimmering Sea (Petrone)
Br: Postum Farm (Cal)
Tr: Buss Jim (—) 1996:(117 7 .06)

L 118

Lifetime Record:	11 M 3 0	$11,157			
1996	8 M 3 0	$11,157	Turf	0 0 0 0	
1995	3 M 0 0		Wet	0 0 0 0	
SA	0 0 0 0		Dist	1 0 0 0	$475

26Sep96-7Fpx fst 1 1/16	:23 :47 1:123 1:462 3↑	Ⓢ Md 32000	66	3	2	21½	31	22	21	Castro J M	LB 115 b	2.70	77-22	Fabulous Heir1201 It's A Screecher1151 My Bettor1153½		9
Lacked room rail 5/16, wide into lane																
18Sep96-6Fpx fst 1 1/16	:223 :463 1:132 1:462 3↑	Md 32000	66	8	3	21½	1hd	21½	22½	Castro J M	LB 115 b	7.10	75-17	Black Pheasant120½ It's A Screecher1153½ Secret Fun1152½	Game inside	10
4Sep96-9Dmr fst 1 1/16	:224 :47 1:114 1:433 3↑	Ⓢ Md 32000	66	6	4	54	55	37	211	Castro J M	LB 118 b	33.20	73-14	Prized Fighter11811 It's A Screecher1185½ Tell The Monk1181¾	Best of rest	9
21Aug96-6Dmr fst 1	:221 :454 1:111 1:382 3↑	Ⓢ Md 28000	55	9	5	53	55	56	59½	Nakatani C S	LB 116 b	15.70	68-21	J. P. Chips1182 Pouring DownRain116hd LibertyTown1203	5 wide 1st turn	9
17Aug96-2Dmr fst 7f	:221 :451 1:111 1:241 3↑	Ⓢ Md 28000	44	4	8	86¼	96	1011	612½	Hunter M T	LB 116 fb	52.10	66-12	Tam's Ice116½ Main Man1184 Mr. Schappacher1185	By tired ones	12
31Jly96-4Dmr fst 6f	:214 :452 :58 1:11 3↑	Ⓢ Md 28000	54	1	10	1011	1010	89¼	76¾	Pedroza M A	LB 116 fb	68.60	77-13	Toby San118½ Buster O'brien118hd Cause I'm Unique120¾	Off slowly	11
17Jly96-9Hol fst 6½f	:221 :451 1:102 1:164 3↑	Md 25000	53	7	7	63½	74½	66½	511	Pedroza M A	LB 117 fb	13.70	71-12	Transonic1225 In Hot Vawter1171 Tell The Monk117½	No rally	9
22Jun96-10Hol fst 6f	:221 :454 :583 1:104 3↑	Ⓢ Md 28000	49	7	9	99¾	86	67	510	Pedroza M A	LB 114 fb	62.30	75-11	Thimbledrone122½ Run The Table116hd T. V. Winner1165½	Crowded start	11
1Sep95-4Dmr fst 6f	:221 :454 :58 1:103	Ⓢ Md 32000	44	2	11	108½	1010	813	69	Douglas R R	LB 118 fb	62.10	79-07	Staged And Ready118nk Tener Suerte1182¾ Engelbert118no	Wide into lane	12
16Aug95-4Dmr fst 6f	:222 :454 :581 1:111	Ⓢ Md 32000	23	6	10	84¼	86½	610	914¾	Pedroza M A	LB 118 fb	13.90	70-10	Romaine1185 StagedAndReady1182 OhSoSpicy1181¾	Steadied after start	12

WORKOUTS: Aug31 Dmr 3f fst :371 H *12/26*

A CLOSER LOOK

2nd Santa Anita

Nino Gatico

Improvement noted from first initial seaside try but what happened last time?; blinker addition sure didn't help; regardless, runner has little speed, little late kick; but when eyeing the opposition he looks very capable of finishing in the money.

It's A Screecher

Runner-up 3 straight, could be his day today; consistent Beyerwise, even has enough speed to get a soft trip; but runner has proven very nondescript, goes for trainer having a brutal year on the major SoCal scene; is runner playable at 6-5?; that's for you to decide.

Power of Prince

Own: Clark Billy

$28,000

SILVA J G (2 0 1 0 .00) 1996:(120 4 .03)

Dk. b or br g. 4
Sire: Johnlee n' Harold (Lord Stapleton)
Dam: Sabra Miss (Restless Native)
Br: J C Hoover & W Williamson (Cal)
Tr: Wicker Lloyd C (—) 1996:(16 0 .00)

L 120

Lifetime Record :	8 M 1 0	$4,590		
1996	2 M 0 0	$1,700	Turf	0 0 0 0
1995	6 M 1 0	$2,890	Wet	0 0 0 0
SA	2 0 0 0		Dist	0 0 0 0

25Sep96-12Fpx fst 6f :221 :46 :584 1:114 3↑ [S]Md 32000 40 1 2 63½ 86¾ 58½ 510½ Silva J G LB 120 16.80 79-09 HevenSent1151 BusterO'brien1151 MnMountinDn1156 Lacked response 8
12Sep96-12Fpx fst 6½f :22 :46 1:113 1:182 3↑ [S]Md 32000 39 7 4 31½ 53¼ 47 515 Silva J G LB 120 13.20 74-09 Jalos1165 My Bettor1159 Caro's Dream1201 Wide trip 10
7Dec95-6Hol fst 6½f :213 :441 1:102 1:164 3↑ Md 25000 38 11 1 31½ 44 78½ 1118 Garcia M S LB 120 b 34.50 67-14 Majestic N Green1204½ Proper Landing1203½ Miraquet1201 Gave way 11
16Nov95-6Hol fst 1 1/16 :232 :472 1:121 1:444 3↑ [S]Md 28000 65 1 1 1hd 1½ 32½ 78 Valdivia J5 LB 112 b 41.80 69-21 Prospective Road1171¼ Agent Double Ex122½ Call MeCoach1172½ Rail trip 11
26Oct95-9SA fst 6½f :214 :45 1:102 1:171 3↑ [S]Md 28000 5 3 3 22½ 45 1015 1029 Silva J G LB 118 b 23.70 57-14 Bold N Bronze1203 Honor Is Power1175½ Mill Shine1204½ Gave way 10
14Oct95-4SA fst 6f :22 :45 :571 1:094 3↑ [S]Md 28000 55 6 4 32½ 43½ 54½ 612½ Berrio O A B 118 31.50 75-11 Chief Ribot1182¾ Waiting Game1181 Juan Colorado1206 Inside trip 9
21Sep95-6Fpx fst 6f :22 :46 :59 1:123 3↑ [S]Md 32000 57 1 1 22½ 21½ 22 21 Silva J G B 114 31.30 85-10 Dasha1091 Power Of Prince114½ Glorious Country114¾ Good effort 8
30Aug95-6Dmr fst 6½f :214 :444 1:111 1:173 3↑ [S]Md 28000 23 9 5 54¾ 67 1015 1019¼ Silva J G B 116 69.40 64-13 Silver Paladin122nk Mt. Sascha1187 Twenty Liters122no Gave way 12

WORKOUTS: Oct5 SLR tr.t 7f fst 1:27 H 1/2 ●Sep21 SLR tr.t 4f fst :464 H 1/8 ●Sep2 SLR tr.t 5f fst 1:00 H 1/5 Aug26 SLR tr.t 7f fst 1:252 H 1/1 Aug20 SLR tr.t 6f fst 1:131 H 3/4 ●Aug13 SLR tr.t 5f fst 1:001 H 1/8

Power Of Prince

Tried routing once last year and fell apart; sprinted thrice since and hasn't shown any lane life either; stretching again, could show some speed yet figures going nowhere during crunch time.

My Bettor

Own: Hanson Stock Farm

$32,000

ESPINOZA V (18 0 5 3 .00) 1996:(719 95 .13)

Dk. b or br g. 3 (May)
Sire: My Habitony (Habitony*GB)
Dam: Happy Bettor (Crazy Kid)
Br: Hanson Stock Farm (Cal)
Tr: Sise Clifford Jr (4 0 0 2 .00) 1996:(154 22 .14)

L 120

Lifetime Record :	6 M 1 2	$9,225		
1996	4 M 1 1	$6,400	Turf	0 0 0 0
1995	2 M 0 1	$2,825	Wet	0 0 0 0
SA	1 0 0 0	$425	Dist	0 0 0 0

26Sep96-7Fpx fst 1 1/16 :23 :47 1:123 1:462 3↑ [S]Md 32000 65 7 5 65¼ 64 33½ 32 Espinoza V LB 115 b 3.30 76-22 Fabulous Heir1201 It's A Screecher1151 My Bettor1153½ Strong late bid 9
12Sep96-12Fpx fst 6½f :22 :46 1:113 1:182 3↑ [S]Md 32000 63 9 8 86¾ 68¾ 36 25 Espinoza V LB 115 b 6.30 84-09 Jalos1165 My Bettor1159 Caro's Dream1201 Awkward start 10
23Aug96-2Dmr fst 6f :214 :45 :572 1:101 3↑ [S]Md 32000 61 2 7 87¾ 77½ 58½ 49 Espinoza V LB 118 b 58.60 79-10 SenorSlewpy1184 NaturllyStn1221 LordBoswell1184 Improved position 9
9Aug96-4Dmr fst 6f :214 :45 :574 1:11 3↑ [S]Md 32000 43 7 5 73½ 107 1111 1112½ Valenzuela P A LB 118 fb 5.40 71-14 Exit1182 Key De Mere1182 Drill Team118nk Gave way 12
29Nov95-4Hol fst 6f :221 :452 :581 1:114 [S]Md 32000 60 8 4 2hd 1hd 1hd 3½ Flores D R LB 119 b 8.40 80-15 J. O. Native119hd Proranger119½ My Bettor119hd Bumped late, gamely 11
10Nov95-9SA fst 6f :22 :452 :574 1:11 [S]Md 32000 46 9 9 88¼ 77½ 58½ 57¼ Flores D R LB 118 17.40 75-14 Variety Voodoo1161 J. O. Native1185½ A Star Is Bruin113½ Wide trip 11

WORKOUTS: Sep5 Dmr 5f fst 1:002 H 10/46 Aug19 Dmr 4f fst :524 H 58/58 Aug7 Dmr 3f fst :361 H 5/31 Aug1 Dmr 6f fst 1:142 H 9/20 Jly26 Dmr 6f fst 1:143 H 12/22 Jly20 Dmr 5f fst 1:021 H 24/38

My Bettor

Seems to be on the upgrade; only 1 behind It's A Screecher at the Fair and could move forward with the route experience under his belt; bred to handle a route, goes for trainer who knows what he's doin'; regular jock still at the helm; consider.

Miscounted

Own: Oakcrest Stable

$28,000

GARCIA J A (12 1 3 1 .08) 1996:(43 11 .26)

B. g. 3 (Mar)
Sire: Summing (Verbatim)
Dam: Miss Believin (Believe It)
Br: Julie McGrath & Susan McGrath (Cal)
Tr: Sadler John W (7 0 1 0 .00) 1996:(211 26 .12)

L 118

Lifetime Record :	4 M 0 0	$2,662		
1996	4 M 0 0	$2,662	Turf	0 0 0 0
1995	0 M 0 0		Wet	0 0 0 0
SA	0 0 0 0		Dist	0 0 0 0

18Sep96-6Fpx fst 1 1/16 :223 :463 1:132 1:462 3↑ Md 32000 54 9 6 52½ 32 35½ 59½ Black C A LB 116 b 6.00 68-17 BlackPheasnt1202½ It'sAScreecher1153½ SecretFun1152½ Lacked response 10
23Aug96-6Dmr fst 6f :22 :451 :573 1:101 3↑ [S]Md 32000 59 7 1 74 64¼ 75½ 49½ Desormeaux K J LB 118 b 11.90 78-10 Keaton'sCarpenter1187 CheckKite118no GladYouAsked1182½ Steadied 1/4 9
9Aug96-4Dmr fst 6f :214 :45 :574 1:11 3↑ [S]Md 32000 49 6 6 41½ 53½ 78 1010 Sorenson D LB 118 b 27.10 74-14 Exit1182 Key De Mere1182 Drill Team118nk 12
Bumped 3 1/2, steadied 1/4
22Jly96-9Hol fst 6f :22 :451 :574 1:102 3↑ [S]Md 32000 56 12 2 31 42½ 47½ 510¾ Sorenson D LB 117 30.20 76-12 Out Of Order1173½ Exit1173½ Spiritofthelaw1201 Lugged out, wide 12

WORKOUTS: Sep30 SA 4f fst :504 H 33/35 Sep14 SA 5f fst 1:05 H 37/37 Sep5 Dmr 4f fst :47 H 2/35 Aug19 Dmr 5f fst 1:011 H 40/68 Aug4 Dmr 5f fst 1:012 H 37/64 Jly19 Hol 5f fst 1:014 Hg 23/32

Miscounted

Light with these Beyerwise, didn't show any real penchant for routing at the Fair; does get a much better post for those looking for playable angles but runner still has to progress considerably to be a legit win-end threat.

continued

Excess Luggage

Own: Futterman & Hilltop Farm $28,000

VERGARA O (3 0 0 0 .00) 1996:(236 19 .08)

Gr. g. 4
Sire: Flying Minstrel (The Minstrel)
Dam: Travelinsaleslady (Verbatim)
Br: Hilltop Farm & Ken Dodge (Cal)
Tr: Perez Dagoberto L (1 0 0 0 .00) 1996:(16 1 .06)

L 120

Lifetime Record: 2 M 0 0

1996	2 M 0 0	Turf	0 0 0 0
1995	0 M 0 0	Wet	0 0 0 0
SA	2 0 0 0	Dist	1 0 0 0

27Mar96-3SA fst 1 1/16 :23 :46⁴ 1:11 1:44³ 4↑ Md 28000 36 5 3 45½ 713 718 726¼ Scott J M LB 118 50.70 46-24 Fleet Flame115⁴½ Plenish120⁶ Mountain's Majesty118⁵ Lugged out 7/8 7
20Mar96-9SA fst 1 :22⁴ :47 1:11⁴ 1:38² 4↑ Md 25000 51 5 8 86½ 88½ 88¾ 713 Scott J M B 120 50.70 64-20 Miswaki Delight118no Indicium120³ Social Climber120³ No rally 9

WORKOUTS: Oct6 Hol 4f fst :48³ H 7/21 Oct2 Hol 6f fst 1:15² H 13/18 Sep25 Hol 6f fst 1:15⁴ H 20/24 Sep13 Hol 5f fst 1:02³ H 25/32 Sep7 Hol 4f fst :48¹ Hg 9/23 Aug31 Hol 4f fst :48³ H 9/21

Mister Preston

Own: Epperson James $32,000

HUNTER M T (18 3 0 1 .17) 1996:(403 55 .14)

Ch. g. 3 (Jan)
Sire: Stanstead (Gummo)
Dam: Maybe This Isit (Splendid Courage)
Br: Jim Epperson (Cal)
Tr: Mayberry Brian A (1 0 0 0 .00) 1996:(78 8 .10)

L 120

Lifetime Record: 4 M 0 1 $1,920

1996	4 M 0 1	$1,920	Turf	0 0 0 0
1995	0 M 0 0		Wet	0 0 0 0
SA	0 0 0 0		Dist	0 0 0 0

22Sep96-5Fpx fst 1 1/16 :23 :46⁴ 1:13 1:47² 3↑ Md 20000 48 5 1 1½ 1hd 31½ 34 Hunter M T LB 115 28.70 69-14 GretWhiteHope115³½ TotllyGrk115½ MistrPrston115¾ Washy post parade 10
5Sep96-9Dmr fst 5½f :21³ :45 :57¹ 1:03² 3↑ Md 25000 28 7 6 75 79½ 1011 1021½ Vergara O LB 118 b 43.20 75-11 H'sARoylHony118hd NtvDsrt118⁸ StrtYrEngns1181¼ Between foes to lane 11
Previously trained by Mitchell Mike
22Jly96-9Hol fst 6f :22 :45¹ :57⁴ 1:10² 3↑ [S]Md 32000 -0 2 7 51¾ 1114 1225 1233½ Nakatani C S LB 117 b 6.50 54-12 Out Of Order117³½ Exit117³½ Spiritofthelaw1201 12
Hustled early, gave way, steadied 1/4
16Jun96-1Hol fst 5½f :22¹ :45⁴ :58³ 1:05 3↑ [S]Md 32000 24 2 8 64¾ 67 813 816½ Nakatani C S B 116 b 2.90 70-13 Rare Champ116hd Kicking Bear122⁶ Medallist116³ Steadied early 8

WORKOUTS: Sep18 SA tr.t 3f fst :36³ H 2/2 Aug31 Dmr 4f fst :47² H 9/51 Aug23 Dmr 5f fst 1:01 H 13/57 Aug12 Dmr 4f fst :47⁴ H 10/49 Jly18 Hol 5f fst 1:01⁴ Hg 26/35 Jly10 Hol 5f fst 1:00⁴ H 6/38

Provide

Own: Moreno Henry $32,000

GLADNEY D (2 0 1 1 .00) 1996:(64 4 .06)

B. c. 3 (Feb)
Sire: Ole' (Danzig)
Dam: Jamaican Gold (Gold Crest)
Br: Henry Moreno (Cal)
Tr: Moreno Henry (4 0 3 0 .00) 1996:(133 16 .12)

115⁵

Lifetime Record: 2 M 0 0 $1,350

1996	2 M 0 0	$1,350	Turf	0 0 0 0
1995	0 M 0 0		Wet	0 0 0 0
SA	0 0 0 0		Dist	1 0 0 0

28Aug96-9Dmr fst 1 :22² :46¹ 1:12¹ 1:37² 3↑ Md 40000 45 3 6 75 75¼ 610 622¼ Douglas R R B 118 18.20 61-22 End Run118¹² StrawberryPatch118² Mr.Schappacher118⁷ Wide into lane 9
15Aug96-9Dmr fst 6½f :22 :44³ 1:10² 1:17 3↑ Md 32000 61 1 8 32 23½ 34 45½ Douglas R R B 118 19.90 81-12 Sri Narayana1181¼ Cub's Folly118hd Proud Danzig118⁴ No late bid 12

WORKOUTS: Sep29 SA 1 fst 1:40⁴ H 2/3 Sep23 SA 7f fst 1:27 H 4/9 Sep17 SA 6f fst 1:14³ H 3/7 Sep11 Dmr 5f fst 1:01 H 7/30 Sep6 Dmr 4f fst :48 H 8/48 Aug27 Dmr 3f fst :36⁴ H 8/15

Excess Luggage

Wheeled back ultra quickly for 2nd career start and showed nothing, with Lasix; coming off an extended vacation now and has no mutuel appeal other than being a fresh face in a weak, weak race.

Mister Preston

Deleted the shades and moved forward at the Fair, albeit in a very slow race for the level; we now know this guy has speed but his staying power is still mighty suspect.

Provide

Could be a viable price play; speed shown in the debut, speed not shown in the route as colt was probably wheeled back too quickly; runner has a decent tab since, probably gets a clear run to the lead with only Mister Preston in hot pursuit; this one only has 2 career losses, hasn't proven void of talent; worth a look regardless.

—Randy Franklin

the best of them and will go off as the favorite, but he's already tried eleven times without winning. No value there. My Bettor has been improving slightly from race to race, but not enough to make me want to bet on him, especially as he's the second choice. He's tried six times and failed, most recently a length behind Screecher. Mister Preston has shown speed competing most recently against even worse animals, but not enough to make a case for himself. Even though his trainer is a friend of mine and very sharp with young horses.

As a general rule, the way you can most quickly establish the quality of a race is by scanning the Beyer figs. Not one contender in here jumps off the page. A second step would be to look for a horse dropping in class or one that has shown some speed while running in no more than two or three races. On this basis, only the bottom horse, Provide, qualifies. Both of his races have been in open company, not limited to animals bred in California. (Kentucky is still where most of the good Thoroughbreds come from; state-breds like these rarely can compete with the Bluegrass aristocrats.) This group is nowhere near as tough as the bunch Provide ran into in his previous efforts, one of which produced a Beyer of 61 from the difficult inside post at Del Mar. Inside posts are particularly treacherous for inexperienced horses, who, unless they can quickly get the lead out of the starting gate, without using themselves up doing so, find themselves hemmed in along the rail with a lot of dirt being kicked back up into their faces. I wouldn't want to run either, if some guy were pelting me with clods all the way.

This time Provide draws the outside post, but that poses a problem, too, because at a mile the outside posts can cost you a lot of ground around the first turn, sometimes as much as two or three lengths. It would take a skilled, experienced rider to overcome such a handicap, but Dihigi Gladney does not qualify. He's an apprentice with a low winning percentage. Randy Franklin likes the horse, but then he wasn't high on Promo Tape, remember? Still, the price is right, a morning line of eight to one that is drawing some support at the windows; by post time, Provide has been backed down to five to one. What now?

SECOND RACE

Santa Anita

OCTOBER 10, 1996

1 MILE. (1.33²) MAIDEN CLAIMING. Purse $18,000. 3-year-olds and upward, bred in California. Weights: 3-year-olds, 120 lbs. Older, 122 lbs. Claiming price $32,000; if for $28,000, allowed 2 lbs.

Value of Race: $18,000 Winner $9,900; second $3,600; third $2,700; fourth $1,350; fifth $450. Mutuel Pool $162,277.30 Exacta Pool $114,271.00 Trifecta Pool $128,461.00 Quinella Pool $21,081.00

Last Raced	Horse	M/Eqt. A.Wt	PP	St	¼	½	¾	Str	Fin	Jockey	Cl'g Pr	Odds $1
28Aug96 9Dmr6	Provide	B	3 115	8	6	4hd	3½	2½	14	17	Gladney D5	32000	5.60
26Sep96 7Fpx2	It's a Screecher	LBb	3 118	2	2	3½	4½	4½½	2½	25	Pedroza M A	28000	1.40
18Sep96 6Fpx5	Miscounted	LB	3 118	5	4	51	51	51	4½½	31½	Garcia J A	28000	13.30
26Sep96 7Fpx3	My Bettor	LBb	3 120	4	5	61	73	6hd	61	41	Espinoza V	32000	2.10
4Sep96 9Dmr4	Nino Gatico	LBb	3 118	1	7	72½	6½	74½	5hd	52½	Garcia M S	28000	7.50
25Sep96 12Fpx5	Power of Prince	LB	4 120	3	1	21½	1½	1½	31	63½	Silva J G	28000	39.40
22Sep96 5Fpx3	Mister Preston	LB	3 120	7	3	11	22	3hd	710	715	Hunter M T	32000	12.40
27Mar96 3SA7	Excess Luggage	Bb	4 120	6	8	8	8	8	8	8	Vergara O	28000	63.60

OFF AT 1:29 Start Good. Won ridden out. Time, :22⁴, :47, 1:12, 1:24², 1:37¹ Track fast.

$2 Mutuel Prices:

8–PROVIDE	13.20	5.00	3.40
2–IT'S A SCREECHER		3.00	2.60
5–MISCOUNTED			5.20

$2 EXACTA 8-2 PAID $33.80 $2 TRIFECTA 8-2-5 PAID $270.40 $2 QUINELLA 2-8 PAID $14.80

B. c, (Feb), by Ole'–Jamaican Gold, by Gold Crest. Trainer Moreno Henry. Bred by Henry Moreno (Cal).

PROVIDE was four wide on the first turn and outside rivals on the backstretch, moved up three deep on the second turn, took the lead outside POWER OF PRINCE leaving the second turn, opened up under some urging and was in hand late. IT'S A SCREECHER raced along the inside to the stretch, came out and was clearly second best. MISCOUNTED between rivals on the first turn and outside NINO GATICO on the backstretch, raced outside IT'S A SCREECHER leaving the second turn and four wide into the lane to pick up the show. MY BETTOR also between rivals on the first turn and outside IT'S A SCREECHER on the backstretch, lacked the needed late response. NINO GATICO saved ground to no avail, was lame after and was vanned off. POWER OF PRINCE set or forced the pace inside MISTER PRESTON for nearly six furlongs, remained inside and weakened. MISTER PRESTON pulled his way up outside POWER OF PRINCE to the lead on the first turn, dueled outside that one until nearing the quarter pole, then gave way. EXCESS LUGGAGE was always outrun.

Owners— 1, Moreno Henry; 2, Dye & J B T T Inc & Wernicke; 3, Oakcrest Stable; 4, Hanson Stock Farm; 5, Granja Vista Del Rio Stable; 6, Clark Billy; 7, Epperson James; 8, Futterman & Hilltop Farm

Trainers— 1, Moreno Henry; 2, Buss Jim; 3, Sadler John W; 4, Sise Clifford Jr; 5, Tinsley J E Jr; 6, Wicker Lloyd C; 7, Mayberry Brian A; 8, Perez Dagoberto L

$2 Daily Double (6–8) Paid $77.20; Daily Double Pool $99,095.

Well, I blew this one. This is a horse I should have taken a small shot with. As you can see, Provide won easily and was "in hand late," meaning that his rider did not have to work at all down the stretch in order to win comfortably by seven lengths. No one else was even competitive, with Screecher lumbering in an unimpressive second. At odds of five and a half to one I should have risked a small amount of money on the winner.

Still, I don't feel too badly and neither should you, when you decide to pass this kind of race. Hindsight is a recurrent racetrack phenomenon that horseplayers torture themselves with. It's also known as the "woulda-coulda-shoulda" syndrome, or variations of same, as in "I woulda bet on the sumbitch, if you don't talk me off him," or "I coulda made a bundle, if I don't get shut out," or "I shoulda hammered him, only I don't like the bug boy on him."

My advice? Put the race behind you. You didn't bet on it, so you didn't lose. Turn the page for the next race.

■   RACE 3: At first glance, this doesn't look like a bettable race either. The favorite is sure to be Costly Frosty, but he'll almost certainly be bet down to even money. He shows Beyer speed ratings of 108 and 107 at this distance at two different tracks. His rider, Pat Valenzuela, was up on him in both of those efforts and is excellent at breaking his mounts quickly out of the gate. The gelding also has enough stamina to win at a mile and his trainer has done very well with him since claiming him the year before. We can disregard his last race at Fairplex, mainly because sprinting is obviously his main talent. What is there not to like about him here? Only his price; we can't bet on him straight.

Who else would seem to have a chance? Moving Tribute has been "declared" off the track program, another way of

3 Santa Anita Park

6½ FURLONGS

6½ Furlongs **(1:14) ALLOWANCE. Purse $46,000. 3-year-olds and upward which have not won $3,000 three times other than maiden or claiming or have never won four races. Weights: 3-year-olds, 120 lbs. Older, 122 lbs. Non-winners of two such races since August 1, allowed 3 lbs. Of such a race since September 1, 5 lbs.**

Guadalcanal

Own: Dizney Donald R & English James

DESORMEAUX K J (21 2 2 3 .10) 1996:(818 147 .18)

B. c. 4
Sire: Copelan (Tri Jet)
Dam: Catch Sunny (Sunny Clime)
Br: Few Ed (Tex)
Tr: Hess R B Jr (7 1 2 1 .14) 1996:(202 36 .18)

L 117

Lifetime Record:	11 3 2 2	$85,165			
1996	3 0 1 0	$13,375	Turf	0 0 0 0	
1995	6 2 1 1	$62,110	Wet	1 0 0 1	$16,110
SA	0 0 0 0		Dist	2 0 1 0	$13,375

22Aug96-7Dmr fst 6½f	:22 :443 1:084 1:151 3↑ Alw 53000N3X	89 5 3 23 21½ 33 46¼	Desormeaux K J	LB 117	7.00	89-13	TomCrusr1193½ MrIcAg1171½ SmmrAtSrtog1171	Between foes, weakened	7
29Jly96-7Dmr fst 7f	:22 :442 1:083 1:21 3↑ Alw 53000N3X	34 6 3 33 31 712 729¼	Desormeaux K J	LB 117	2.70	66-10	BoundlssMomnt1193½ TrbIntDncr1172 MrIcAg1193	Drifted out, gave way	7
6Jun96-8Hol fst 6½f	:22 :441 1:083 1:143 3↑ Alw 47000N3X	101 4 4 22 21 11½ 21½	Desormeaux K J	LB 116	8.30	92-11	Bold Capital1181½ Guadalcanal1164 First Intent1181¾	Outfinished	8
28May95-9Bel fst 1⅛	:453 1:094 1:36 1:50 Peter Pan-G2	63 4 3 32½ 34 1012 1022¼	Alvarado F T	115	34.00	60-22	Citadeed112½ Pat N Jac113nk Treasurer1152½	Wide, gave way	10
23Apr95-8Kee sly 1⅛	:224 :462 1:113 1:45 Lexington-G2	88 1 1 1hd 2hd 21½ 35¾	Bailey J D	L 115	6.60	79-27	Star Standard1152¼ Royal Mitch1183 Guadalcanal1158½	Pace, weakened	5
Previously trained by Perry William W									
25Mar95-8Aqu fst 1	:232 :464 1:121 1:364 Gotham-G2	64 2 5 61½ 73¾ 914 724¾	Migliore R	114	9.80	60-25	Talkin Man1227 Da Hoss1172 Devious Course1175½	Wide turn, no rally	11
24Feb95-8Aqu fst 1⅛ ⊡	:241 :483 1:134 1:453 Alw 34000N2X	89 4 2 1½ 11 14 17	Migliore R	119	*.90	77-29	Guadalcanal1197 Candy Cone1172 Larchmont117hd	Kept to task	7
29Jan95-8Aqu fst 1⅛ ⊡	:234 :49 1:144 1:482 Alw 32000N1X	83 8 5 2hd 1½ 14 17½	Migliore R	117	*1.95	63-35	Guadalcanal1177½ Elk Basin1173 Is Sveikatas117nk	Wide trip	9
15Jan95-8Aqu fst 1⅛ ⊡	:24 :474 1:13 1:46 Alw 32000N1X	71 6 2 22 22 25 26½	Migliore R	117	2.55	68-27	Paragallo's Hope1176½ Guadalcanal117nk Conduit Street112hd	Held place	7
30Dec94-5Suf fst 6f	:23 :47 1:00 1:123 Md Sp Wt	90 1 1 12½ 18 111 118	Caraballo J C	122	*.40	85-26	Guadalcanal12218 Two Across122nk Jojo Bo122hd	In hand	8

WORKOUTS: Oct6 SA 3f fst :362 H 8/19 Sep30 SA 4f fst :481 H 8/35 Sep22 SA 5f fst :594 H 6/46 Sep16 SA 5f fst 1:003 H 6/29 Sep9 Dmr 4f fst :501 H 25/31 Sep2 Dmr 4f fst :49 Hg 29/66

Costly Frosty

Own: Keh & Knudson & Martinez

VALENZUELA P A (33 2 5 4 .06) 1996:(491 60 .12)

B. g. 4
Sire: Frosty the Snowman (His Majesty)
Dam: Karen R. (Riva Ridge)
Br: Appleton Arthur I (Fla)
Tr: Marshall Robert W (3 1 1 0 .33) 1996:(139 25 .18)

L 119

Lifetime Record:	15 5 2 1	$135,850			
1996	4 2 1 0	$60,250	Turf	3 0 0 0	
1995	11 3 1 1	$75,600	Wet	0 0 0 0	
SA	2 1 0 0	$14,250	Dist	2 1 1 0	$29,750

29Sep96-11Fpx fst *1⅛	:483 1:13 1:381 1:503 3↑ PomonaInvtlH150k	94 5 1 1½ 1hd 31 64¼	Douglas R R	LB 114 b	3.20	91-15	Region113hd Misnomer1171 Windy's Halo1112	Inside duel	9
7Sep96-7Dmr fst 1	:221 :453 1:102 1:352 3↑ Alw 50000N2X	102 4 5 52½ 31½ 31 14	Valenzuela P A	LB 117 b	*1.60	93-14	Costly Frosty1174 Elmhurst117hd Flick117¾	Waited 1/4, split foes	8
25Aug96-3Dmr fst 6½f	:221 :444 1:091 1:152 3↑ Alw 47000N2X	108 3 6 21½ 21 2hd 2nk	Valenzuela P A	LB 117 b	1.90	94-15	Patrick117nk Costly Frosty1172 Contender1173½	Bid, outgamed	6
20Jly96-5Hol fst 6½f	:22 :442 1:084 1:15 3↑ Alw 37000N1X	107 4 6 31½ 3½ 13 110	Valenzuela P A	LB 118 b	2.90	91-11	Costly Frosty11810 Devon Dancer118¾ Plenish1183	Ridden out	8
23Sep95-11Fpx fst 1⅛	:224 :452 1:11 1:454 Ⓡ Derby Trial48k	71 4 4 44½ 55½ 57 34½	Berrio O A	LB 122 b	*1.60	76-15	To Be Khaled1193 Trophy Time1191½ CostlyFrosty1221	Bit wide into lane	5
4Sep95-7Dmr fst 1	:22 :451 1:10 1:36 Clm c-50000	89 3 1 13½ 12½ 14 13½	Berrio O A	LB 115 fb	8.00	90-11	CostlyFrosty1153½ HrdWorkn'Gy1143½ Thrtydollrcowboy117¾	Speed, held	8
Claimed from Delima Jose E, Delima Jose E Trainer									
24Aug95-7Dmr fm 1 Ⓣ	:223 :464 1:113 1:361 Clm 62500	65 10 5 41½ 52¾ 76¼ 811	Berrio O A	LB 115 fb	7.50	78-11	Time For Sacrifice1172¼ FrenchWine116hd TwoPunchGlen1172	Weakened	10
3Aug95-3Dmr fst 6f	:212 :441 :563 1:09 3↑ Alw 42000N1X	90 1 8 53½ 53 33 23¼	Berrio O A	LB 114 fb	3.70	92-12	Suggest1163¼ Costly Frosty114no Getting Enough114¾	Inside bid	8
12Jly95-8Hol fst 6f	:214 :443 :563 1:09 Playa DelRey71k	91 6 5 62¾ 63¼ 53½ 43¾	Berrio O A	LB 115 fb	12.20	91-11	FlyingStndby115½ DesertPirte1192½ BoundlessMomnt118¾	5 wide to turn	6
25Jun95-3Hol fst 6f	:212 :44 :56 1:083 Clm 32000	98 7 2 31½ 32½ 2hd 13½	Berrio O A	LB 115 fb	*2.00	97-06	Costly Frosty1153½ Rivermeritsdream116¾ Big Em1157	Steady handling	8

WORKOUTS: Sep23 Hol 5f fst 1:003 H 7/36 Sep17 Hol 4f fst :483 H 12/31 Sep3 Dmr 4f fst :491 H 28/35 Aug18 Dmr 4f fst :473 H 8/58 Jly29 Dmr 5f fst 1:012 H 35/69 Jly14 Hol 7f fst 1:251 H 2/6

A CLOSER LOOK

3rd Santa Anita

Guadalcanal

Comebacker at Hollywood sure was nifty but maybe that was the max as subsequents nowhere near as good; colt has speed, suspect staying power; but he doesn't look completely outgunned at this level, has some lick in affair without much of that commodity signed on; chance.

Costly Frosty

Wasn't impressed with the triple digit Beyer earned over Devon Dancer, was impressed with the fig when getting necked by the capable Patrick; what happened at the Fair?; runner might not have liked the surface, the opposition, the distance......; tons better as a sprinter regardless and probably one of the ones to strongly consider winwise.

Moving Tribute

Own: Farish & Relatively Stable

DELAHOUSSAYE E (17 4 2 6 .24) 1996:(800 134 .17)

Ch. c. 4
Sire: Zilzal (Nureyev)
Dam: Fold the Flag (Raja Baba)
Br: Farish William S (Ky)
Tr: Drysdale Neil (3 0 2 0 .00) 1996:(136 18 .13)

L 117

Lifetime Record :	9 2 4 2	$89,360			
1996	4 0 2 1	$28,850	Turf	1 0 0 0	$3,300
1995	5 2 2 1	$60,510	Wet	0 0 0 0	
SA	2 1 1 0	$27,750	Dist	1 0 0 1	$6,750

12Aug96-8Dmr fst 1 :223 :453 1:10 1:352 3↑ Alw 50000N2X 97 4 2 2hd 2hd 2hd 2nk Delahoussaye E LB 117 *2.00 93-13 Sovereign Sage117nk Moving Tribute117nk Flick1171 Game try 6
4Jly96-2Hol fm 1 Ⓣ :233 :464 1:103 1:341 3↑ Alw 44000N2X 84 1 6 65 63½ 55 45¼ Delahoussaye E LB 116 *1.70 87-08 Khorz1163½ ArrivederciBby1161 HundredDollrkiss116¾ On rail to 2nd turn 6
15Jun96-8Hol fst 1 1/16 :231 :454 1:093 1:421 3↑ Alw 44000N2X 98 9 3 2½ 2hd 1½ 2½ Delahoussaye E B 116 *1.90 89-14 Lloydminister116½ Moving Tribute116½ Briartic Heir116no Led, caught 10
27May96-2Hol fst 6½f :22 :442 1:09 1:152 3↑ Alw 45000N2X 97 3 3 42½ 43 41½ 31 Delahoussaye E B 116 5.80 88-11 First Intent117¾ Boundless Moment116hd Moving Tribute116hd Willingly 6
2Oct95-6Bel fst 1⅛ :492 1:141 1:392 1:522 3↑ Alw 36000N2X 81 2 1 2hd 2½ 22 37¾ Stevens G L 115 *.70 62-31 Hunting Hard113nk Jo Ran Express1167½ MovingTribute115¾ Dueled, tired 5
4Sep95-3Bel fst 7f :224 :452 1:094 1:223 3↑ Alw 34000N2X 95 2 3 41¾ 52½ 1hd 2¾ Stevens G L 113 *1.05 87-08 FlyingChvron112¾ MovingTrbut113no GoodbyDony1162½ Four wide, game 7
14May95-3Hol fst 1 1/16 :231 :46 1:10 1:413 Alw 40000N1X 99 2 2 22 2½ 1½ 12¾ Delahoussaye E B 116 *.40 93-08 Moving Tribute1162¾ Can't Decipher1163½ Conquest1165½ Steady urging 5
15Apr95-6SA fst 6f :22 :45 :563 1:084 Md Sp Wt 100 4 2 2hd 1hd 11½ 13¼ Valenzuela P A B 118 *.60 93-14 Moving Tribute1183¼ Short Freeze1183 Clover Rover1184 Handily 8
19Mar95-6SA fst 6f :212 :44 :56 1:082 Md Sp Wt 88 4 4 63¾ 56 45 27 Delahoussaye E B 118 8.80 88-06 Paying Dues1187 Moving Tribute1181¾ Impulse1182½ Wide into lane 10

WORKOUTS: Oct6 Hol 5f fst 1:014 H 9/16 Oct1 Hol 6f fst 1:172 H 16/17 Sep25 Hol 5f fst 1:02 H 15/30 Sep19 Hol 4f fst :511 B 20/20 ●Sep7 Hol 6f fst 1:124 H 1/6 Aug31 Hol 3f fst :364 H 5/14

Summer At Saratoga

Own: Red Oak Stables

MCCARRON C J (18 4 3 3 .22) 1996:(680 157 .23)

Dk. b or br c. 4
Sire: Saratoga Six (Alydar)
Dam: Ann's Roberto (Roberto)
Br: Red Oak Farm Inc (Fla)
Tr: McAnally Ronald (11 1 0 3 .09) 1996:(333 61 .18)

L 117

Lifetime Record :	11 3 4 1	$111,425			
1996	1 0 0 1	$7,950	Turf	0 0 0 0	
1995	10 3 4 0	$103,475	Wet	0 0 0 0	
SA	5 1 1 0	$39,625	Dist	7 1 3 1	$58,400

22Aug96-7Dmr fst 6½f :22 :443 1:084 1:151 3↑ Alw 53000N3X 91 2 6 74¾ 53 43 35¼ Almeida G F LB 117 b 6.50 90-13 TomCruiser1193½ MrIceAge1171¾ SummerAtSrtog1171 Bit awkward start 7
26Dec95-3SA fst 6½f :222 :45 1:091 1:153 3↑ Alw 47000N2X 98 2 2 41 31½ 31 2½ McCarron C J LB 115 b 5.40 93-11 [D]TheExeterMan117½ SummerAtSrtog115¾ GrceOfDrby1174½ Inside trip 8
Placed first through disqualification.
12Nov95-5SA fst 6½f :212 :442 1:084 1:151 3↑ Alw 40000N2X 93 4 5 42½ 41¾ 32 43¼ McCarron C J LB 114 b 4.50 92-07 High Stakes Player1162 Son Of A Pistol1191¼ TeamLeader116nk 4 wide turn 10
14Oct95-3SA fst 6½f :213 :44 1:092 1:16 3↑ Alw 40000N2X 95 6 4 52½ 44 51¾ 2hd Delahoussaye E LB 120 b 1.90 92-11 Juiceberry117hd SummerAtSrtog1202½ OcnOrbit1171½ Lugged in 1/8 & 1/16 7
1Sep95-7Dmr fst 6f :213 :441 :563 1:09 3↑ Alw 42000N1X 93 8 3 52¾ 42½ 21 11¾ McCarron C J LB 116 b 3.90 96-07 SummerAtSrtog1161¾ TheExtrMn116½ MintChocolt118¾ 5 wide into lane 9
5Aug95-9Dmr fst 6f :22 :444 :571 1:091 3↑ Md Sp Wt 96 7 1 43 42½ 2½ 1½ McCarron C J LB 118 b *.70 95-09 SummerAtSrtog118½ SonOfAPistol118hd FirstWtch1186½ 4 wide into lane 11
23Jly95-4Hol fst 6½f :222 :451 1:092 1:16 3↑ Md Sp Wt 90 4 8 3½ 11 1hd 22½ McCarron C J LB 116 b *.70 87-11 MinistroGrande1222½ SummerAtSrtog1163 Boiserie1169 Ducked in start 8
25Jun95-10Hol fst 6f :22 :444 :564 1:09 3↑ Md Sp Wt 89 10 3 31½ 31 2hd 21½ McCarron C J LB 116 b 2.50 94-06 Suggest1161½ SummerAtSaratoga1169 ChevalSauvge116½ Bid, outkicked 10
29May95-10Hol fst 6½f :214 :443 1:091 1:153 3↑ Md Sp Wt 87 9 7 74½ 52¼ 32 23 Almeida G F LB 115 b 5.40 88-07 TresParaiso1153 SummerAtSrtog1152½ Pirte'sGulch116nk Forced in start 11
Previously trained by Eurton Peter
15Apr95-6SA fst 6f :22 :45 :563 1:084 Md Sp Wt 73 5 1 1hd 31 45 410¼ Antley C W LB 118 b 9.80 82-14 MovingTribute1183¼ ShortFreeze1183 CloverRovr1184 Dueled, weakened 8

WORKOUTS: Oct8 SA 4f fst :474 H 6/24 Oct2 SA 4f fst :482 H 19/32 Sep25 SA 6f fst 1:143 H 18/28 Sep18 SA 5f fst 1:003 H 14/52 Sep12 Dmr 5f fst 1:013 H 6/11 Sep6 Dmr 5f fst :594 H 5/46

Moving Tribute

This guy's missed a few times at low odds; but he's seem some pretty rugged sprinters also; proven capable fresh, retains his regular jock; distancewise 6 1/2 looks just right; all in all, this is probably a major player- although he doesn't hold any advantage when noting he's racing one notch above his conditions.

Summer At Saratoga

Only one race this year, that's cause for concern; but his Beyer didn't drop that much, and trainer keeps him at this level; colt has always shown some promise, had success with Chris M. at the helm; worktab isn't exactly stellar but at least with a consistency to it; adds to the exotics mix.

continued

Tres Paraiso

Own: Auerbach Ernest

NAKATANI C S (20 5 5 0 .25) 1996:(866 191 .22)

B. g. 4
Sire: Honest Pleasure (What a Pleasure)
Dam: Belledoux (Barachois)
Br: Auerbach Ernest (Cal)
Tr: Vienna Darrell (2 1 0 0 .50) 1996:(126 27 .21)

L 117

Lifetime Record :	10 3 3 0	$96,675			
1996	5 2 1 0	$58,825	Turf	1 0 0 0	
1995	5 1 2 0	$37,850	Wet	0 0 0 0	
SA	0 0 0 0		Dist	3 1 1 0	$32,700

14Sep96- 9BM fst 6f :214 :441 :562 1:084 3↑ BM BCSprintH192k 78 11 5 8 6½ 85 11 8¾ 11 8¾ Lopez A D LB 116 39.40 88-10 Boundless Moment1161 Concept Win115½ Paying Dues119½ Raced wide 11
22Aug96- 7Dmr fst 6½f :22 :443 1:084 1:151 3↑ Alw 53000N3X 66 1 7 6 4¾ 7 5½ 78 7 15¾ Antley C W LB 117 *2.10 79-13 Tom Cruiser119¾ Mr Ice Age1171¾ Summer At Saratoga1171 7
Hopped in air start, 5 wide
21Jly96- 2Hol fst 6½f :214 :441 1:091 1:152 3↑ [S]Answer Do71k 93 3 6 4 1½ 4 3½ 34 25 Desormeaux K J LB 120 2.50 84-12 Letthebighossroll1245 TrsPriso1201¾ WildGold1222 Late outside for 2nd 6
20Jun96- 7Hol fst 6f :22 :444 :562 1:082 3↑ Alw 41500N2X 107 4 3 21 2hd 2hd 12 McCarron C J LB 119 10.90 97-10 Tres Paraiso1192 Ambivalent1131¼ VenusGenus1161¾ Dueled, kicked clear 8
10May96- 7Hol fst 7f :222 :451 1:09 1:211 3↑ [S]Alw 40000N1X 94 6 5 2hd 2hd 11 1no Stevens G L LB 120 *1.30 96-12 Tres Paraiso120no Ambivalent1156¼ Woodman's Kris120no Just held 10
26Jly95- 5Dmr fm 1 (T) :224 :471 1:112 1:353 [R]Oceanside80k 80 1 2 21 5 2¼ 5 3¾ 6 5½ Desormeaux K J LB 116 14.00 87-05 LkeGeorge1162 ScoreQuick116no PrivteInterview116hd Inside, weakened 7
Run in divisions
14Jly95- 3Hol fst 7½f :22 :442 1:091 1:28 3↑ Alw 40000N1X 90 6 2 2hd 1hd 2hd 2 2½ Desormeaux K J LB 116 *1.00 91-10 Mint Green1182½ Tres Paraiso1163¾ Gunnys Gold118nk Well wide early 6
21Jun95- 8Hol fst 1 1/16 :23 :461 1:104 1:432 3↑ [S]Alw 43000N1X 85 2 1 1hd 1hd 11 23 Desormeaux K J LB 116 1.80 81-17 T. J.'s Gold1163 Tres Paraiso1162 Dresser115nk Inside duel 8
29May95-10Hol fst 6½f :214 :443 1:091 1:153 3↑ Md Sp Wt 94 5 1 2½ 2hd 1½ 13 Desormeaux K J LB 115 *2.90 91-07 TresParaiso1153 SummerAtSaratoga1152½ Pirte'sGulch116nk Clearly best 11
30Apr95- 9Hol fst 6f :22 :443 :57 1:093 3↑ Md Sp Wt 72 4 8 55 45 4 7½ 4 7¼ Desormeaux K J LB 116 6.20 85-11 Bank Code1152¼ Deep Power1223 Grace Of Darby1152 Off slowly, wide 8

WORKOUTS: Oct8 SA tr.t 3f fst :363 H 1/1 Sep28 SA 5f fst 1:004 H 16/43 Sep23 SA tr.t 3f fst :364 H 1/2 Sep9 Dmr 6f fst 1:133 B 3/10 Sep3 Dmr 5f fst 1:04 H 29/29 Aug29 Dmr 3f fst :35 H 2/22

Off The Tee

Own: Lupica Louis A

ANTLEY C W (2 0 0 0 .00) 1996:(699 106 .15)

B. g. 5
Sire: London Bells (Nijinsky II)
Dam: Knight's Promise (Sir Ivor)
Br: Mira Loma Thoroughbred Farm (Cal)
Tr: Buc John R (—) 1996:(52 11 .21)

L 117

Lifetime Record :	19 9 2 3	$72,095			
1996	6 3 0 0	$65,415	Turf	2 0 0 1	$490
1995	9 6 1 1	$5,310	Wet	1 1 0 0	$540
SA	0 0 0 0		Dist	1 0 1 0	$680

14Sep96- 9BM fst 6f :214 :441 :562 1:084 3↑ BM BCSprintH192k 96 5 7 43 5 2½ 4 1¾ 42 Gonzalez R M LB 115 8.50 95-10 BoundlessMoment1161 ConcptWin115½ PyingDus119½ Raced wide turn 11
30Aug96- 8BM fst 6f :214 :441 :562 1:084 3↑ West12RanchH35k 97 7 4 33 3 2½ 1hd 14 Gonzalez R M LB 115 10.70 97-10 Off The Tee1154 Big Red Irishman1143 LilSneeker115¾ Wide stretch run 9
6Jly96-10Pln fst 6f :214 :442 :561 1:092 3↑ SamJWhitingH37k 94 3 4 4 1½ 65 54 1nk Gonzalez R M LB 115 10.00 94-09 Off The Tee115nk Big Fat Jack1161 Go Bux113hd Shuffled back turn 8
14Jun96- 6GG fst 6f :212 :433 :56 1:091 3↑ Clm 50000 91 3 5 3 1½ 32 31 1 1½ Gonzalez R M LB 115 11.30 93-08 Off The Tee1151½ Pharaoh's Heart118hd Governor Elect1172½ Off slowly 5
Previously trained by Bergen Paul D
5May96- 5GG fst 6f :212 :433 :554 1:084 3↑ Clm 75000 84 6 5 76 7 6¾ 6 6¼ 64 Tohill K S LB 115 58.10 91-09 [DH]Lil Sneeker117 [DH]Lookin' Groovy1151 Juan's Boy117½ Outrun 7
8Mar96- 7BM fst 6f :221 :452 :58 1:112 4↑ Alw 25000N1X 54 10 4 6 4¼ 9 8¾ 11 12 11 12¾ Olguin G L LB 118 12.00 71-20 Swing's Lew118hd Osceola Lad1181½ Saltwater Sharpie118no Outrun 11
Previously trained by Clark Ray P
30Sep95-12TuP fm 1 1/16 (T) :232 :463 1:11 1:432 3↑ Bienvenidos13k 51 2 6 6 7½ 5 6½ 6 13 6 17¾ Bridges K M L 115 8.80 82-06 Passiano117¾ Walk Point1211½ Kemper1213 Tired thru stretch 10
Previously trained by Brunson Phil A
20Aug95- 9Wyo fst 6f :231 :434 1:08 3↑ Alw 1500NC 94 4 4 21 3 1½ 11 1 1½ Guymon T F LB 124 *1.10 102-13 Off The Tee1241½ Desert Dasher1243 Jaminjerry1243 Late speed 5
13Aug95-12Wyo fst 6f :214 :434 1:091 3↑ Alw 1500NC 83 3 5 2½ 21 2½ 1½ Black K LB 124 *.30 96-12 Off The Tee124½ Golden Courage1246 NaturalTwilight124hd Pressed pace 6
29Jly95- 7Wyo fst 6f :22 :442 1:094 3↑ Alw 1300N4L 74 3 2 33 2 1½ 1 1½ 1 5½ Black K LB 124 *.60 93-15 Off The Tee1245½ Diana's Reggie1243½ Golden Courage1241½ Pressed pace 6

WORKOUTS: Sep29 BM 5f fst 1:002 H 3/30 Aug23 BM 5f fst 1:023 H 10/18 Aug16 Bmf 5f fst 1:031 H 17/20 Jly20 GG 5f fst 1:00 H 5/26

Tres Paraiso

Looked like an up-and-comer when beating the talented Ambivalent twice at Hollypark; regressed some in the Answer Do, really regressed since; no local experience to fall back on yet many will embrace when eyeing the jock aloft, trainer's stats for the year; we're inclined to be very wary.

Off The Tee

Healthy Beyers for the most part, consistency noted also; gelding was only 2 off Boundless Moment up north as well; does he fit with this bunch classwise?; will he like this main track?; tough to say; and stylewise this guy is used to racing behind :21 4/5 quarters; will the pace be faster here?; maybe not, but when the hustlin' starts this guy will have a different brand of hoss to chase.

Pumpkin House

Own: Lewis Charlie & McCaslin Robert F

Dk. b or br c. 4
Sire: Pirate's Bounty (Holst the Flag)
Dam: Halloween Baby (Naskra)
Br: Wygod Mr & Mrs Martin J (Cal)
Tr: Keen Dallas E (3 2 0 1 .67) 1996:(204 42 .21)

SOLIS A (30 5 5 6 .17) 1996:(1087 198 .18)

L 117

		Lifetime Record :	8 3 2 2		$144,750		
1996	3 0 0 2	$16,050	Turf	1 0 0 0		
1995	5 3 2 0	$128,700	Wet	1 1 0 0		$22,000
SA	2 1 1 0	$30,400	Dist	2 1 1 0		$30,400

5Sep96-8Dmr fst 1 .223 .461 1:102 1:351 3↑ Alw 51300N3x   81 1 3 2° 39½ 35½ 39½ Solis A   LB 117   2.40   84-13 Patrick117½ Sovereign Sage117° Pumpkin House117   Rail trip 4

10Aug96-5Dmr fm 1 ⊕.223 .47 1:11 1:351 3↑ Alw 57000N3x   89 8 5 5³½ 6³½ 6⁹½ 7⁷ Delahoussaye E   LB 117   7.70   87-11 Gastown117ⁿᵏ Beau Jingles117³½ Expelled117½   Between foes, weakened 9

26Jly96-6Dmr fst 1 .223 .461 1:101 1:354 3↑ Clm c-62500   87 5 5 5½ 5³½ 31 31½ McCarron C J   LB 117   *1.80   90-17 I'm Checkin'Out117½ NaturalSwinger117½ PumpkinHouse117²½   Willingly 8

Claimed from Wygod Mr & Mrs Martin J, Ellis Ronald W Trainer

2Jly95-8Hol fst 1¹⁄₁₆ .234 .471 1:112 1:421   Affirmed H-G3   90 5 3 31 31½ 22 29 Stevens G L   LB 115   2.50   87-04 Mr Purple120⁹ Pumpkin House115²½ Oncefortheroad114ⁿᵈ   6

Bobbled start, 4 wide into lane

4Jun95-7Hol fst 7½f .221 .443 1:093 1:282 3↑ SⒶAlw 45000N2x   97 9 3 8⁸ 7⁷½ 31½ 1² Stevens G L   LB 114   *2.10   92-10 Pumpkin House114² Saros° Triumph115² Desert Pirate114³   Clearly best 9

6May95-7Hol fst 1¹⁄₁₆ .233 .464 1:111 1:431   SⒶSnow Chief66k   92 8 7 7⁵½ 4⁴½ 2ⁿᵈ 1ʰᵈ Valenzuela P A   LB 117   3.20   85-17 Pumpkin House117ʰᵈ Gastown115⁶ Canyon Crest114¹½   Game inside 8

5Apr95-7SA fst 6½f .212 .44 1:093 1:16   SⒶAlw 42000N1X   88 8 1 7⁷ 7⁴½ 3² 2½ Stevens G L   LB 120   *1.00   91-10 Tank Ya Folks120½ Pumpkin House120ⁿᵏ Twice Shy117¹½   Outkicked late 8

11Mar95-10SA wf 6f .214 .44 1:093 1:16   SⒶMd Sp Wt   86 3 3 4¹½ 2²½ 21 1½ Stevens G L   LB 118   *1.90   92-07 PumpkinHouse118½ MojiveRed113⁹ GoldenPretens118¹½   Steady handling 7

WORKOUTS: Oct5 Hol 4f fst :493 H 19/20   Sep26 Hol 6f fst 1:123 H 2/21   Sep18 Hol 4f fst :474 H 4/17   Sep1 Dmr 4f fst :88 H 10/44   Aug24 Dmr 5f fst :09 H 7/51   Aug5 Dmr ⊕ 4f fm :501 H (d) 8/10

Pumpkin House

*Former trainer hung out a
monstrous 'for sale' sign
July 26 after this one's
year layoff and the bait
and hoss were taken;
efforts since rarther drab
and a bit surprised that
sharp Keen keeps this
one at this level; maybe
colt will find his old form
at this track but he won't
find the legs he used to
have.*

—Randy Franklin

saying he's been scratched. Summer At Saratoga has ability, but he's had only one race since December and shows just one win in seven tries at the distance. Off The Tee can run, but his races have all been up north against easier competition and his highest Beyer is a 97. Pumpkin House is not the horse he once was and was horrified in his last effort at Del Mar by Patrick, who barely edged out Costly Frosty there on August 25.

We're now left with two more horses to consider, Guadalcanal and Tres Paraiso. The former looks chancy at best, but shows one race, with a Beyer of 101, that would make him a contender. It came after a layoff, as does this race, though only about six weeks instead of a year. The colt obviously has problems, as he's had to add Lasix and Butazolidin for his last three efforts. But he's fast, is ridden by a top jockey, is trained by a man who likes to win races, and shows a nice steady workout pattern for his return. Best of all, his price will be high. I'd like to be able to throw him out, but it might be dangerous to do so.

Tres Paraiso is a more interesting possibility. That Beyer of 107 jumps off the page at you, even though his three subsequent efforts have failed to repeat. If we take a closer look, though, we can make a case for disregarding them. His try on July 21 was not bad and came in a minor stakes race. On August 22 he eliminated himself at the start and lost more ground going wide on the turn. On September 14 he was clearly competing over his head against much better animals, as you can tell from his price, $39.40 to the dollar. He shows three nice works since that race and is back among his friends, a horseman's way of saying that he's now competing at his proper level of ability. His trainer wins over a fifth of his races, a very high percentage, and his new jockey, Corey Nakatani, is always among the top five riders at every meet.

Shall we bet this race or not? And if so, how?

THIRD RACE

Santa Anita

OCTOBER 10, 1996

6½ FURLONGS. (1.14) ALLOWANCE. Purse $46,000. 3-year-olds and upward which have not won $3,000 three times other than maiden or claiming or have never won four races. Weights: 3-year-olds, 120 lbs. Older, 122 lbs. Non-winners of two such races since August 1, allowed 3 lbs. Of such a race since September 1, 5 lbs.

Value of Race: $46,000 Winner $25,300; second $9,200; third $6,900; fourth $3,450; fifth $1,150. Mutuel Pool $236,146.50 Exacta Pool $187,677.00 Quinella Pool $33,195.00

Last Raced	Horse	M/Eqt. A.Wt	PP St	¼	½	Str Fin	Jockey	Odds $1
14Sep96 9BM11	Tres Paraiso	LB 4 117	4 6	5⁴	4hd	2½ 1½	Nakatani C S	6.00
14Sep96 9BM4	Off The Tee	LB 5 117	5 1	4hd	5³	3½ 2²	Antley C W	4.00
29Sep96 11Fpx6	Costly Frosty	LBb 4 119	2 4	3½	1hd	1½ 3⁶	Valenzuela P A	1.20
5Sep96 8Dmr3	Pumpkin House	LB 4 117	6 2	6	6	6 4¹	Solis A	9.90
22Aug96 7Dmr3	Summer At Saratoga	LBb 4 117	3 5	1hd	2hd	4¹ 5²	McCarron C J	4.00
22Aug96 7Dmr4	Guadalcanal	LB 4 117	1 3	2hd	3½	5¹ 6	Desormeaux K J	8.60

OFF AT 1:57 Start Good. Won driving. Time, :21⁴, :44³, 1:08⁴, 1:15 Track fast.

$2 Mutuel Prices:

4–TRES PARAISO	14.00	6.60	3.00
5–OFF THE TEE		5.40	2.80
2–COSTLY FROSTY			2.20

$2 EXACTA 4–5 PAID $71.80 $2 QUINELLA 4–5 PAID $43.20

B. g, by Honest Pleasure–Belledoux, by Barachois. Trainer Vienna Darrell. Bred by Auerbach Ernest (Cal).

TRES PARAISO was four wide early, continued off the rail behind the dueling leaders, found room to rally into the stretch, took the lead outside COSTLY FROSTY in midstretch and pulled clear under urging, then held sway under a strong hand ride. OFF THE TEE was five wide early, dueled four wide on the backstretch, drifted out a bit when outside the winner on the turn, came four wide into the stretch and went willingly to the wire. COSTLY FROSTY set or forced the pace between rivals to the stretch, inched away from foes into the stretch but could not match the top pair. PUMPKIN HOUSE broke alertly, then dropped back and angled in, raced a bit off the rail throughout and passed a pair of tiring rivals. SUMMER AT SARATOGA dueled between rivals on the backstretch and three deep on the turn, then weakened. GUADALCANAL forced the pace along the inside to the stretch and gave way.

Owners— 1, Auerbach Ernest; 2, Lupica Louis A; 3, Keh & Knudson & Martinez; 4, Lewis Charlie & McCaslin Robert F; 5, Red Oak Stables; 6, Dizney Donald R & English James

Trainers— 1, Vienna Darrell; 2, Buc John R; 3, Marshall Robert W; 4, Keen Dallas E; 5, McAnally Ronald; 6, Hess R B Jr

Scratched— Moving Tribute (12Aug96 8DMR2)

$3 Pick Three (6–8–4) Paid $808.50; Pick Three Pool $93,555.

Before we analyze the result of this race and I tell you how I wound up betting it, you'll note that we've been handicapping the card without looking also at the official program published by the track. This is because most of the time you will be looking at the *Racing Form* before you ever get to the track or a wagering satellite. It is important for you to be able to analyze a race, even quickly, without having to resort to or being influenced by the morning line, which you should pay attention to only *after* you've made your own selections. The odds assigned to each entry by the track handicapper represent only his own opinion. One of the golden rules, remember, is not to base your action at the races on other people's opinions, however expert they may appear to be. If you've done your homework and know how to read and interpret the statistics, you're as likely to pick a winner as anybody else around you.

This third race is a case in point. I had decided I could not wager on it straight, because I thought both Costly Frosty and Tres Paraiso would go off at low odds. To my surprise, the public ignored Tres Paraiso and let him go at six to one from his morning line of three to one. I wavered. I thought about betting on him straight, but then decided his odds might drop again before the start. This often happens, as the public, influenced by the morning line or some tout sheet, decides to pour money in at the last minute. Then, too, I was afraid of Guadalcanal, knocked down to eight to one from a morning line of ten. I thought seriously about passing again, but decided instead to get into the game.

This was because I had already handicapped the next two races and knew that the odds on all the horses in both of them would be high enough to justify taking a chance on my favorite parlay, the pick-three. Even if Costly Frosty won, at his odds of six to five, I'd almost certainly show a nice profit without risking much. I invested thirty-six dollars in two one-dollar pick-threes, using only Costly Frosty and Tres Paraiso to three horses in each of the next two races.

I should have stopped there, but I still had this gut feeling that Guadalcanal might run a big one, so I used him by boxing him in exactas to my two top selections. If he had run second to one of them, I'd have made a nice hit, while still finding myself in action with the pick-three. If he'd won, with either of my other horses running second, I've have lost the pick-three bet, but cashed a very sizable exacta ticket to compensate for it. Another golden rule, remember? Every wager you make must show a profit; never bet just to get your money back.

Guadalcanal ran for half the race, then stopped as if shot, and Tres Paraiso was not bet down. I felt a little foolish at the end of this race for not having cashed on him, but I was alive in what might become a lucrative pick-three. A third of the day gone and I had lost eighteen dollars, not too bad at my level of action.

Let's suppose we are not going into this next race with an interest in a pick-three. How would it work out as a fresh betting proposition? Poorly. Why? Let's have a look at pages 126–128.

■   RACE 4: First of all, the conditions of the race indicate that these are among the weakest of the two-year-old fillies on the grounds, as untalented a group as you will ever find at a major racetrack. Their owners have so little confidence in them that they have entered them at the rock-bottom price at this track for the category. None of them has a speed rating of any significance and the logical contenders will almost certainly go off at odds too low to warrant a straight bet. Let's find these contenders.

Royal Wish has been declared out of the race, but had showed nothing to recommend her anyway. Good riddance. Flying Hostess showed a brief turn of speed at Fairplex, but stopped to a walk for no apparent reason; she ran her first race on Lasix, so had no obvious excuse for giving up. Sparkling Meeting displayed such a serious case of the slows, a Beyer fig of 49, that even the addition of blinkers probably won't help. (Read the *Form*'s comment on her.) Boomshacalaca should obviously be pulling a milk wagon in some Third World country.

Of the first-time starters, about whom we know less than the others, we have to do a little guessing. In this kind of

4 — Santa Anita Park

6 Furlongs (1:07¹) **MAIDEN CLAIMING. Purse $17,000. Fillies, 2-year-olds bred in California. Weight, 120 lbs. Claiming price $32,000, if for $28,000, allowed 2 lbs.**

6 FURLONGS

Bud's Pet
Own: Wacken Caesar
$32,000

Dk. b or br f. 2 (Mar)
Sire: Neptune*ARG (Ahmad)
Dam: Volage (Pretense)
Br: Wacken Caesar (Cal)
Tr: Mitchell Mike (7 2 2 0 .29) 1996:(306 69 .23)

STEVENS G L (9 3 1 1 1 .33) 1996:(553 115 .21)   L 120

	Lifetime Record:	2 M 1 0	$4,050		
1996	2 M 1 0	$4,050	Turf	0 0 0 0	
1995	0 M 0 0		Wet	0 0 0 0	
SA	0 0 0 0		Dist	0 0 0 0	

4Sep96-6Dmr fst 5½f :22 :45³ :58⁴ 1:05¹ ⊕Md 3200 4.60 80-10 Run For B.And W118½ Prized Peaches116¹ Moose118¾ 4 wide trip 11
21Aug96-4Dmr fst 5½f :22² :46³ :58⁴ 1:05¹ ⊕Md 3200 *2.30 82-13 Hot Baby118½ Bud's Pet118ⁿᵏ Forgotten Woman118½ Bid, outfinished 11
WORKOUTS: Oct5 Hol5f fst 1:02³ H 22/25 ●Sep27 Hol4f fst :48² H 1/15 Sep20 Hol3f fst :37⁴ H 9/17 ●Sep14 Hol3f fst :35⁴ H 1/12 Aug30 Dmr3f fst :37⁴ H 16/20 Aug16 Dmr3f fst 1:02 Hg4/59

Judyjudyjudy
Own: Cardiff Stud Farm & Hi Card Ranch
$32,000

Gr/ro f. 2 (Mar)
Sire: Desert Wine (Damascus)
Dam: Lady Hawkins (Hawkin's Special)
Br: Hi Card Ranch & Cardiff Stud Farm (Cal)
Tr: Dollase Wallace (20 5 1 0 .25) 1996:(101 23 .23)

NAKATANI C S (20 5 5 0 .25) 1996:(866 191 .22)   120

	Lifetime Record:	0 M 0 0			
1996	0 M 0 0		Turf	0 0 0 0	
1995	0 M 0 0		Wet	0 0 0 0	
SA	0 0 0 0		Dist	0 0 0 0	

WORKOUTS: Oct3 Hol6f fst 1:14⁴ H 8/15 Sep26 Hol5f fst 1:03² H 25/20 Sep20 Hol5f fst 1:02³ H 20/21 Sep13 Hol4f fst :50¹ H 12/25 Aug26 Dmr4f fst :49 H 46/74
Aug19 Dmr3f fst :35⁴ H 5/33 Aug2 Dmr3f fst :37 H 17/26 Jly27 Dmr3f fst :38 H 26/74

Flying Hostess
Own: Valpredo John
$32,000

B. f. 2 (Jun)
Sire: Flying Victor (Flying Paster)
Dam: Yankee Hostess (Dimaggio)
Br: Valpredo John (Cal)
Tr: Olguin Ulises (—) 1996:(150 8 .05)

BLANC B (18 2 2 4 .11) 1995:(1022 104 .10)   L 120

	Lifetime Record:	1 M 0 0	$600		
1996	1 M 0 0	$600	Turf	0 0 0 0	
1995	0 M 0 0		Wet	0 0 0 0	
SA	0 0 0 0		Dist	1 0 0 0	$600

23Sep96-3Fpx fst 6f :21⁴ :46² :59¹ 1:12² ⊕Md Sp Wt *1.40 65-09 Guthr115¹⁰ Doub'lWnnr116⁸ Woodford'contyMs116½ Early foot, gave way 6
WORKOUTS: Sep30 Fpx3f fst 1:03¹ H 8/10 ●Sep19 Fpx3f fst :34¹ H 1/12 Aug30 Dmr5f fst 1:00⁹ H 2/12

A CLOSER LOOK
4th Santa Anita

Bud's Pet
Disappointed in her last start after a promising debut; may bounce back with an improved performance given her recent works; training exceptionally well; top-notch trainer and jock adds to her appeal.

Judyjudyjudy
Sire is adequate with first timers, connecting at a 15% clip; dam has dropped 2 winners; filly's works have been inconsistent; she's record several decent drills, and several sluggish ones as well; attracts Nakatani; tough call.

Flying Hostess
Hit a wall after 4f in her debut; you never want to see a horse fade like that, especially at Fpx where the track favors speed; suspect in the stamina department.

Sparkling Meeting
Own: Iron County Farms Inc
$32,000
ANTLEY C W (2 0 0 0 .00) 1996:(699 106 .15)

B. f. 2 (Apr)
Sire: General Meeting (Seattle Slew)
Dam: Sparkling Star (Lyphard)
Br: Mabee John C Mr & Mrs (Cal)
Tr: Lewis Craig A (4 0 1 0 .00) 1996:(157 20 .13)
120

Lifetime Record: 1 M 0 0 $450

1996	1 M 0 0 $450	Turf	0 0 0 0
1995	0 M 0 0	Wet	0 0 0 0
SA	0 0 0 0	Dist	0 0 0 0

2Sep96- 2Dmr fst 5½f :222 :46 :584 1:052 [F][S]Md c-32000 49 1 10 10⁸½ 99¾ 68½ 55½ Antley C W LB 118 2.80 80-09 MssEnchntmnt118½ Prls'npnths1184 JmnJmMcQ116¾ Drifted well wide 12
Claimed from Golden Eagle Farm, Dollase Wallace Trainer

WORKOUTS: Sep27 SA 6f fst 1:16 H 16/18 Sep21 SA 6f fst 1:151 H 19/24 Aug30 Dmr 4f fst :484 Hg 15/36 Aug25 Dmr 6f fst 1:15 H 15/22 Aug18 Dmr 5f fst :592 H 9/54 Aug11 Dmr 5f fst 1:02 H 40/55

Moose
Own: McGrath Edward T
$32,000
HUNTER M T (18 3 0 1 .17) 1996:(403 55 .14)

Dk. b or br f. 2 (Mar)
Sire: Pirate's Bounty (Hoist the Flag)
Dam: Maybe the Best (Irish Ruler)
Br: Wygod Martin J Mr & Mrs (Cal)
Tr: Greenman Walter (4 2 0 0 .50) 1996:(243 42 .17)
120

Lifetime Record: 3 M 0 1 $4,275

1996	3 M 0 1 $4,275	Turf	0 0 0 0
1995	0 M 0 0	Wet	0 0 0 0
SA	1 0 0 0 $975	Dist	1 0 0 0 $600

28Sep96- 7BM fst 6f :223 :454 :581 1:104 [F][S]Md Sp Wt 58 4 2 2½ 2hd 23 57 Nakatani C S LB 117 *1.10 80-15 Billie's Babe1173 Fair Mims1171 Rulina1172 Gave way 10
4Sep96- 6Dmr fst 5½f :22 :453 :584 1:051 [F]Md 32000 60 9 5 74½ 56½ 55½ 32¼ Flores D R B 118 7.10 85-10 Run For B And W1181¼ Prized Peaches1161 Moose1181½ 4 wide turn 11
10Apr96- 1SA fst 2f :213 [F][S]Md Sp Wt — 2 2 5¾ 52¼ Delahoussaye E B 118 12.80 — — TheresEilen118nk ExcllntHlf1181¾ RndisPrimvr118hd Dueled between foes 10

WORKOUTS: Sep25 SA 5f fst 1:022 H 31/37 Sep19 SA 6f fst 1:151 H 12/15 Sep13 Dmr 4f fst :501 H 3/10 Aug31 Dmr 5f fst 1:012 H 33/63 Aug26 Dmr 6f fst 1:14 H 10/25 Aug20 Dmr 6f fst 1:134 H 8/21

Royal Wish
Own: Jackson & Sahadi
$32,000
SORENSON D (2 0 0 0 .00) 1996:(208 21 .10)

Ch. f. 2 (Apr)
Sire: Magesterial (Northern Dancer)
Dam: Keep Hoping*GB (Busted*GB)
Br: Duffel Joseph A (Cal)
Tr: Jackson Bruce L (—) 1996:(90 7 .08)
L 120

Lifetime Record: 0 M 0 0

1996	0 M 0 0	Turf	0 0 0 0
1995	0 M 0 0	Wet	0 0 0 0
SA	0 0 0 0	Dist	0 0 0 0

WORKOUTS: Sep27 SA 4f fst :471 Hg 4/30 Sep14 SA 3f fst :354 Hg 3/18 Sep8 Hol 5f fst 1:011 H 8/19 Aug28 Hol 5f fst 1:003 H 9/15 Aug21 Hol 5f fst 1:014 Hg 12/24 Aug14 Hol 5f fst 1:032 H 13/18
Aug6 Hol 4f fst :493 H 12/24 Jly31 Hol 4f fst :493 H 18/24 Jly22 Hol 4f fst :483 H 6/25 Jly16 Hol 4f fst :484 H 10/35 Jun23 Hol 4f fst :494 Hg 41/54 Jun16 Hol 4f fst :49 H 16/44

Slewpy's Bad Habit
Own: Manzani Ronald
$32,000
PEDROZA M A (23 4 3 1 .17) 1996:(1021 125 .12)

Dk. b or br f. 2 (Feb)
Sire: Slewpy (Seattle Slew)
Dam: Habit Ann (Habitony*GB)
Br: Manzani Ronald (Cal)
Tr: Spawr Bill (5 2 0 0 .40) 1996:(345 54 .16)
120

Lifetime Record: 0 M 0 0

1996	0 M 0 0	Turf	0 0 0 0
1995	0 M 0 0	Wet	0 0 0 0
SA	0 0 0 0	Dist	0 0 0 0

WORKOUTS: Sep30 SA 4f fst :50 H 28/35 Sep18 SA 6f fst 1:132 H 2/12 Sep11 Dmr 5f fst 1:023 H 22/30 Sep4 Dmr 5f fst 1:03 H 60/67 Aug29 Dmr 5f fst 1:031 H 57/68 Aug24 Dmr 4f fst :492 H 26/53
Aug16 Dmr 5f fst 1:013 H 33/59 Aug11 Dmr 4f fst :494 H 35/58 Aug6 Dmr 3f fst :384 H 12/14 Aug1 Dmr 3f fst :394 H 35/37 Jly15 Hol 3f fst :361 H 2/14

Sparkling Meeting

Joins a new barn after a decent closing effort in her debut; new connections add blinkers to her equipment, hoping to sharpen her speed; could be dangerous if she comes out more aggressively at the start.

Moose

Didn't run poorly at BM; in fact, she ran her race from a Beyer standpoint; caught a talented NoCal crew that came home in extremely good time; loses Nakatani but picks up an underrated jock in Hunter; major player.

Royal Wish

Makes her first start off a number of short drills; trainer and jock both have poor win percentages on this circuit; sire gets 9% first-out winners; dam has dropped one winner; prefer to see a race.

Slewpy's Bad Habit

Not much breeding info to go on; Slewpy gets 9% winners with first timers; this is the dam's first foal; as a racehorse she was a disappointment, retiring a maiden after just one start; some of her siblings went on to do some things, though; from a good barn.

continued

Julies Desert Star

Own: Young Stephen A
$32,000
VALENZUELA P A (33 2 5 4 .06) 1996:(491 60 .12)

B. f. 2 (Mar)
Sire: Desert Wine (Damascus)
Dam: Morningstar Lane (Maheras)
Br: Steve Young & Robert Scherman (Cal)
Tr: Aguirre Paul G (1 0 0 0 .00) 1996:(74 11 .15)
120

Lifetime Record :	2 M 0 1	$2,700			
1996	2 M 0 1	$2,700	Turf	0 0 0 0	
1995	0 M 0 0		Wet	0 0 0 0	
SA	0 0 0 0		Dist	1 0 0 1	$2,700

11Sep96-4Dmr fst 6f :22^1 :45^4 :58^2 1:11^1 [S]Md 32000 60 1 3 3^1 2^2 2$^{2\frac12}$ 3$^{8\frac12}$ Valenzuela P A B 116 b 23.10 74–15 Red Phone118^5 Native Sculpture118$^{3\frac12}$ Julies Desert Star116$^{1\frac34}$ Inside trip 10
29Aug96-6Dmr fst 6½f :22^1 :45^2 1:11 1:18 Ⓕ[S]Md 32000 46 2 9 8$^{3\frac34}$ 8$^{5\frac12}$ 8^{11} 7$^{10\frac12}$ Berrio O A B 118 19.20 70–14 Message Of Honey118^{nk} Miss Lawless118^5 Lady Integrity118^1 No late bid 12
WORKOUTS: Sep28 Hol 5f fst 1:01^1 H *18/31* Sep22 Hol 4f fst :48^3 H *6/15* Aug15 Dmr 4f fst :48^2 Hg*30/64* Aug10 Dmr 6f fst 1:13^2 H *6/24* Aug4 Dmr 5f fst 1:00^3 H *18/64* Jly23 Hol 5f fst 1:02^4 H *18/25*

Boomshacalaca

Own: Marchosky Rubin
$32,000
VALENZUELA F H (7 0 0 0 .00) 1996:(473 25 .05)

B. f. 2 (Feb)
Sire: Saros*GB (Sassafras*Fr)
Dam: Live to Love (Regalberto)
Br: Perez Mag (Cal)
Tr: Valenzuela Martin Jr (2 0 0 0 .00) 1996:(20 0 .00)
L 120

Lifetime Record :	2 M 0 0	$340			
1996	2 M 0 0	$340	Turf	0 0 0 0	
1995	0 M 0 0		Wet	0 0 0 0	
SA	0 0 0 0		Dist	1 0 0 0	$340

19Sep96-12Fpx fst 6f :22^1 :46^4 :59^3 1:12^2 Ⓕ[S]Md 32000 23 10 9 10$^{8\frac34}$ 9$^{8\frac34}$ 7^{11} 6^{16} Gonzalez S Jr LB 116 82.70 71–09 Filaree116$^{2\frac12}$ Unaflame116^1 Progressive Party116$^{3\frac12}$ Very wide 1st turn 10
29Aug96-6Dmr fst 6½f :22^1 :45^2 1:11 1:18 Ⓕ[S]Md 32000 4 11 6 12^{10} 12^{13} 12^{23} 12$^{28\frac34}$ Valenzuela F H LB 118 81.80 52–14 Message Of Honey118^{nk} Miss Lawless118^5 Lady Integrity118^1 Outrun 12
WORKOUTS: Oct5 SA 5f fst 1:03^1 H *22/23* Sep15 SA tr.t 5f fst 1:04^3 H *2/4* Aug25 Dmr 4f fst :50^1 Hg*44/60* Aug18 Dmr 5f fst 1:02^1 H *42/54* Aug11 Dmr 5f fst 1:02^4 Hg*52/55* Aug4 Dmr 5f fst 1:02^2 H *56/64*

Lady in the Hall

Own: Kenis & 3 Plus U Stable
$32,000
GARCIA J A (12 1 3 1 .08) 1996:(43 11 .26)

Ch. f. 2 (Apr)
Sire: Wheatly Hall (Norcliffe)
Dam: Womanoftheeighties (Foreign Power)
Br: Van Berg Jack C (Cal)
Tr: Van Berg Jack C (—) 1996:(384 48 .13)
120

Lifetime Record :	0 M 0 0			
1996	0 M 0 0		Turf	0 0 0 0
1995	0 M 0 0		Wet	0 0 0 0
SA	0 0 0 0		Dist	0 0 0 0

WORKOUTS: Oct3 Hol 5f fst 1:00^4 Hg*2/27* Sep23 Hol 5f fst 1:05^4 H *36/36* Sep15 Hol 4f fst :52^1 H *29/29* Aug18 Hol 4f fst :48^4 Hg*8/17* Aug11 Hol 4f fst :49^2 H *17/20* Aug5 Hol 4f fst :51^1 H *14/19* Jly25 Hol 3f fst :37^3 H *3/6* Jly8 Hol 3f fst :39 H *26/29*

Julies Desert Star

Took a major step forward in her last start after being equipped with blinkers; also seemed to benefit from the addition of P.Val; lightly-raced and therefore still eligible for further progress.

Boomshacalaca

Beaten 45 lengths in her 2 career starts; has yet to earn better than a 23 Beyer; nothing to like.

Lady In the Hall

The sire isn't much when it comes to first time starters (just 6% winners); came back with a good work on October 3 after 2 slow drills in Sept.; why just 3 published works since mid-August? best to see a race.

–Byron King

situation, it is essential to scan the "A Closer Look" column, this one written by Byron King, for clues. Factual clues, not opinions. On that basis, we can immediately eliminate Lady in the Hall. King waffles a bit on Slewpy's Bad Habit, but the statistics on her breeding are discouraging enough to warrant elimination. Only Judyjudyjudy seems to have enough going for her to make her a threat, but not much of one, mainly because all of her works but one have been glacially slow.

We are now left with Bud's Pet, Moose, and Julies Desert Star, the three entries I used in my pick-three. It is almost impossible to separate them. Bud's Pet was beaten by Moose on September 4, but shows two excellent works since that race, picks up a stronger rider for this category, and is trained by Mike Mitchell, who wins more claiming races than anyone. After having failed up north in an open maiden event, Moose has dropped back in with her friends and is running for the second time on Lasix. If I had to pick out only one horse to use in this race, however, it would have to be Julies Desert Star. She broke from the inside post in her last race and, with the addition of blinkers, showed far more speed than previously before tiring. Or did she bleed? The *Form* doesn't tell us, so we'll have to wait for the program or the track announcer to enlighten us.

We still have nothing to warrant risking money on a straight bet, much less an exotic. Do we pass?

As you can tell from the chart on page 130, Bud's Pet won easily, paying the astonishingly good price of $10.20, well above her morning line of five to two. When I arrived at the track, I also discovered from my program that Julies Desert Star was indeed adding Lasix. (Information on changes in medication doesn't always make it into the *Form* on time, so that you will need always to check your program, where the addition of Lasix is indicated either by the symbol Ⓛ or L1.)

FOURTH RACE

Santa Anita
OCTOBER 10, 1996

6 FURLONGS. (1.07¹) MAIDEN CLAIMING. Purse $17,000. Fillies, 2-year-olds bred in California. Weight, 120 lbs. Claiming price $32,000, if for $28,000, allowed 2 lbs.

Value of Race: $17,000 Winner $9,350; second $3,400; third $2,550; fourth $1,275; fifth $425. Mutuel Pool $301,159.00 Exacta Pool $216,198.00 Trifecta Pool $247,020.00 Quinella Pool $37,900.00

Last Raced	Horse	M/Eqt. A.Wt	PP	St	¼	½	Str	Fin	Jockey	Cl'g Pr	Odds $1
4Sep96 6Dmr5	Bud's Pet	LB 2 120	1	4	6⁴	4²	34½	11½	Stevens G L	32000	4.10
11Sep96 4Dmr3	Julies Desert Star	LBb 2 120	7	2	1ʰᵈ	2½	1ʰᵈ	24½	Valenzuela P A	32000	3.50
	Slewpy's Bad Habit	LB 2 120	6	1	2½	1ʰᵈ	21½	3²	Pedroza M A	32000	8.00
28Sep96 7BM5	Moose	LB 2 120	5	3	5ʰᵈ	51½	5¹	4³	Hunter M T	32000	3.30
	Lady in the Hall	Bf 2 120	2	6	8¹	7½	72½	5½	Garcia J A	32000	18.90
	Judyjudyjudy	LBb 2 120	2	9	7ʰᵈ	6³	62½	6½	Nakatani C S	32000	
2Sep96 2Dmr5	Sparkling Meeting	LBb 2 120	4	6	31½	3ʰᵈ	4ʰᵈ	7⁶	Antley C W	32000	
19Sep96 12Fpx6	Boomshacalaca	LB 2 120	8	7	9	8	8	8	Valenzuela F H	32000	
23Sep96 3Fpx6	Flying Hostess	LB 2 120	3	8	4½	—	—	—	Blanc B	32000	

OFF AT 2:32 Start Good. Won driving. Time, :22¹, :45⁴, :58¹, 1:10⁴ Track fast.

$2 Mutuel Prices:

1–BUD'S PET	10.20	5.20	3.80
7–JULIES DESERT STAR		4.60	3.20
6–SLEWPY'S BAD HABIT			6.60

$2 EXACTA 1–7 PAID $44.20 $2 TRIFECTA 1–7–6 PAID $398.60 $2 QUINELLA 1–7 PAID $20.00

Dk. b. or br. f, (Mar), by Neptuno*ARG–Volage, by Pretense. Trainer Mitchell Mike. Bred by Wackeen Caesar (Cal).

BUD'S PET saved ground on the backstretch and turn, angled out into the stretch, made the lead under urging a sixteen and proved best under steady handling late. JULIES DESERT STAR went up outside SLEWPY'S BAD HABIT to duel for command on the backstretch, regained a short lead outside that one in upper stretch, could not match the winner but clearly bested the rest. SLEWPY'S BAD HABIT sprinted to the early lead and angled in, dueled inside JULIES DESERT STAR to midstretch and weakened but held the show. MOOSE was pulling under a tight hold outside the winner on the backstretch, continued off the rail on the turn and lacked the needed rally. LADY IN THE HALL raced well off the rail on the backstretch and outside BOOMSHACALACA leaving the turn and improved position in the stretch. JUDYJUDYJUDY hesitated and was off slowly, saved ground and also improved position. SPARKLING MEETING was taken outside early, raced three deep into the turn and outside the winner leaving the bend, then weakened. BOOMSHACALACA angled in early and saved ground but never menaced. FLYING HOSTESS stumbled a step out of the gate, drifted out when the rider lost the right iron, had the saddle slip on the backstretch and was pulled up.

Owners— 1, Wackeen Caesar; 2, Young Stephen A; 3, Manzani Ronald; 4, McGrath Edward T; 5, Kenis & 3 Plus U Stable; 6, Cardiff Stud Farm & Hi Card Ranch; 7, Iron County Farms Inc; 8, Marchosky Ruben; 9, Valpredo John

Trainers— 1, Mitchell Mike; 2, Aguirre Paul G; 3, Spawr Bill; 4, Greenman Walter; 5, Van Berg Jack C; 6, Dollase Wallace; 7, Lewis Craig A; 8, Valenzuela Martin Jr; 9, Olguin Ulises

Scratched— Royal Wish

$3 Pick Three (8–4–1) Paid $671.40; Pick Three Pool $47,113.

Had I not been alive in my pick-three to both horses, I might have boxed them in an exacta, with perhaps a straight bet on Bud's Pet as well. Or I might have begun my pick-three with this race, as the next two contests looked equally wide open. I chose to do nothing and so found myself still in action with my parlay bet to three horses in the next race and a potential small killing.

Actually, I did choose to become involved in this race in another way. At Santa Anita, the fourth on a normal nine-race card marks the beginning of the pick-six. I might not have become involved in it at all, as I don't play it every day, but for two factors: the pool would be huge, with a two-day carry-over of $342,122, and I thought it might not take a very big ticket to hit it, because I liked two horses in the last two races well enough to single them in the sequence.

I eventually came up with a play costing forty-eight dollars, using three horses in the fourth race, two in each of the next three, and one in the last two: three by two by two by two by one by one times two dollars. Because even such a modest investment pushed me over my limit for this type of bet, I persuaded a friend of mine to buy half the ticket with me. I now had risked another twenty-four dollars of my working capital of three hundred for the day.

In my pick-six, I used Bud's Pet and Julies Desert Star, but decided to drop Moose for Judyjudyjudy, the only other horse in the race I thought had a chance. She was eliminated at the start, but had she won I at least would have found myself still in action in the pick-six with a long shot, some consolation for having lost my pick-three.

We've now come to the halfway point of the day and I'm still down eighteen dollars, but much will now depend on what happens in the fifth. Usually, on every racing day, there will be one contest that decides your fate, one race on which everything rides. If I lose this next one, I could find myself down at least fifty-four dollars and perhaps as much as seventy-eight. Not disastrous, but discouraging. Shall we have a look?

■ RACE 5: Along with the requisite number of cheap maiden races, this is exactly the sort of contest you are likely to come up against on any weekday at the track. The best

5 Santa Anita Park

1$\frac{1}{16}$ MILES. (1:39) CLAIMING. Purse $13,000. 3-year-olds. Weight, 120 lbs. Non-winners of two races at one mile or over since August 1, allowed 3 lbs. Of such a race since September 1, 5 lbs. Claiming price $12,500; if for $10,500, allowed 2 lbs. (Maiden or races when entered for $10,000 or less not considered.)

Don's Memory

Own: Carrillo Mr & Mrs Fred W — $12,500

Dk. b or br g. 3 (Mar)
Sire: Roman Majesty (His Majesty)
Dam: Top Quality (Golden Eagle II*Fr)
Br: Holt Lester (Cal)
Tr: Spawr Bill (5 2 0 0 .40) 1996:(345 54 .16)

PINCAY L JR (19 4 0 6 .21) 1996:(754 98 .13) — L 115

Lifetime Record:	11 3 0 2	$51,886		
1996	5 1 0 1	$18,355	Turf	0 0 0 0
1995	6 2 0 1	$33,531	Wet	0 0 0 0
SA	5 2 0 0	$33,786	Dist	0 0 0 0

15Sep96-2Fpx	fst 6½f	:22 :46 1:11^{2} 1:18^{2}	Clm 16000	73 4 5 3^{3} 3^{1} 3^{2½} 3^{1}	Flores D R	LB 116 b	*1.70	88-11	SettleSouth114½ SunsetBoulevrd114½ Don'sMemory116½	Bumped break	7
4Sep96-5Dmr	fst 6f	:22^{1} :45^{2} :57^{3} 1:10^{1}	Clm 20000	61 9 3 6^{2¾} 7^{3¾} 7^{4¾} 5^{9½}	Douglas R R	LB 116 b	18.60	78-10	Jestersluckyone116½ Sneaky Guy116no Syn's Way117^{4}	Broke thru gate	9
14Feb96-3SA	fst 6½f	:22^{3} :45^{3} 1:10^{2} 1:17	Clm 32000	64 4 6 5^{2½} 6^{3¼} 5^{5½} 7^{8}	Nakatani C S	LB 120	4.50	77-18	Discard The Five120hd Open River120^{2} Cee A Natural1181¾	Bumped early	9
28Jan96-2SA	fst 6f	:21^{4} :44^{4} :57^{2} 1:10^{4}	Clm c-25000	64 3 5 5^{4} 4^{4} 4^{3½} 5^{5}	Atkinson P	B 121	2.70	79-15	Bowled Over116½ Primero Del Anno119½ Justin's Jewel119^{3}	Inside trip	11
Claimed from Lester Holt Family Trust, Stute Warren Trainer											
1Jan96-4SA	fst 6f	:22 :45^{2} :57^{4} 1:10^{4}	Clm 25000	77 2 7 3^{2½} 2½ 2hd 1nk	Atkinson P	B 121	7.60	84-14	Don's Memory121nk Sams Market121½ Tener Suerte1211¾	Game inside	9
6Dec95-6Hol	fst 7f	:22^{2} :45^{1} 1:10^{2} 1:23	Clm 50000	23 9 4 4^{1¾} 5^{6½} 10^{16} 10^{28½}	Valenzuela F H	B 116 b	17.30	59-14	Discard The Five115^{4} Romaine116^{2} Baffling Baffert117hd	Gave way	10
21Oct95-8SA	fst 7f	:22^{4} :45^{3} 1:10 1:22^{4}	ⓡCal Stallion70k	53 5 1 4^{1½} 6^{4} 6^{7¾} 5^{15}	Atkinson P	B 115 b	11.00	73-12	Cavonnier119^{2} Ready To Order1171¼ Romaine1172¾	Gave way	6
13Oct95-7SA	fst 6f	:22 :45^{1} :57^{4} 1:10^{2}	Clm 35000	74 4 3 5^{2} 4^{2} 3^{2} 1nk	Atkinson P	B 118 b	9.40	85-11	Don'sMemory118nk Romine1201¾ BowledOver115^{1}	Lacked room into lane	9
24Sep95-8Fpx	fst 6f	:22 :46 :58 1:10^{2}	Clm 32000	59 3 10 5^{5} 6^{6½} 5^{9½} 3^{12}	Atkinson P	B 116 b	4.80	85-08	KingJitters109^{7} StgedAndRedy114^{5} Don'sMemory116no	Off slow, jostled	10
9Aug95-7Dmr	fst 5½f	:22 :45 :56^{4} 1:03	Clm 62500	61 7 8 9^{5½} 9^{5½} 8^{5¾} 7^{9¼}	Atkinson P	B 118 b	26.80	89-07	JimmyHoof118½ SingulrVison118½ ZppdThMssg118^{3}	Fractious paddock	10

WORKOUTS: Oct1 SA 4f fst :50^{2} H *21/26* Aug31 Dmr 5f fst 1:01^{1} H *30/63* Aug22 Dmr 6f fst 1:15 H *21/32* Aug15 Dmr 5f fst 1:01^{1} H *34/72* Aug8 Dmr 5f fst 1:01^{4} H *30/54* Aug1 Dmr 4f fst :48^{4} H *26/47*

Gibby's Value

Own: Lemalu Stables — $12,500

Ch. g. 3 (May)
Sire: Present Value (Halo)
Dam: Edgewater (Verbatim)
Br: Jay Bligh (Cal)
Tr: Avila A C (3 0 0 0 .00) 1996:(76 8 .11)

BERRIO O A (5 0 0 0 .00) 1996:(434 25 .06) — L 117

Lifetime Record:	12 3 1 1	$30,838		
1996	11 3 1 1	$30,838	Turf	1 0 0 0
1995	1 M 0 0		Wet	0 0 0 0
SA	3 0 0 0		Dist	5 2 1 0 $17,950

28Sep96-4Fpx	fst 1$\frac{1}{16}$	:23 :46^{3} 1:12^{1} 1:45^{2}	Clm c-10000	59 5 6 6^{7} 6^{5½} 4^{3} 4^{8}	Espinoza V	LB 120 f	*1.30	75-10	Engelbert114^{1} Rowdy Ryan115^{6} Work 'n' Man114^{1}	Wide early, rail lane	6
Claimed from Bligh Jay W, Young Steven W Trainer											
14Sep96-3Fpx	fst 1$\frac{1}{16}$	:23^{3} :48 1:13^{4} 1:47^{2}	Clm 12500	66 1 3 3^{3½} 3^{3} 1½ 1^{3}	Garcia J A	LB 114	*1.60	73-16	Gibby's Value114^{3} ⒹProfitable Music114nk Engelbert1132½	Rallied wide	6
18Jly96-3Hol	fst 1$\frac{1}{16}$	:23^{2} :47^{2} 1:12^{2} 1:45	Clm 12500	64 1 4 4^{2½} 4^{3} 3^{1½} 2¾	Antley C W	LB 116 b	*1.60	75-24	Rush Springs116¾ Gibby's Value1161¼ Mollys Giant116^{2}	4 wide into lane	6
3Jly96-5Hol	fst 7f	:22^{1} :45^{4} 1:11^{1} 1:23^{4}	Clm 16000	67 5 11 11^{8} 9^{6¼} 4^{2¾} 3^{6}	Antley C W	LB 118 b	11.50	77-15	Silver Bandit1185½ Flex N Go117½ Gibby's Value1183½	Late bid	11
15Jun96-7Hol	fst 7½f	:22^{2} :45^{3} 1:10^{1} 1:29^{3}	Clm 20000	68 8 11 9^{7½} 9^{5½} 5^{4½} 4^{6¾}	Antley C W	LB 115 b	21.80	79-13	Boysville1151¼ Predetermined115^{1} Silver Bandit1154½	Squeezed start	11
Previously trained by Arterburn Lonnie											
25May96-5GG	fst 1	:22^{3} :45^{3} 1:11^{2} 1:38^{3}	Clm 15000N2X	66 7 7 7^{9½} 5^{4} 1½ 1¾	Baze R A	LB 118 b	*1.40	77-17	Gibby's Value118¾ Pontranco118^{4} Timeforachill118^{2}	Wide late run	8
13May96-7GG	fm 1$\frac{1}{16}$ ⓣ	:23^{3} :48 1:12^{3} 1:44^{4}+	Clm 25000	55 1 3 3^{4} 4^{3} 5^{8½} 7^{10½}	Baze R A	LB 117 b	3.20	71-18	Blue Sky1182½ Once A Friend115^{2} Jillem117^{2}	Steadied early stages	8
27Apr96-1GG	fst 1$\frac{1}{16}$	:23 :46^{3} 1:11^{1} 1:44	3↑ Md 13500	72 6 7 6^{6¾} 4^{4½} 3^{2} 1^{1}	Baze R A	LB 116 b	4.00	83-13	Gibby's Value116^{1} Referee120^{2} Ghostly Spirits120^{5}	Rallied wide	7
Previously trained by Young Steven W											
16Mar96-6BM	fst 1	:22^{2} :46 1:11^{2} 1:36^{4}	ⓢMd Sp Wt	43 3 5 5^{7½} 6^{6¾} 6^{10} 4^{19½}	Valdivia J^{5}	LB 113 b	20.60	65-13	Hello Heller118½ Talk That Walk118^{8} Skywire1181^{1}	No rally	6
7Feb96-8SA	fst 1	:23 :47 1:11^{3} 1:37^{4}	ⓢMd 32000	23 5 8 9^{9¾} 9^{12} 10^{19} 10^{30½}	Solis A	LB 117 b	10.00	49-17	Te Atua117^{2} Bit Of Summing112¾ March Of Kings1175½	Stumlbed start	10

WORKOUTS: Oct4 SA 4f fst :46^{4} H *5/33* Aug29 Dmr 4f fst :48^{2} H *12/48* Aug11 Dmr 6f fst 1:14^{1} H *13/22*

A CLOSER LOOK

5th Santa Anita

Don's Memory

Hasn't worked out like Spawr would have hoped, but at least this gelding enters this race off a fairly good effort; may be ready to peak in his 3rd start back from a layoff; has never been in this cheap; benefits from the return to his favorite track (2 for 5 at SA); the obvious question mark is how he adapts to a route.

Gibby's Value

Moves up in price following being claimed at Fpx; lacks the lofty speed figures of some of these opponents, although he does at least possess a good overall record; may not be fast enough to take home the top prize.

Bombay

Own: Brown Rubin $12,500

ATKINSON P (3 0 0 0 .00) 1996:(330 19 .06)

B. g. 3 (Apr)
Sire: Procida (Mr. Prospector)
Dam: Enfante (Northern Baby)
Br: Hancock Arthur B III (Ky)
Tr: Lewis Craig A (4 0 1 0 .00) 1996:(157 20 .13)

L 115

Lifetime Record:	11 2 3 2	$54,289			
1996	10 2 2 2	$53,329	Turf	4 0 0 2	$8,680
1995	1 M 1 0	$960	Wet	0 0 0 0	
SA	0 0 0 0		Dist	2 2 0 0	$38,669

12Sep96-10Fpx fst *1⅛ :472 1:121 1:38 1:511 3↑ Alw 12500s 71 2 10 1011 910 1011 912½ Atkinson P LB 116 b 17.40 79-14 Moondust1143 Gavel Gate1161½ Mr. Lucky Junction1142 Wide into lane 10

25Aug96-4Dmr fst 1 1/16 :222 :453 1:11 1:454 Clm 12500 71 2 7 613 35 1½ 14¼ Atkinson P LB 116 b 3.90 73-27 Bombay1164¼ PhntomProspector1167 JustCllmePirte1161 Clear, driving 8

1Aug96-7Dmr fst 1 :22 :452 1:102 1:362 Clm 40000 31 4 10 1016 1013 918 930 Antley C W LB 116 b *3.30 58-13 BitOfSumming1142 NerlyPerfect116½ Hchro1162½ Crowded start, outrun 10

23Jun96-8Hol fm 1 1/16 Ⓣ :232 :471 1:111 1:42 Clm 62500 68 8 12 1215 129¾ 108¾ 98¾ Solis A LB 116 7.80 77-11 Doman Lore1161 Shady Link116½ A Honey Of A Ship119no Off slowly 12

2Jun96-8Hol fm 1½ Ⓣ :481 1:123 2:032 2:281 3↑ Alw 43000N1X — 2 8 — — — — Desormeaux K J LB 116 b 4.20 — 21 Shanawi12213 Royal Regatta1202 Deydamar1221¼ Pulled up, walked off 8

17May96-4Hol fm 1 1/16 Ⓣ :241 :483 1:122 1:424 Clm c-62500 81 5 7 65½ 64½ 63½ 3½ Antley C W B 116 b 9.10 82-12 Grumpy Gramps117nk Doman Lore116hd Bombay116hd Closed gamely 8

Claimed from Weir D E & J E, Greenman Walter Trainer Previously trained by Lewis Kevin

27Apr96-13TuP fst 1 :224 :453 1:094 1:353 Tempe H25k 75 5 10 97½ 76½ 63½ 2¾ Baze D 120 b *1.10e 87-12 J V Bennett117¾ Bombay120nk Hit Man Mackee1183½ Angled wide, gamely 10

23Mar96-7TuP fm 1 1/16 Ⓣ :234 :484 1:13 1:46 Mr Too Long14k 68 5 6 54 41 52½ 3¾ Gann S L 117 b *1.50 71-28 Frankster117¾ Little Red Caboose117no Bombay117no 5-wide into lane 7

18Feb96-14TuP fst 1 1/16 :22 :444 1:094 1:441 Ariz Derby58k 70 3 10 912 910 64½ 1¾ Gann S L 122 b *1.30e 85-20 Bombay122¾ J V Bennett122hd Broadway Charlie122no Driving 11

19Jan96-5TuP fst 1 :242 :483 1:132 1:383 Md Sp Wt 61 4 6 67¾ 64 44 24 Desilva A J 118 *.50 69-20 Axe The Affair1174 Bombay118¾ DFourrollsatforty1172½ 7

Wide into lane, ducked in near 1/16

WORKOUTS: Oct4 SA 4f fst :482 H *17/33* Sep27 Fpx 5f fst 1:00 H *1/3* Sep22 Fpx 5f fst 1:02 H *6/14* Sep4 Dmr 7f fst 1:264 H *1/1* Aug16 Dmr 5f fst 1:012 H *30/59* Aug9 Dmr 5f fst 1:011 H *29/68*

Bombay

Flopped in his last start; that was to be expected under the circumstances; he faced a tough field of older starter allowance horses, and got spanked as a result; wisely returns to his proper level following that fiasco; should respond with better.

B. T.'s Gold

Own: Keh L Steve $12,500

SORENSON D (2 0 0 0 .00) 1996:(208 21 .10)

Dk. b or br c. 3 (Feb)
Sire: Rare Brick (Rare Performer)
Dam: Siena Slew (Slew o' Gold)
Br: Miller Eleanor & Rowland Eleanor, et al. (Ky)
Tr: Stutts Charles R (—) 1996:(29 0 .00)

L 115

Lifetime Record:	13 1 4 0	$14,520			
1996	8 1 1 0	$7,320	Turf	2 0 0 0	$170
1995	5 M 3 0	$7,200	Wet	2 0 0 0	$1,650
SA	0 0 0 0		Dist	2 1 0 0	$3,725

21Sep96-4BM fm 1 1/16 Ⓣ :232 :47 1:113 1:44 Alw 13500s 47 4 9 87½ 712 715 714¾ Tohill K S LB 117 b 71.00 69-16 Chocolate High117no Skip A Stream117½ Shining Paster1173 Outrun 9

12Sep96-5BM fst 1 1/16 :231 :464 1:113 1:451 Md 8000 60 3 5 43½ 2hd 11½ 14 Tohill K S LB 118 fb 3.90 79-12 B. T.'s Gold1184 Adjustable Note118hd DoublePistachio11814 Rallied wide 6

6Sep96-7BM fst 1 :222 :463 1:103 1:343 3↑ Md 18000 48 5 8 86¾ 810 718 729½ Tohill K S LB 114 f 19.60 66-14 Skip A Stream11619 Hunstanton1163 D C Express1162 Outrun 8

10Aug96-5Bmf fm 1 Ⓣ :23 :47 1:114 1:364 3↑ Clm 12500 68 3 7 109¾ 87½ 78¾ 77¾ Tohill K S LB 113 fb 57.20 81-11 Minks Law1171 Redenham117½ High Drama1151 Outrun 10

Previously trained by Stutts Charles R

27Mar96-8GG fst 1 :23 :462 1:104 1:371 Md 18500 46 4 9 99½ 811 712 614¾ Hummel C R LB 118 b 8.50 69-17 Whobeashobe1181 Roll Tide1186 Impact Player118nk Outrun 9

31Jan96-4BM my 1 :221 :461 1:114 1:371 Md 20000 56 7 8 76¾ 55 57 411 Warren R J Jr LB 118 b 11.30 72-14 Farma Green1181 Jillem1189½ Courageous Wonder118½ No rally 8

15Jan96-6BM sly 1 :23 :471 1:121 1:381 Md 20000 51 4 6 56½ 44½ 36 48 Warren R J Jr LB 118 b 3.30 70-16 All The Music1182 Excellante1185 NotNowFred1181 Drifted out 1st turn 8

3Jan96-4BM fst 1 :224 :471 1:122 1:383 Md 20000 62 3 6 74¾ 64 42 2nk Hummel C R LB 118 b 4.00 76-19 Motion Machine118nk B. T.'s Gold1181 Not Now Fred118½ Rallied wide 7

21Dec95-6Hol fst 1 1/16 :222 :454 1:113 1:423 Md 32000 44 7 10 1013 84 69¾ 522½ Antley C W LB 119 b 7.40 65-12 Star's Thee Law11411 Predetermined1194 Red Mischief1111½ 10

Steadied sharply start; wide into lane

1Dec95-1GG fst 1 :23 :47 1:121 1:39 Md c-13500 56 1 5 1½ 1hd 21½ 22½ Schvaneveldt C P 118 b *1.00 72-25 Code M. D.1182½ B. T.'s Gold1185½ Jeblad1165 7

Bumped start, steadied 1st turn Claimed from Bierig & Oetman & Prato, Birch D Alan Trainer

WORKOUTS: Oct5 SA 1f fst 1:404 H *1/3* Sep30 SA 6f fst 1:152 H *16/22* Aug31 BM 4f fst :503 H *26/32* Aug24 BM 5f fst 1:043 H *33/36* Aug2 BM 5f fst 1:041 H *26/29* Jly26 BM 5f fst 1:04 H *15/16*

B. T.'s Gold

Returns to the main track after having no luck on the turf; not crazy about his main track form; he's just 1 for 11 on dirt; has yet to prove the ability to compete against winners; shaky.

continued

Rush Springs

Own: Charles Ronald L $12,500

B. g. 3 (Feb)
Sire: Persevered (Affirmed)
Dam: Sweet Vendor (Restless Wind)
Br: Cook Robert J. (Ky)
Tr: Shulman Sanford (6 0 0 0 .00) 1996:(268 29 .11)

						Lifetime Record:	18	4	5	3	$38,087
1996	13	4	3	3	$31,995	Turf	1	1	0	0	$4,500
1995	5 M	0	0		$6,092	Wet	4	0	0	0	
SA	0	0	0	0		Dist	4	1	0	2	$14,435

L 115

ESPINOZA V (18 0 5 3 .00) 1996:(719 95 .13)

19Sep96- 8Fpx fst 1¹⁄₁₆	:23 :46⁴ 1:21 1:45				Clm 25000		Flores D R	3.90
7Sep96- 3Dmr fst 1¹⁄₁₆	:23² :47² 1:12 1:43⁴				Clm c-16000		Espinoza V	2.10

Claimed from Weir D E & J E, Greenman Walter Trainer

11Aug96- 7Dmr fst 1	:23 :46³ 1:11¹ 1:38	Clm 16000		Espinoza V	
18Jly96- 3Hol fst 1¹⁄₁₆	:23² :47² 1:12 1:45	Clm 12500		Espinoza V	
27Jun96- 5Hol fst 1¹⁄₁₆	:23² :47² 1:12 1:45	Clm 16000		Espinoza V	
31May96- 7Hol fst 6¹⁄₂f	:22¹ :44⁴ 1:10¹ 1:16³	Clm 16000		Gladney D5	

Previously trained by Lewis Kevin

4May96- 5 A11uP fm 7¹⁄₂f ⑦	:24¹ :48¹ 1:12³ 1:31⁴	Clm 12500		Gann S L	
10Apr96- 3TuP fst 1	:23 :47 1:12 1:38¹	Clm 10000		Gann S L	
26Mar96- 11TuP fst 6¹⁄₂f	:21⁴ :44 1:09⁴ 1:16²	Clm 10000		Gann S L	
8Mar96- 3TuP fst 6f	:21⁴ :44² :59¹ 1:09⁴	Alw 6500N2L		Gann S L	

WORKOUTS: ...

Get to the Truth

Own: Weismann Stephen B $12,500

Dk. b or br g. 3 (Mar)
Sire: Fred Astaire (Nijinsky II)
Dam: Sweet Little Lies (Raise a Native)
Br: Bendabout Farm (Ky)
Tr: Whittingham Charles (3 1 0 0 .33) 1996:(115 14 .12)

						Lifetime Record:	7	1	0	0	$10,650
1996	7	1	0	0	$10,650	Turf	3	0	0	0	
1995	0 M	0	0			Wet	0	0	0	0	
SA	2	0	0	0	$975	Dist	1	0	0	0	$1,425

L 115

SOLIS A (30 5 5 6 .17) 1996:(1087 198 .18)

15Aug96- 8Dmr fm 1¹⁄₈ ⑦	:47⁴ 1:12¹ 1:37 1:49²	3↑ Alw 46000N1X		Almeida G F	58.90
27Jly96- 9Dmr fm 1¹⁄₁₆ ⑦	:48³ 1:13 1:38² 1:50³	Alw 46000N1X		Pincay L Jr	31.10
14Jly96- 1Hol fm 1¹⁄₁₆ ⑦	:47² 1:11³ 1:35 1:54¹	3↑ Alw 35500N1X		Pincay L Jr	18.80
6Jun96- 6Hol fst 1¹⁄₄	:47¹ 1:21¹ 1:38¹ 2:04⁴	3↑ Md 25000		Pincay L Jr	*1.40
17May96- 3Hol fst 1¹⁄₁₆	:23 :47¹ 1:13 1:43¹	3↑ Md 32000		Pincay L Jr	2.00
20Apr96- 5SA fst 1	:23 :47 1:13 1:37	Md Sp Wt		Valenzuela F H	10.60
31Mar96- 2SA fst 1	:23⁴ :48 1:12⁴ 1:37⁴	Md Sp Wt		Valenzuela F H	10.60

WORKOUTS: Oct13 SA 6f fst 1:13⁴ H 2/14 Sep29 SA 11 fst 1:27² H 5/9 Sep24 SA 7f fst 1:27 H 2/6 Sep19 SA 6f fst 1:14² H 4/15 Sep14 SA 5f fst 1:00³ H 4/27 Sep8 Dmr 4f fst :49³ H 25/40

Rush Springs

Made a strong bid to go after the leaders last time out, but failed to quicken down the lane; still only missed 3rd by a nose; a consistent, honest gelding that gives his all every time he steps on the track; a logical contender.

Get to The Truth

The Bald Eagle wisely drops this gelding in class following a series of poor efforts on the lawn; owns good speed figures, but don't care for his running style; he's a plodder - the kind that likes to race far back and mount a late rally; needs to get in gear earlier if he is to threaten for the top prize.

Engelbert

Own: Bizal & Longnecker & Whitehouse — $12,500
PEDROZA M A (23 4 3 1 .17) 1996:(1021 125 .12)

Dk.b or br g. 3 (Mar)
Sire: Fast Account (Private Account)
Dam: Avrila (Skywalker)
Br: Hat Ranch West (Cal)
Tr: Stephen Craig (—) 1996:(5 1 .20)

L 115

Lifetime Record: 24 2 5 6 $66,622												
1996	13	1	4	3	$37,122	Turf	0	0	0	0		
1995	11	1	1	3	$29,500	Wet	1	0	0	1		$4,350
SA	9	1	3	1	$28,700	Dist	9	1	2	3		$26,460

28Sep96-4Fpx fst 1 1/16 :23 :46³ 1:12¹ 1:45² Clm 10000 73 3 4 5⁶ 5⁴½ 1½ 1¹ Pedroza M A LB 114 4.10 83-10 Engelbert114¹ Rowdy Ryan115⁶ Work 'n' Man114¹ Inside rally 6
14Sep96-3Fpx fst 1 1/16 :23³ :48 1:13⁴ 1:47² Clm 10500 61 2 4 4³½ 4⁴ 3²½ 3³¾ Pedroza M A LB 113 6.00 70-16 Gibby's Vlue114³ D ProfitbleMusic114nk Engelbert113²½ Steadied 1st turn 6
Placed second through disqualification.
18Jly96-3Hol fst 1 1/16 :23² :47² 1:12² 1:45 Clm 12500 — 6 5 6⁹ 6¹⁶ — — Toscano P R LB 116 4.50 — 24 RushSprings116½ Gibby's Vlu1161¼ MollysGint116² Pulled up, walked off 6
3Jly96-5Hol fst 7f :22¹ :45⁴ 1:11¹ 1:23⁴ Clm 16000 53 10 3 8³½ 11⁷¾ 11⁷ 7¹²½ Toscano P R LB 116 b 8.00 70-15 Silver Bandit118⁵½ Flex N Go117½ Gibby's Value118³½ Wide trip 11
15Jun96-7Hol fst 7½f :22² :45³ 1:10¹ 1:29³ Clm 20000 68 10 2 4¹½ 4¹½ 4⁴ 5⁷ Douglas R R LB 115 8.90 79-13 Boysville115¹¼ Predetermined115¹ Silver Bandit115⁴½ Weakened 11
19May96-3Hol fst 1 1/16 :23⁴ :47² 1:11² 1:43² Clm c-16000 71 2 4 4³½ 5³ 4⁵ 3⁷ Solis A LB 116 3.70 77-16 CourageousWonder116²½ Wltz'nM.D.116⁴½ Engelbert116¾ 4 wide 2nd turn 6
Claimed from The Hat Ranch, Stute Melvin F Trainer
2May96-1Hol fst 1 1/16 :22⁴ :46³ 1:12¹ 1:45² Clm 20000 73 2 6 6⁸½ 4⁵½ 3²½ 3²½ Solis A LB 116 2.50 71-26 BearToBeKrafty121½ CourgeousWonder116² Engelbert116²⁶ Inside trip 6
10Apr96-2SA fst 1 :22⁴ :47¹ 1:12² 1:38³ Clm 20000 73 5 5 6⁵¼ 5¹½ 2²½ 2² Solis A LB 117 4.70 74-25 Bear To Be Krafty120² Engelbert117¹½ Boysville112¹¾ 4 wide 2nd turn 6
24Mar96-7SA fst 7f :22¹ :45¹ 1:10 1:23¹ Clm 20000 71 4 9 9¹¹ 9⁸¾ 4⁶½ 2⁵ Solis A LB 117 9.30 81-12 Type Ryder120⁵ Engelbert117no Boysville113⁶½ Off bit slow 9
7Mar96-3SA fst 1 1/16 :23² :47² 1:12¹ 1:45 Clm 20000 56 2 3 3²½ 4²½ 6⁹ 8¹⁷½ Solis A LB 117 3.80 53-26 BearToBeKrafty120½ BafflingBaffert112² Predetermined117¹½ Gave way 8

WORKOUTS: Sep8 Fpx 4f fst :49³ H 3/9 Sep2 Hol 4f fst :48² H 9/16 Aug22 Hol 5f fst 1:03¹ H 10/12 Aug14 Hol 5f fst 1:02³ H 9/18 Jly15 SA 4f fst :48 H 4/13

Engelbert

Benefited from a ground-saving trip at Fpx; appears to be back on his game after going off form at Hol; runs well at this track and consistently hits the boards; a candidate for a top-3 finish.

Linger

Own: John H Deeter Trust — $12,500
BLANC B (18 2 2 4 .11) 1996:(1022 104 .10)

B. c. 3 (Feb)
Sire: Houston (Seattle Slew)
Dam: Infringe (Irish River*Fr)
Br: Hibbert R E (Ky)
Tr: Benedict Jim (—) 1996:(97 12 .12)

L 115

Lifetime Record: 10 1 0 3 $23,755												
1996	10	1	0	3	$23,755	Turf	2	0	0	0		$855
1995	0	M	0	0		Wet	0	0	0	0		
SA	4	1	0	1	$14,000	Dist	6	1	0	3		$22,400

22Sep96-4BM fst 1 :23 :46³ 1:11¹ 1:37⁴ Clm 20000 70 5 2 2hd 2½ 4²½ 5⁶ Baze R A LB 117 3.30 74-22 Candi's Craft117½ CourageousPete117³ TcticlAlert117½ Wide, weakened 5
6Sep96-2BM fm 1 1/16 ① :23² :47³ 1:12¹ 1:43⁴ Clm 25000 65 7 3 3¹½ 4² 5⁷½ 5⁷½ Baze R A LB 117 5.50 77-15 Falcon Force117¹ Airborne Shuttle119⁴ Lil Man Can115no Wide trip 8
18Aug96-9Bmf fm 1 1/16 ① :24¹ :47⁴ 1:11² 1:41⁴ 3↑ Clm 25000 78 3 3 2² 4¹½ 6⁵¾ 7⁶¾ González R M LB 115 18.50 88-03 Leap To The Lead117¹½ Stone Cold117no Sekondi117¹ Gave way late 9
28Jly96-1Dmr fst 1 1/16 :22³ :46² 1:11³ 1:44² Clm c-20000 66 1 6 5² 6²½ 4²½ 5³½ Solis A LB 116 2.20 76-17 Dialingfordollars115½ Coyote Canyon116¹½ Ali Brat116½ Wide into lane 7
Claimed from Hibbert Robert E, Cecil B D A Trainer
10Jly96-7Hol fst 1 1/16 :23¹ :46³ 1:10⁴ 1:44³ Clm 25000 74 5 6 6⁴½ 5³¾ 5⁷½ 3³½ Solis A B 116 3.70 74-18 Courageous Wonder116¹½ Nearly Perfect116² Linger116¹¼ Late for 3rd 9
23May96-1Hol fst 1 1/16 :23² :46⁴ 1:10⁴ 1:42² Clm 25000 82 4 4 4² 3¹ 3¹½ 3²½ Solis A B 116 6.30 86-19 Bear To Be Krafty116² Candelotto116½ Linger116⁵ Bid, outfinished 6
11Apr96-7SA fst 1 1/16 :22² :46² 1:11² 1:44¹ Clm 40000 37 2 6 7⁶ 8⁷½ 8⁹¾ 8²⁶½ Solis A B 117 26.70 48-24 Te Atua117⁶½ Westo117¹ March Of Kings117³½ Stumbled start 9
13Mar96-2SA gd 1 1/16 :23¹ :47 1:11³ 1:44¹ Md 32000 73 5 3 2¹½ 2¹ 1hd 1hd Solis A B 117 5.10 74-22 Linger117hd Forge117⁷½ Far East Ridge115hd Stiff drive 8
Previously trained by Rash Rodney
16Feb96-2SA fst 1 1/16 :22⁴ :46⁴ 1:12¹ 1:44² Md 32000 70 9 8 7⁹ 6⁴½ 5⁵½ 3⁶ Solis A B 117 12.70 67-19 Victorious Type117½ Bit Of Summing117⁵½ Linger117no Bothered start 12
5Jan96-8SA fst 6½f :22 :45 1:10² 1:17 Md 32000 61 12 8 8⁷½ 6⁵½ 5⁴½ 6⁵¾ Black C A B 119 4.30 79-12 Candi's Craft119½ Soviet Square119¹¼ Lively Jet119³ Wide into lane 12

WORKOUTS: Oct6 BM 3f fst :39¹ H 19/20 Sep15 BM 4f fst :47¹ H 2/45 ● Aug30 BM 5f fst :59⁴ H 1/23 Aug10 Bmf 4f fst :49 H 16/25 Jly24 Dmr 5f fst 1:00² H 10/53

Linger

Has yet to respond for his new connections but should fare better with the drop to the $12,500 level; didn't run too badly in his last start, pressing the pace for 6f; capable.

continued

Ricks Pride

Own: Anson Ronald & Susie — $12,500

Dk. b or br g. 3 (Jan)
Sire: Raymond Earl (Loom)
Dam: Miss Rubmeabout (Against the Snow)
Br: Papac Ranch (Cal)
Tr: Peterson Douglas R (1 1 0 0 1.00) 1996:(71 15 .21)

GARCIA M S (10 0 1 0 .00) 1996:(464 37 .08) — L 115

Lifetime Record:	8 1 0 0	$10,175		
1996	8 1 0 0	$10,175	Turf	0 0 0 0
1995	0 M 0 0		Wet	0 0 0 0
SA	2 0 0 0		Dist	0 0 0 0

26Sep96-8Fpx fst 6½f $:21^4$ $:45^4$ 1:11 $1:17^2$ Clm 16000 **45** 6 6 4^3 $7^{6½}$ 9^{10} $9^{15½}$ Garcia M S LB 114 b 24.10 79-12 Shaquielle114^2 Cutlass Crusader115^{no} Singular Vision116^{nk} Tired badly 9
29Aug96-5Dmr fst 6f $:21^4$ $:44^3$ $:57^1$ $1:10^1$ Clm 32000 **45** 7 6 $7^{4¾}$ $8^{8¾}$ 8^{11} 8^{17} Hunter M T LB 116 b 35.70 71-14 Reef Reef116¾ [D]Invictus116^{nk} Celtic Boy116^6 No threat 8
3Jly96-5Hol fst 7f $:22^1$ $:45^4$ $1:11^1$ $1:23^4$ Clm c-16000 **60** 2 1 1^1 $1^{½}$ 1^{hd} $4^{9½}$ McCarron C J LB 115 b 2.60 73-15 Silver Bandit$118^{5½}$ Flex N Go117½ Gibby's Value$118^{3½}$ Dueled, weakened 11
Claimed from Papac Andrew & Andrew G, Inda Eduardo Trainer
13Jun96-6Hol fst 7f $:22^2$ $:45^2$ 1:10 1:23 3↑ Md 25000 **78** 12 1 $1^{1½}$ $1^{1½}$ $1^{3½}$ 1^3 McCarron C J LB 116 b *1.90 87-09 Ricks Pride116^3 Deep Seat Gambler116^4 Our Irishman116¾ Clearly best 12
31May96-6Hol fst 7f $:22^1$:45 $1:09^1$ $1:22^3$ 3↑ [S]Md 32000 **34** 3 8 $5^{2¼}$ $2^{2½}$ 9^{16} $9^{21¾}$ Garcia M S B 115 b 5.70 67-11 TochdownMm$115^{4½}$ AbsoltRlr117^4 OgtBGood$122^{3½}$ Bumped start,rail trip 12
8May96-9Hol fst 7f :22 $:44^4$ 1:10 $1:22^4$ 3↑ [S]Md 32000 **70** 11 4 $7^{2¾}$ $5^{4½}$ $4^{1½}$ $4^{3½}$ Garcia M S B 115 b 23.20 84-13 Candelotto110^{hd} Touchdown Miami115^1 Nearly Perfect$117^{2½}$ 11
Angled in sharply 1/4 pole, came out 1/8 pole.
20Apr96-4SA fst 6f $:21^3$ $:45^2$:58 $1:11^1$ [S]Md 32000 **48** 7 7 $6^{4¾}$ $8^{6¾}$ $6^{8½}$ 6^8 Toscano P R B 118 23.70 74-14 Solid As Gold113½ Twelfth Knight116^3 Proud$118^{3½}$ Blocked into lane 10
24Mar96-6SA fst 5½f $:22^1$ $:45^4$ $:58^1$ $1:04^4$ Md 32000 **31** 4 8 4^2 6^5 $8^{9½}$ 9^{14} Toscano P R B 118 12.90 72-12 YnkeeCstle$113^{1½}$ TwelfthKnight$116^{1¾}$ DepStGmblr118^2 Forced wide turn 10

WORKOUTS: Sep11 Dmr 5f fst $1:00^3$ H *3/30* Aug23 Dmr 4f fst $:50^2$ H *38/46* Aug17 Dmr 3f fst $:39^1$ H *16/16*

Ricks Pride

Hasn't put it together since being claimed; in fact, he's beaten just one horse in his last two starts; expected to flash more speed with the stretch out; needs to shake loose early to have a realistic shot of winning.

—Byron King

horses run mainly on weekends and holidays, when more people go to the races and the handles are larger. Every day of the week, however, the racing associations have to find enough animals to fill their programs and the result is a race like this one, the lowest of the low. "Never knock a horse until it's dead," Charlie Whittingham once observed, on the sound principle that many horses, especially young ones, can be improved, occasionally even turned into champions. The great Cigar, remember, was a mediocre performer as a three-year-old, when he was competing exclusively on grass. It wasn't until his trainer put him on the dirt that he realized his enormous potential and became the dominant horse of his era, winning nineteen races and just under ten million dollars in purses. What we are looking at here is three-year-olds, so perhaps, on the Whittingham principle, we should be wary of condemning them too early in their careers.

Unfortunately, the Cigars of racing are the rare exceptions that prove the rule. Strictly from a bettor's standpoint, these horses are established bums, so untalented that even this late in the year they can only compete in their own age group. They are so bad that we can't even begin handicapping the race by throwing out the obvious losers. The only one I gave no chance to was B. T.'s Gold, whose highest Beyer on the dirt is a 62, way back in January. Luckily, I don't have to bet at all. I've used three horses in my pick-three—Don's Memory, Linger, and Ricks Pride. Why? Don's Memory has had only two races since February, is dropping one notch in class in a search for "friends," is stretching out for the first time from a sprint, is breaking from a good post for the distance, has had a work since his last effort, benefits from a favorable trainer-jockey combination, and has actually managed to win three times in his inglorious career. Linger has fewer positive factors in his favor but is also dropping in class, showed a bit of speed against much better animals in his last attempt, and sports the best Beyer fig of the bunch, an 82. Ricks Pride is perched outside, a bad place to be here, but is also stretching out, has speed, and is dropping in class. His morning line is a delicious fifteen to one, a poor estimate of his chances by the track handicapper. It might persuade a lot of bettors to overlook him, which makes him an interesting play for me. In our search for value, it's always important to find horses being ignored by the experts. In my pick-six, however, I've used only Don's Memory and Linger, in order to stay within my money-management guidelines.

Would I have bet this race if I had not been alive in my parlays? Not solely on the race itself. Since we can only eliminate one horse from the field of nine, I could not have made a straight bet. The only wager I could have risked was to start another pick-three, using my top trio of horses in the sixth and seventh contests, also wide-open affairs.

As I was sitting there that day, watching these untalented beasts lumbering toward the starting gate, I received a tip on Bombay from a well-meaning friend of mine, who assured me that Craig Lewis, the animal's trainer, was high on his horse. I checked my *Form* but did not budge from my seat. Sure, Bombay, a plodder who would rally from at least ten lengths out at the half, could win here, as he already had against a similar field on August 25. But he's exactly the kind of horse you would do well never to risk money on ever at any price; for him to win, he would need a fast pace up front in the early stages and a clear trip around the final turn. Too chancy. The hallmark of all such races is inconsistency. The cheaper the horse, the more inconsistent he's likely to be. If racing is to be merely a blind gamble, then forget it and go play the lottery.

As most often happens in horse racing, one of the logical

FIFTH RACE

Santa Anita

OCTOBER 10, 1996

1 1/16 MILES. (1.39) CLAIMING. Purse $13,000. 3-year-olds. Weight, 120 lbs. Non-winners of two races at one mile or over since August 1, allowed 3 lbs. Of such a race since September 1, 5 lbs. Claiming price $12,500; if for $10,500, allowed 2 lbs. (Maiden or races when entered for $10,000 or less not considered.)

Value of Race: $13,000 Winner $7,150; second $2,600; third $1,950; fourth $975; fifth $325. Mutuel Pool $326,006.10 Exacta Pool $236,818.00 Trifecta Pool $278,854.00 Quinella Pool $40,459.00

Last Raced	Horse	M/Eqt. A.Wt	PP	St	1/4	1/2	3/4	Str	Fin	Jockey	Cl'g Pr	Odds $1
15Sep96 2Fpx3	Don's Memory	LBb 3 117	1	1	2^2	2^{hd}	2^{hd}	2^1	$1^{\frac{1}{2}}$	Pincay L Jr	12500	2.30
21Sep96 4BM7	B. T.'s Gold	LBb 3 116	4	7	$5^{\frac{1}{2}}$	5^1	$6^{2\frac{1}{2}}$	$4^{\frac{1}{2}}$	2^{nk}	Sorenson D	12500	72.30
15Aug96 8Dmr7	Get to the Truth	LBb 3 115	6	8	8^1	8^{hd}	$7^{1\frac{1}{2}}$	$3^{1\frac{1}{2}}$	3^{nk}	Solis A	12500	4.50
12Sep96 10Fpx9	Bombay	LBb 3 116	3	9	9	9	9	6^{hd}	$4^{2\frac{3}{4}}$	Atkinson P	12500	6.80
28Sep96 4Fpx4	Gibby's Value	LBf 3 117	2	5	7^6	7^6	5^1	1^{hd}	5^1	Berrio O A	12500	14.50
19Sep96 8Fpx4	Rush Springs	LBb 3 115	5	2	$4^{1\frac{1}{2}}$	4^2	4^{hd}	5^2	6^6	Espinoza V	12500	4.50
28Sep96 4Fpx1	Engelbert	LB 3 115	7	6	$6^{1\frac{1}{2}}$	6^{hd}	8^1	$7^{\frac{1}{2}}$	$7^{1\frac{1}{2}}$	Pedroza M A	12500	12.20
22Sep96 4BM5	Linger	LB 3 115	8	4	3^4	$3^{4\frac{1}{2}}$	$3^{2\frac{1}{2}}$	8^1	$8^{\frac{3}{4}}$	Blanc B	12500	8.50
26Sep96 8Fpx9	Ricks Pride	LBb 3 115	9	3	$1^{2\frac{1}{2}}$	$1^{3\frac{1}{2}}$	$1^{\frac{1}{2}}$	9	9	Garcia M S	12500	6.10

OFF AT 3:01 Start Good. Won driving. Time, :22⁴, :45⁴, 1:10⁴, 1:37³, 1:44² Track fast.

$2 Mutuel Prices:

1–DON'S MEMORY	6.60	4.80	3.20
4–B. T.'S GOLD		36.40	14.60
6–GET TO THE TRUTH			3.40

$2 EXACTA 1–4 PAID $256.80 $2 TRIFECTA 1–4–6 PAID $1,910.40 $2 QUINELLA 1–4 PAID $174.40

Dk. b. or br. g, (Mar), by Roman Majesty–Top Quality, by Golden Eagle II*Fr. Trainer Spawr Bill. Bred by Holt Lester (Cal).

DON'S MEMORY came off the rail early on the backstretch, bid between rivals on the second turn, came four wide into the stretch, drifted in under right handed urging after taking a short lead inside the eighth pole and held sway. B. T.'S GOLD was taken well off the rail on the backstretch, moved up outside on the second turn and six wide into the stretch and finished well. GET TO THE TRUTH had a rail trip and also continued willingly to the wire. BOMBAY was a bit slow into stride and unhurried to the second turn, raced a bit wide into the stretch and closed gamely late. GIBBY'S VALUE was a bit washy at the gate, saved ground, moved up inside leaving the second turn to gain a short lead into the stretch, battled between foes in deep stretch and weakened late. RUSH SPRINGS bobbled slightly at the start, raced outside the winner on the first turn and off the rail on the backstretch, went outside GET TO THE TRUTH into the stretch and lacked the needed late kick. ENGELBERT was outside B. T.'S GOLD early and outside GIBBY'S VALUE on the backstretch, continued off the rail and did not rally. LINGER angled in early, went outside the winner on the backstretch and three deep on the second turn, came five wide into the stretch and weakened. RICKS PRIDE sped to the early lead, angled in when clear, dueled inside on the second turn, drifted out a bit into the stretch and had little left.

Owners— 1, Carrillo Mr & Mrs Fred W; 2, Kehl L Steve; 3, Weissman Stephen B; 4, Brown Rubin; 5, Lemalu Stables; 6, Charles Ronald L; 7, Bizal & Longnecker & Whitehouse; 8, John H Deeter Trust; 9, Anson Ronald & Susie

Trainers— 1, Spawr Bill; 2, Stutts Charles R; 3, Whittingham Charles; 4, Lewis Craig A; 5, Avila A C; 6, Shulman Sanford; 7, Stephen Craig; 8, Pinelli Laura; 9, Peterson Douglas R

Overweight: Don's Memory (2), B. T.'s Gold (1), Bombay (1).

Don's Memory was claimed by Enlow & Valenta; trainer, Carava Jack.,

Gibby's Value was claimed by Bligh Jay W; trainer, Young Steven W.

$3 Pick Three (4–1–1) Paid $449.70; Pick Three Pool $67,466.

choices, Don's Memory, won. I had hoped that the crowd, stimulated by a morning line of three to one, would make Rush Springs the favorite. He was a horse I had thrown out, mainly because his Beyers were low, his trainer and jockey were winless at the meet, and I thought he might be overbet. But these days it's harder to fool even unsophisticated horseplayers, or at least the ones with the most money to bet. Don's Memory paid only $6.60 to win, well below his early line of four to one.

My other two horses ran poorly, with the outside post most certainly contributing to Ricks Pride's defeat. He went very fast around the first turn, which exhausted him, and he was finished three quarters of the way through the race. Linger, too, showed speed but stopped. Don's Memory, however, had the perfect trip and made me a comfortable winner for the afternoon. My two pick-threes paid a total of $299.80, minus the cost of the tickets, thirty-six dollars, leaving me with a profit on the race of $263.80. Now we subtract the eighteen dollars I'm behind for the day, which leaves me showing a net profit of $245.80.

Before we bask in the warm glow of how easy all this may seem, let's check this chart again. Rush Springs ran dismally and Bombay also failed to score, but look at who finished second, B. T.'s Gold, the one entry in the race I had dismissed as an impossibility. At huge odds, he ran the race of his life and could easily have won, if he hadn't had to go six wide on the turn for home. My margin of success was barely half a length, with the first four finishing all within a length of one another. I could just as easily have found myself down for the day and also out of the pick-six. So when this happens to you, remember that luck is also a prime ingredient of any winning day. Rejoice in your success, but don't take it for granted.

With a solid profit of $245 tucked safely in my wallet,

the temptation now is to wrap up, to make merely token bets the rest of the day and be certain of taking home at least two hundred dollars in winnings. Especially since my pick-six is still alive. But is this the right way to play the game? No, not when your luck is running. Ride the streak for as long as you can. Winners often come in bunches, just like losers. The rule in all forms of gambling is to press a winning streak and to lay off when you're losing. You'll know soon enough when it's over.

To press a streak does not mean that I'm advocating recklessness. In a casino game like craps or blackjack, luck is the dominant factor. In horse racing, as in poker, skill prevails. What we have to do now, assuming that you've been betting along with me, is handicap the last four races, then decide how seriously we need to press. If the last four races on the card present us with real opportunities, then our task is to exploit them with confidence, in the form of solid plays.

■ RACE 6: Unfortunately this sixth event is not one to take a real shot on. As you can see from the conditions, it's the same race as the fourth. What makes it mildly attractive is the probability that Aglo Darling will be a heavily overbet favorite, opening up possibly lucrative opportunities on other entries. Aglo Darling hasn't run since August 1, when she went off against a similar field at forty to one. She shows only three works since then, none of them outstanding. Still, she could easily win. She picks up a top jockey and she'll be hard to beat, especially as she may be adding Lasix, a possibility confirmed later by the program. I had to use her in my pick-six, but I did so reluctantly. She qualifies as a Dummy God horse, the sort of animal Gerry Okuneff identifies as favored by the God of the dummies who will bet heavily on her. When the Dummy God horses win, Gerry and the other pros must lose. It happens often enough to keep them humble.

6 Santa Anita Park

6 Furlongs (1:071) **MAIDEN CLAIMING. Purse $17,000. Fillies, 2-year-olds bred in California. Weight, 120 lbs. Claiming price $32,000, if for $28,000, allowed 2 lbs.**

6 FURLONGS (START / FINISH)

Audene's Kite

Own: Murphy William J — $32,000
TOSCANO P R (7 0 0 1 .00) 1996:(525 43 .08)

Ch. f. 2 (Feb)
Sire: Shanekite (Hoist Bar)
Dam: Audene's Bid (Dance Bid)
Br: Murphy William J (Cal)
Tr: Hendricks Dan L (7 0 0 1 .00) 1996:(157 28 .18)

L 120

Lifetime Record:	1 M 0 0	$450		
1996	1 M 0 0	$450	Turf	0 0 0 0
1995	0 M 0 0		Wet	0 0 0 0
SA	0 0 0 0		Dist	0 0 0 0

6Sep96- 6Dmr fst 5½f :214 :453 :584 1:053 ⒻMd 32000 20 8 7 6¾ 76 5½ 513½ Toscano P R LB 118 4.40 71-12 Sparkling Ripple118½ Iza Bay116no Magic Remedy1189 4 wide to turn 8

WORKOUTS: Oct2 SA 6f fst 1:162 H 15/19 Sep26 SA 5f fst 1:012 H 23/42 Sep20 SA 4f fst :493 H 16/32 Sep1 Dmr 4f fst :491 Hg32/44 Aug27 Dmr 6f fst 1:144 H 9/19 Aug22 Dmr 5f fst 1:004 H 11/56

Tappin Her Toes

Own: Thimigan & Van Berg — $32,000
GARCIA J A (12 1 3 1 .08) 1996:(43 11 .26)

B. f. 2 (Mar)
Sire: Prince Colony (Pleasant Colony)
Dam: Catchy Little Tune (Daryl's Joy)
Br: Robert M Snell & Jack Van Berg (Cal)
Tr: Van Berg Jack C (—) 1996:(384 48 .13)

L 120

Lifetime Record:	7 M 0 2	$11,806			
1996	7 M 0 2	$11,806	Turf	0 0 0 0	
1995	0 M 0 0		Wet	0 0 0 0	
SA	0 0 0 0		Dist	2 0 0 1	$3,030

12Sep96- 6Fpx fst 6f :221 :46 :591 1:123 Ⓕ[S]Md Sp Wt 41 6 7 77 77 811 79¼ Garcia J A LB 116 5.90 77-09 Echoes Of Spring1163¼ TutaNiche116½ DoubleWinner116½ Wide thru out 9
29Aug96- 6Dmr fst 6½f :221 :452 1:11 1:18 Ⓕ[S]Md 32000 56 8 1 51¼ 21½ 23½ 46¼ Almeida G F LB 118 2.90 75-14 MessageOfHoney118nk MissLawless1185 LdyIntegrity1181 4 wide to turn 12
15Aug96- 2Dmr fst 6f :221 :452 :58 1:111 Ⓕ[S]Md 32000 54 7 4 32 32 22½ 34½ Almeida G F LB 118 3.80 78-12 Jackpot Justice1184 Busy Lizzy118½ Tappin Her Toes1184 Lost 2nd late 12
28Jly96- 6Dmr fst 5½f :213 :444 :573 1:042 Ⓕ[S]Md Sp Wt 27 6 9 1011 1118 1117 1116½ Almeida G F LB 118 6.50 74-07 Granja Realeza1182½ Kamali118½ Explosive Linda1182½ Forced out start 11
17Jly96- 4Hol fst 5f :221 :463 :582 Ⓕ[S]Md 40000 66 3 2 2½ 3½ 31 41¼ Almeida G F B 118 7.30 92-12 SexyFres118½ EchosOfSpring118½ PrfctStp118nk Between foes,willingly 10
27Jun96- 2Hol fst 5½f :224 :462 :59 1:052 Ⓕ[S]Md Sp Wt 49 2 1 2½ 22 23 44 Espinoza V B 118 8.30 80-11 Fairness1182 Busy Lizzy1181 Aquarellist1181 Weakened 7
12Jun96- 6Hol fst 4½f :22 :453 :514 ⒻMd 50000 48 5 2 54 46½ 36 Espinoza V B 118 13.10 87-09 CrisTheSwimmer1185 BeutifulFc1181 TppinHrTos1181 Lugged out 3 1/2 10

WORKOUTS: Oct1 Hol 4f fst :484 H 10/24 Sep23 Hol 3f fst :372 H 3/7 ●Sep7 Dmr 5f fst :584 H 1/31 Aug25 Dmr 4f fst :472 H 2/60 Aug12 Dmr 5f fst 1:013 H 43/54 Jly11 Hol 5f fst 1:032 H 40/43

Sunny Holiday

Own: Cavanagh Marguerite F & Thomas M — $32,000
SOLIS A (30 5 5 6 .17) 1996:(1087 198 .18)

B. f. 2 (Mar)
Sire: Fatih (Icecapade)
Dam: Dreamer's Holiday (Tree of Knowledge)
Br: Cavanagh Marguerite & Thomas Family Trust (Cal)
Tr: Matlow Richard P (1 0 0 1 .00) 1996:(23 4 .17)

L 120

Lifetime Record:	1 M 0 0	$1,350		
1996	1 M 0 0	$1,350	Turf	0 0 0 0
1995	0 M 0 0		Wet	0 0 0 0
SA	0 0 0 0		Dist	0 0 0 0

2Sep96- 2Dmr fst 5½f :222 :46 :584 1:052 Ⓕ[S]Md 32000 50 4 12 84¾ 76¾ 46½ 45¼ Solis A LB 118 4.40 81-09 Miss Enchantment118½ Pearls'npantyhose1184 Jamin Jaime Mc Q116¾ 12
Off bit slow; in tight 3/8

WORKOUTS: Oct3 Hol 6f fst 1:16 H 15/15 Sep27 Hol 5f fst 1:024 H 23/30 Sep20 Hol 5f fst 1:024 H 22/31 Sep13 Hol 4f fst :50 H 12/25 Aug25 Dmr 5f fst 1:003 H 13/59 Aug19 Dmr 6f fst 1:144 H 9/22

A CLOSER LOOK

6th Santa Anita

Audene's Kite

Trainer does excellent job with 2nd-time starters in maiden-claiming races, including some who didn't perform well in first start; full sis to $28,100 earner Tamalito Dulce; despite the low Beyer, trainer analysts won't be surprised to see her in either exacta slot.

Tappin Her Toes

Took scenic route in Pomona and came away with nothing; half to $88,653 earner Mr. Zippity Do Dah and $45,900 earner Big Gate; sometimes shows speed; pattern so far is to run 3rd or worse at moderate odds.

Sunny Holiday

Barn does well with lightly raced horses and is 2 for 11 overall with 2yo on SA-Hol-Dmr circuit since start of '95; most horses improve in 2nd start; half to $68,868 earner Dreamer's Star; dam made $44,260; Solis is willing to try again; mixed signals.

Aglo Darling

Own: Schuth Harold L

$32,000

Dk. b or br. f. 2 (Feb)
Sire: My Habitony (Habitony*GB)
Dam: Tony's Darling (Nashaglo)
Br: Pejsa Anton W (Cal)
Tr: Bloomquist Charles E (—) 1996:(48 8 .17)

120

				Lifetime Record :	1 M 0 1	$2,700
	1996	1 M 0 1	$2,700	Turf	0 0 0 0	
	1995	0 M 0 0		Wet	0 0 0 0	
	SA	0 0 0 0		Dist	0 0 0 0	

STEVENS G L (9 3 11 .33) 1996:(553 115 .21)

1Aug96–2Dmr f5t 5½f :221 :459 :58 1:043 89–09 Cashcheckorcharge118no Morell'sLove118¾ AgloDrling118⁵ Finished well 12

WORKOUTS: Sep27 SA 5f fst 1:013 H 7/18 Sep22 SA 5f fst 1:143 H 7/19 Sep22 SA 5f fst 1:013 H 26/46 Jly25 LA 4f fst :484 Dg2/4 Jly10 LA 5f fst 1:01 H 1/2

My Sister Jane

Own: Ridgeley Farm

$32,000

B. f. 2 (Apr)
Sire: Iam the Iceman (Pirate's Bounty)
Dam: Julienne'Mex (First Amendment)
Br: Ridgeley Farm (Cal)
Tr: Stute Warren (2 0 0 0 .00) 1996:(62 11 .18)

120

				Lifetime Record :	0 M 0 0	
	1996	0 M 0 0		Turf	0 0 0 0	
	1995	0 M 0 0		Wet	0 0 0 0	
	SA	0 0 0 0		Dist	0 0 0 0	

DELAHOUSSAYE E (17 4 2 5 .24) 1996:(800 134 .17)

WORKOUTS: Oct5 SA 5f fst 1:012 H 12/23 Sep29 SA 6f fst 1:153 Hg28/39 Sep23 SA 5f fst 1:012 H 19/52 Sep12 SA 5f fst 1:01 H 9/52 Sep6 Dmr 4f fst :472 H 9/55
Sep2 Dmr 3f fst :384 H 29/34 Aug28 Dmr 3f fst :351 H 2/21 Jly21 Hol 4f fst :482 H 8/27 Jly15 Hol 4f fst :361 Hg2/14 Jly9 Hol 4f fst :501 H 24/35

Granjacita

Own: Granja Vista Del Rio Stable

$32,000

Ch. f. 2 (Mar)
Sire: Debonair Roger (Raja Baba)
Dam: Almocita (Flying Paster)
Br: Granja Vista Del Rio (Cal)
Tr: Tinsley J E Jr (1 0 0 0 .00) 1996:(24 7 .08)

120

				Lifetime Record :	1 M 0 0	$340
	1996	1 M 0 0	$340	Turf	0 0 0 0	
	1995	0 M 0 0		Wet	0 0 0 0	
	SA	0 0 0 0		Dist	1 0 0 0	

GARCIA M S (10 0 1 0 .00) 1996:(464 37 .08)

23Sep96–12Fpx 1st 6f :229 :464 :591 1:121 75–09 BeyondRedemption11634 TimlyViw1162 GtuRoug1163 Passed tiring foes 10

WORKOUTS: Sep13 Fpx 3f fst 1:021 H 5/8 Sep4 Fpx 4f fst :501 H 4/10 Aug15 SLR tr.t 4f fst :484 H 7/12 Aug10 SLR tr.t 4f fst :493 H 10/12 Jly3 SLR tr.t 4f fst :51 H 3/6 Jly25 Fpx 3f fst :394 H 5/6

Acadiana

Own: Cesena Laurie M

$32,000

Dk. b or br. f. 2 (May)
Sire: Regal and Royal (Vaguely Noble*GB)
Dam: Princess Don B. (Don B.)
Br: Wild Oak Ranch (Cal)
Tr: Desormeaux J Keith (1 0 0 1 .00) 1996:(50 9 .18)

120

				Lifetime Record :	1 M 0 0	$340
	1996	1 M 0 0	$340	Turf	0 0 0 0	
	1995	0 M 0 0		Wet	0 0 0 0	
	SA	0 0 0 0		Dist	1 0 0 0	

DESORMEAUX K J (21 2 2 3 .10) 1996:(818 147 .18)

21Sep96–9Fpx 1st 6f :222 :462 :591 1:13 B 116 78–10 Hunny Now116⁵ I'm Quick N'cool116⁵ Sunshine Gal116¾ No factor 10

WORKOUTS: Oct5 SA 4f fst :493 H 4/14 Sep18 SA 5f fst 1:033 H 49/52 Sep10 Dmr 6f fst 1:152 H 4/4 Sep5 Dmr 4f fst :493 Hg 17/35 Aug31 Dmr 5f fst 1:004 H 24/63 Aug27 Dmr 4f fst :493 H 17/30

Aglo Darling

Made good first impression and comes into this heat with the best speed figure in the bunch; fact Stevens takes mount is a plus; full sis to $50,030 earner No Ice; obvious threat.

My Sister Jane

Limited, positive data on sire with firsters; barn can get them to fire in debut, too (has won with 3 of last 14 first-out 2yo at major SoCal tracks); half to $68,845 earner Irish Recruit; dam made $135,141; maybe.

Granjacita

Career literally got off to a slow start in Pomona, as she was last after a quarter-mile in debut; half to $67,420 earner Hachero; like barn more with horses older than 2; lean toward others.

Acadiana

Spent debut running in midpack; nothing special from figure standpoint; half to $16,850 earner Prince Silver; cost $5,500 in Jan.; barn is zip for 7 with 2yo on SA-Hol-Dmr circuit since start of '95, but has good overall stats this year; like others more.*

continued

Reconvene

Own: Mamakos & Mcanally — $32,000

ALMEIDA G F (14 0 2 1 .00) 1996:(272 18 .07)

b. f. 2 (Mar)
Sire: Classic Fame (Nijinsky II)
Dam: Light a Charm (Majestic Light)
Br: Mamakos J & McAnally R (Cal)
Tr: McAnally Ronald (11 1 0 3 .09) 1996:(333 61 .18)

120

Lifetime Record:	0 M 0 0			
1996	0 M 0 0		Turf	0 0 0 0
1995	0 M 0 0		Wet	0 0 0 0
SA	0 0 0 0		Dist	0 0 0 0

Elegant Grace

Own: Gordy Gwen G — $28,000

VALENZUELA P A (33 2 5 4 .06) 1996:(491 60 .12)

Dk. b or br f. 2 (Mar)
Sire: Summing (Verbatim)
Dam: Ayleen (Coursing)
Br: Fuqua Gwen (Cal)
Tr: Cecil B D A (5 0 1 1 .00) 1996:(117 17 .15)

118

Lifetime Record:	1 M 0 0			
1996	1 M 0 0		Turf	0 0 0 0
1995	0 M 0 0		Wet	0 0 0 0
SA	0 0 0 0		Dist	1 0 0 0

25Aug96–6Dmr fst 6f :22 :45^1 :58^1 1:12^1 [F][S]Md Sp Wt 29 8 3 8$^{4\frac{3}{4}}$ 9^{14} 9^{14} 9$^{14\frac{1}{2}}$ Carr D B 118 40.60 63–15 Chilldown118$^{1\frac{3}{4}}$ Inexcessivelylucky118$^{\frac{1}{2}}$ Aquarellist118$^{1\frac{3}{4}}$ 5 wide, gave way 9

WORKOUTS: ●Oct7 Hol 3f fst :35^3 H *1/17* Oct2 Hol 5f fst 1:03^1 H *29/33* Sep27 Hol 5f fst 1:01^2 H *15/30* Sep21 Hol 4f fst :49^3 H *6/19* Sep15 Hol 4f fst :49 H *15/29* Aug19 Dmr 4f fst :47^3 Hg *9/58*

Lebec

Own: Valpredo John — $32,000

BLANC B (18 2 2 4 .11) 1996:(1022 104 .10)

B. f. 2 (Mar)
Sire: Savona Tower (Somethingfabulous)
Dam: Scarpina (Nantequos)
Br: Valpredo John (Cal)
Tr: Olguin Ulises (—) 1996:(150 8 .05)

120

Lifetime Record:	3 M 0 1	$3,230			
1996	3 M 0 1	$3,230	Turf	0 0 0 0	
1995	0 M 0 0		Wet	0 0 0 0	
SA	0 0 0 0		Dist	1 0 0 0	$1,190

28Sep96–12Fpx fst 6½f :22^1 :46^2 1:12^1 1:18^4 [F]Md 32000 52 6 2 4$^{2\frac{1}{4}}$ 3^5 2^6 3$^{6\frac{1}{4}}$ Scott J M B 116 10.80 81–12 Loves Pure Light116^6 Tahiti Tease116^{nk} Lebec116^1 Just lost 2nd 10

19Sep96–12Fpx fst 6f :22^1 :46^4 :59^3 1:12^2 [F][S]Md 32000 46 1 3 3^2 3^1 4^5 4^7 Scott J M B 116 6.10 80–09 Filaree116$^{2\frac{1}{2}}$ Unaflame116^1 Progressive Party116$^{3\frac{1}{2}}$ Inside, tired 10

2Sep96–2Dmr fst 5½f :22^2 :46 :58^4 1:05^2 [F][S]Md 32000 48 8 7 9$^{6\frac{1}{2}}$ 8$^{8\frac{1}{4}}$ 7^9 7^6 Blanc B B 118 44.50 80–09 MissEnchntment118$^{\frac{1}{2}}$ Perls'npntyhose118^4 JminJimMcQ116$^{\frac{3}{4}}$ No threat 12

WORKOUTS: Sep26 Fpx 3f fst :35^4 H *7/9* Sep15 Fpx 5f fst 1:02^1 H *10/20* Sep9 Fpx 5f fst 1:01^4 H *3/15* Aug30 Dmr 3f fst :38^4 H *20/20* Aug24 Dmr 5f fst 1:02^1 H *42/61* Aug18 Dmr 5f fst 1:00^3 Hg *21/54*

Reconvene

McAnally with 2yo maiden claimers on SA-Hol-Dmr circuit since start of '95: 1 for 5; barn's best work in 2yo division in last couple years has been with experienced runners; limited, negative data on sire with firsters; half to $5,847 earner Twice a Charm; moderate appeal.

Elegant Grace

Half to $176,745 earner Eddie Champion; saw all the heels in debut and returns at more reasonable level; for fans of the maiden-to-maiden-claiming angle.

Lebec

Earned some minor checks in Pomona; as a group, 2yo who made their previous start at Fairplex don't fare too well at Oak Tree; half to $41,675 earner Noble Boss.

-Mart Kolvastik

Who else could win here? Let's throw out Granjacita and Acadiana (no speed), Reconvene (dull works, distance breeding), Elegant Grace (no apparent ability), and Lebec (established mediocrity). I couldn't quite eliminate Tappin Her Toes, mainly because she has shown some zip in previous efforts and is dropping in class. Let's consider her a long-shot possibility.

This leaves us with Sunny Holiday and My Sister Jane. Sunny Holiday lost her only try, at Del Mar, in slow time, but was well bet, keeps her top jockey, and is trained by Richard Matlow, whose winning percentage is high. My Sister Jane shows several decent workouts, draws Eddie Delahoussaye, a fine rider, for her debut, and is trained by Warren Stute, another high-percentage winner.

What do we do?

This race ended my pick-six hopes. I had wanted to use another horse in addition to the darling of the Dummy God, but settled on Sunny Holiday over My Sister Jane, mainly because she seemed to have a bit more going for her than the first-time starter. I was obviously wrong about that, but, as the account of the race makes clear, the Dummy God was not sitting on his throne that afternoon. Aglo Darling was extremely unlucky to lose, after having been fouled at the start and all but eliminated. Even so, she was beaten by less than a length, though it might as well have been a mile, as far as I was concerned.

Because I was ahead and pressing my luck a bit, I had also started another pick-three, this one using the favorite, Tappin Her Toes, and Sunny Holiday. In hindsight, I obviously should have used the winner in my pick-three, thus ensuring the survival of at least one of my parlay wagers. But I allowed myself to be put off My Sister Jane when she received

	SIXTH RACE	6 FURLONGS. (1.07¹) MAIDEN CLAIMING. Purse $17,000. Fillies, 2-year-olds bred in California.

Santa Anita
OCTOBER 10, 1996

Value of Race: $17,000 Winner $9,350; second $3,400; third $2,550; fourth $1,275; fifth $425. Mutuel Pool $226,466.80 Exacta Pool $224,262.00 Trifecta Pool $285,259.00 Quinella Pool $34,101.00

Last Raced	Horse	M/Eqt. A.Wt	PP	St	1/4	1/2	Str	Fin	Jockey	Cl'g Pr	Odds $1
	My Sister Jane	B 2 120	4	5	6³	6¹½	2ʰᵈ	1¾	Delahoussaye E	32000	7.10
1Aug96 2Dmr³	Aglo Darling	LB 2 120	3	8	7ʰᵈ	7³	5½	2⁴¼	Stevens G L	32000	0.80
25Aug96 6Dmr⁹	Elegant Grace	B 2 118	8	1	2²½	2¹½	1¹	3¹	Valenzuela P A	28000	9.80
2Sep96 2Dmr⁴	Sunny Holiday	LB 2 120	2	9	5¹½	4¹½	3½	4½	Solis A	32000	4.30
24Sep96 9Fpx⁶	Acadiana	B 2 120	6	3	3¹	3ʰᵈ	4¹	5¹	Desormeaux K J	32000	18.10
23Sep96 12Fpx⁶	Granjacita	B 2 120	5	6	8¹½	8½	8ʰᵈ	6ⁿᵏ	Garcia M S	32000	63.50
28Sep96 12Fpx³	Lebec	B 2 120	9	7	9	9	9	7½	Blanc B	32000	17.60
12Sep96 6Fpx⁷	Tappin Her Toes	LB 2 120	1	4	4ʰᵈ	5½	7²	8⁵¼	Garcia J A	32000	9.70
	Reconvene	B 2 120	7	2	1ʰᵈ	1ʰᵈ	6ʰᵈ	9	Almeida G F	32000	42.80

OFF AT 3:30 Start Good For All But AGLO DARLING. Won driving. Time, :22², :46², :59¹, 1:11⁴ Track fast.

$2 Mutuel Prices:	4—MY SISTER JANE	16.20	5.20	4.00
	3—AGLO DARLING		2.80	2.60
	8—ELEGANT GRACE			4.80

$2 EXACTA 4–3 PAID $40.40 $2 TRIFECTA 4–3–8 PAID $342.20 $2 QUINELLA 3–4 PAID $15.80

B. f, (Apr), by Iam the Iceman–Julienne*Mex, by First Amendment. Trainer Stute Warren. Bred by Ridgeley Farm (Cal).

MY SISTER JANE came in a bit after the start, raced outside TAPPIN HER TOES early and off the rail leaving the backstretch, went four wide on the turn and five wide into the stretch, gained the lead just past midstretch and held off AGLO DARLING under urging. AGLO DARLING stumbled and broke a bit outward, then was squeezed back to lose position, moved up inside GRANJACITA leaving the backstretch, came wide into the stretch and finished well. A claim of foul by the rider of AGLO DARLING against the winner for alleged interference at the start was not allowed by the stewards, who ruled the winner was not the cause of AGLO DARLING'S trouble. ELEGANT GRACE dueled outside RECONVENE to the stretch, inched away from that one in midstretch and had the rider lose the whip, then could not match the top pair. SUNNY HOLIDAY was forced out and squeezed back at the start, sprinted up inside down the backstretch, remained inside and could not offer the needed late response. ACADIANA raced off the rail on the backstretch and outside SUNNY HOLIDAY on the turn, came four wide into the stretch to loom a threat and could not sustain her bid. GRANJACITA raced well off the rail and passed tiring rivals. LEBEC raced wide and was not a threat. TAPPIN HER TOES came out at the start and lugged out a bit early, raced just off the inside to the stretch and weakened. RECONVENE sprinted to a slim early lead, dueled inside ELEGANT GRACE to the stretch and weakened in the final furlong.

Owners— 1, Ridgeley Farm; 2, Gelgin & Schreter Trust & Schwartz; 3, Gordy Gwen G; 4, Cavanagh Marguerite F & Thomas M; 5, Cesena Laurie M; 6, Granja Vista Del Rio Stable; 7, Valpredo John; 8, Thimigan & Van Berg; 9, Mamakos & McAnally

Trainers— 1, Stute Warren; 2, Olivares Frank; 3, Cecil B D A; 4, Matlow Richard P; 5, Desormeaux J Keith; 6, Tinsley J E Jr; 7, Olguin Ulises; 8, Van Berg Jack C; 9, McAnally Ronald

Scratched— Audene's Kite (6Sep96 6DMR⁵)

$3 Pick Three (1–1–4) Paid $516.30; Pick Three Pool $81,531.

---

so little support at the parimutuel windows, going off at seven to one, twice her morning-line odds. With first-time starters, a clue to their ability or lack of it can often be found on the tote board, where some sizable bets and consequent lower odds may reflect on the confidence a horse's connections have in their champion. When no one apparently was risking any serious money on My Sister Jane, I couldn't make myself use her over Sunny Holiday. A mistake I would pay for.

I was not staring at a disaster, but clearly I had taken a step backward in my pursuit of the giant pot at the end of the rainbow. I could still hope for a pick-five, which might pay a couple of hundred dollars, but I had lost thirty-six, bringing my profit down to $209.80.

Three races to go, what now?

RACE 7: These horses may not have much of a future, but at least they've all won at least once. This means that we can handicap the seventh race without having to do as much guessing as in the maiden contests. A quick scan of the Beyer figs, however, is not reassuring; no horse appears to be a standout, with only two in the field having achieved the not so exalted level of 70. Whom can we throw out?

Let's scrap Hunny Now, who comes off a very unimpressive maiden win with a Beyer of 56. Goodbye to Sparkling Ripple and Progressive Party, who don't even have early speed to go with their unimpressive figs. At first glance, Loves Pure Light looks like a possible contender, but her only win was at Fairplex, not a major track, and against maidens. Horses coming off maiden triumphs often wilt when thrown in for the first time with winners. The same observation can be made about Beyond Redemption, so let's eliminate both of them.

Of the remaining four, Run for B and W seems an unlikely choice, but she does come out of a stakes race and shows two decent works. I can't quite put a line through her, especially at her price, eight to one on the program and seventeen to one by post time. Tuta Niche took ten races to break her maiden, but she has some speed and sports the two highest Beyers in the field. And she will also be a long shot. At low

7 Santa Anita Park

6 Furlongs (1:07^1) CLAIMING. Purse $30,000. Fillies, 2-year-olds. Weight, 120 lbs. Claiming price $40,000, if for $35,000, allowed 2 lbs.

Run for B and W

Own: DeLima Jose E — $40,000
TOSCANO P R (7 0 0 1 .00) 1996:(525 43 .08)

B. f. 2 (Apr)
Sire: Bet Twice (Sportin' Life)
Dam: Giubilante (Chieftain)
Br: Muirfield Ventures (Md)
Tr: DeLima Jose E (3 0 0 0 .00) 1996:(53 7 .13)

L 120

Lifetime Record :	4 1 0 1	$17,475			
1996	4 1 0 1	$17,475	Turf	0 0 0 0	
1995	0 M 0 0		Wet	0 0 0 0	
SA	1 0 0 0		Dist	0 0 0 0	

12Sep96-9Fpx fst 6½f :21^4 :46^3 1:10^4 1:17^1 Ⓕ Bustles&Bows48k 52 4 5 4^{2½} 4^{5½} 3^{7½} 3^{16} Berrio O A LB 116 b 16.20 79-09 Silken Magic115^1 CleverPrincess116^{15} RunForBAndW116^8 Bore out 4 1/2 5
4Sep96-6Dmr fst 5½f :22 :45^3 :58^4 1:05^1 Ⓕ Md 32000 66 5 7 3^{½} 3^1 3^2 1^{1¼} Berrio O A LB 118 b 18.70 87-10 RunForBAndW118^{1¼} PrizedPeaches116^1 Moose118^{1½} Gamely kicked clear 11
22May96-6Hol fst 4½f :22^3 :46^3 :53 Ⓕ Md 40000 34 4 5 4^6 3^5 4^4 Berrio O A LB 118 b 5.40 83-11 Princess Year118^1 Lil Miss Romance118^{2½} Beyond Belief118^{½} No late bid 7
17Apr96-1SA fst 2f :21^4 Ⓕ Md Sp Wt — 2 9 7^{3½} 7^{7¾} Linares M G 118 f 41.20 — — UltimateHonor118^{¾} QuietCaller118^{1¼} Slew'sHigh118^{2¾} Off slow, drifted in 10

WORKOUTS: Oct1 SA 5f fst 1:01^2 H *9/25* Sep24 SA 4f fst :48 H *5/20* Aug29 Dmr 5f fst 1:00^2 Hg *8/68* Aug22 Dmr 5f fst 1:00 H *5/56* Aug15 Dmr 5f fst 1:02^3 H *58/72* Aug8 Dmr 4f fst :49^2 H *31/52*

Hunny Now

Own: Cox Donald Lee — $40,000
HUNTER M T (18 3 0 1 .17) 1996:(403 55 .14)

Dk. b or br f. 2 (Mar)
Sire: Noble Monk*IRE (African Sky*GB)
Dam: Madam Avie (Lord Avie)
Br: Cox Donald Lee (Cal)
Tr: Dutton Jerry (5 0 0 0 .00) 1996:(110 19 .17)

L 120

Lifetime Record :	2 1 0 0	$10,700			
1996	2 1 0 0	$10,700	Turf	0 0 0 0	
1995	0 M 0 0		Wet	0 0 0 0	
SA	0 0 0 0		Dist	1 1 0 0	$9,350

24Sep96-9Fpx fst 6f :22^2 :46^2 :59^4 1:13 Ⓕ Ⓢ Md 32000 55 9 4 1^1 1^1 1^{½} 1^1 Hunter M T LB 116 b *.90 84-10 Hunny Now116^1 I'mQuickN'cool116^{1½} SunshineGal116^{½} Responded drive 10
4Sep96-6Dmr fst 5½f :22 :45^3 :58^4 1:05^1 Ⓕ Md 32000 56 11 1 1^{½} 1^1 1^2 4^{3¾} Valenzuela P A LB 118 b 8.20 83-10 Run For B And W118^{1¼} Prized Peaches116^1 Moose118^{1½} 5 wide to turn 11

WORKOUTS: Oct2 SA 4f fst :48 H *14/32* Sep19 SA 5f fst 1:03^1 H *26/31* Sep12 SA 4f fst :47^1 H *4/13* Aug28 Dmr 5f fst 1:00^3 Hg *10/51* Aug21 Dmr 5f fst 1:00^3 Hg *25/74* Aug15 Dmr 5f fst :59^4 Hg *9/72*

Sweet And Lowdown

Own: Busby & Plumley — $40,000
PEDROZA M A (23 4 3 1 .17) 1996:(1021 125 .12)

Dk. b or br f. 2 (Apr)
Sire: Stalwart (Hoist the Flag)
Dam: Twice Regal (King Pellinore)
Br: White Oak Ranch (Cal)
Tr: Mayberry Brian A (1 0 0 0 .00) 1996:(78 8 .10)

L 120

Lifetime Record :	3 1 0 1	$27,025			
1996	3 1 0 1	$27,025	Turf	0 0 0 0	
1995	0 M 0 0		Wet	0 0 0 0	
SA	0 0 0 0		Dist	1 1 0 0	$13,750

18Sep96-11Fpx fst 6½f :21^2 :45^2 1:11^3 1:18^4 Ⓕ Ⓡ Barretts Deb102k 60 7 2 3^2 3^3 4^{4½} 3^{2¼} Pedroza M A LB 113 7.30 85-11 CallingYou115^{nk} Justdrling116^2 SweetAndLowdown113^{½} Wide final turn 8
26Aug96-3Dmr fst 6f :22^1 :45^3 :58^3 1:12^1 Ⓕ Md 50000 61 7 2 2^{hd} 2^{½} 3^{½} 1^{hd} Solis A LB 118 *1.10 78-17 Sweet And Lowdown118^{hd} WoodfordcountyMis118^2 Guthrie118^{hd} Gamely 8
28Jly96-6Dmr fst 5½f :21^3 :44^4 :57^3 1:04^2 Ⓕ Ⓢ Md Sp Wt 56 8 10 6^{5¼} 5^{8½} 4^{7½} 5^6 Pedroza M A LB 118 2.20 85-07 GranjaRealeza118^{2¼} Kamli118^{½} ExplosiveLind118^{2½} Bumped, took up start 11

WORKOUTS: Oct3 SA 4f fst :49 H *19/33* Sep10 SA tr.t 3f fst :36^1 H *4/7* Jly21 Dmr 4f fst :47^4 H *4/26* ●Jly10 SA 5f fst :59^4 H *1/33*

A CLOSER LOOK

7th Santa Anita

Run for B and W

Split field in Fairplex stake, but was far behind the exacta horses; reasonably competitive in terms of best Beyer; nonetheless, will side with others.

Hunny Now

Showed some speed vs. maidens; was the superior horse (odds-on) in Pomona, but gets a harsher test here; barn is 10 for 70 (14% wins) with juveniles on SA-Hol-Dmr circuit since start of '95.

Sweet and Lowdown

Showed competitive spirit in diploma run and gave a decent account of herself in the 100-grander; enough speed to get striking position; Mayberry with 2yo on SA-Hol-Dmr circuit since start of '95: 7 for 55, or 13% wins; can't fault those taking optimistic view.

Sexy Fresa

Own: Granja Mexico

ESPINOZA V (18 0 5 3 .00) 1996:(719 95 .13) — $35,000

Dk. b or br f. 2 (May)
Sire: Slew's Royalty (Seattle Slew)
Dam: Sexy Drive (Inverness Drive)
Br: Granja Mexico (Cal)
Tr: Palma Hector O (3 0 1 0 .00) 1996:(87 12 .14)

L 118

Lifetime Record:	3 2 0 1	$39,375			
1996	3 2 0 1	$39,375	Turf	0 0 0 0	
1995	0 M 0 0		Wet	0 0 0 0	
SA	0 0 0 0		Dist	0 0 0 0	

6Sep96-3Dmr	fst	5½f	:214	:452	:574	1:043	ⒻClm 40000	60	4	3	2hd	2hd	21	3¾	Espinoza V	LB 120	*1.40	85-12	Morell's Love1204 JckpotJustice120¾ SexyFrs120½	Dueled between foes	6
14Aug96-3Dmr	fst	5½f	:22	:451	:58	1:044	ⒻClm 50000	68	5	3	3nk	2½	1hd	12	Espinoza V	LB 120	*1.00	89-12	SexyFres1202 PrciousPc1131 CCLovsDimonds120¾	Gamely kicked clear	6
17Jly96-4Hol	fst	5f	:221	:463		:582	Ⓕ[S]Md 40000	70	4	4	3½	2½	1hd	1½	Espinoza V	LB 118	*3.10	93-12	Sexy Fresa118½ Echoes Of Spring118½ Perfect Step118nk	4 wide, gamely	10

WORKOUTS: Sep28 SA 5f fst 1:013 H 23/43 Sep20 SA tr.t 4f fst :502 H 3/3 Aug30 Dmr 5f fst 1:011 H 21/52 Aug23 Dmr 4f fst :472 H 2/46 Aug6 Dmr 4f fst :474 H 5/40 Jly31 Dmr 4f fst :48 H 23/70

Sparkling Ripple

Own: Reinsch & Weissman

VALENZUELA P A (33 2 5 4 .06) 1996:(491 60 .12) — $40,000

Dk. b or br f. 2 (Jan)
Sire: Desert Wine (Damascus)
Dam: Pink Positive (Lord At War*Arg)
Br: Bobby George & Connie George (Cal)
Tr: Orman Mike (1 0 0 0 .00) 1996:(115 12 .10)

L 120

Lifetime Record:	3 1 0 2	$15,300			
1996	3 1 0 2	$15,300	Turf	0 0 0 0	
1995	0 M 0 0		Wet	0 0 0 0	
SA	0 0 0 0		Dist	1 0 0 1	$2,700

6Sep96-6Dmr	fst	5½f	:214	:453	:584	1:053	ⒻMd 32000	57	2	8	53¼	54	33	1½	Valenzuela P A	LB 118	*1.00	85-12	Sparkling Ripple118½ Iza Bay116no Magic Remedy1189	Closed gamely	8
16Aug96-5Dmr	fst	6f	:222	:46	:582	1:111	Ⓕ[S]Md 32000	48	5	5	66¼	66	47	39	Valenzuela P A	B 118	2.90	74-11	Morell'sLove1188 TahitiTease1181 SprklingRipple1181	In bit tight early	9
2Aug96-2Dmr	fst	5½f	:22	:454	:584	1:052	Ⓕ[S]Md 32000	50	8	1	32½	33	32½	33	Black C A	B 118	4.20	83-08	PerfctStp1181½ MissEnchntmnt1181¼ SprklingRippl1182	Veered out start	8

WORKOUTS: Oct4 SA 5f fst 1:013 H 31/49 Sep26 SA 5f fst 1:012 H 23/42 Aug11 Dmr 3f fst :354 H 7/23 Jly26 Dmr 3f fst :371 H 13/27

Progressive Party

Own: Charles & Clear Valley Stables

PINCAY L JR (19 4 0 6 .21) 1996:(754 98 .13) — $40,000

B. f. 2 (Mar)
Sire: Romantic Prince*Ire (Henbit)
Dam: Party in Progress (Stalwart)
Br: Clear Valley Stable (Cal)
Tr: Shulman Sanford (6 0 0 0 .00) 1996:(268 29 .11)

L 120

Lifetime Record:	8 1 0 1	$15,740			
1996	8 1 0 1	$15,740	Turf	0 0 0 0	
1995	0 M 0 0		Wet	0 0 0 0	
SA	0 0 0 0		Dist	3 1 0 1	$12,740

26Sep96-3Fpx	fst	6f	:221	:461	:594	1:124	ⒻMd 32000	56	6	7	57	22½	11	13	Espinoza V	LB 116	2.20	85-12	ProgressiveParty1163 OutOfTaxes1163 WhiteOcen1162	Drew clear drive	7
19Sep96-12Fpx	fst	6f	:221	:464	:593	1:122	Ⓕ[S]Md 32000	54	4	10	86¾	43	34	33½	Flores D R	LB 116	7.90	83-09	Filaree1162½ Unaflame1161 Progressive Party1163½	Wide into lane	10
29Aug96-6Dmr	fst	6½f	:221	:452	1:11	1:18	Ⓕ[S]Md 28000	49	6	11	95¾	108	69	69¼	Atkinson P	LB 116	19.30	72-14	MessageOfHoney118nk MissLwless1185 LdyIntegrity1181	Wide into lane	12
16Aug96-5Dmr	fst	6f	:222	:46	:582	1:111	Ⓕ[S]Md 32000	46	2	9	76¾	77½	57	410	Pedroza M A	LB 118	7.30	73-11	Morell's Love1188 Tahiti Tease1181 Sparkling Ripple1181		9
Came in start; steadied early & 3/8																					
1Aug96-2Dmr	fst	5½f	:221	:453	:58	1:043	Ⓕ[S]Md 28000	56	12	1	66½	65½	57	45½	Pedroza M A	LB 116	6.70	84-09	Cashcheckorchrge118no Morell'sLove118½ AgloDrling1185	5 wide to turn	12
10Jly96-4Hol	fst	5½f	:221	:461	:592	1:054	ⒻMd 28000	38	1	8	810	712	77½	57¾	Pedroza M A	LB 116	15.30	74-16	Ardent Moment1183½ Pete'sCupid118hd ThatsaKnightsGal1184	Inside trip	11
23Jun96-4Hol	fst	5f	:223	:463		:594	ⒻMd 32000	40	6	7	78½	67¾	57¼	42½	Pedroza M A	LB 118	23.50	84-11	LilMissRomnce118¾ ArdentMoment118nk StrLgu1181½	Improved position	10
5Jun96-6Hol	fst	5f	:222	:461		:583	ⒻMd 32000	22	2	8	52½	74¾	87¾	813½	Pedroza M A	B 118	21.60	79-11	[D]Firness118½ DontFerTheHet1185 Pt'sCupid1182	Used early, gave way	8

WORKOUTS: Oct4 SA 4f fst :492 H 23/33 Sep8 Dmr 4f fst :483 H 18/40 Aug23 Dmr 3f fst :354 H 4/24 Aug9 Dmr 3f fst :363 H 15/22 Jly27 Dmr 3f fst :354 H 9/34 Jly20 Hol 4f fst :473 H 3/24

Sexy Fresa

Lone member of the field with more than one career win; only Tuta Niche, who has raced 10 times, has exceeded her top Beyer; has early speed and room to develop; running lines of first 2 races show she doesn't mind a pace battle; barn with 2yo at major SoCal tracks since start of '95: 4 for 32 (13% wins); big player.

Sparkling Ripple

Got diploma in her first start with Lasix; a key issue is whether she can use that effort as a springboard to better things; barn is 3 for 19 with 2yo this year on major SoCal circuit; mixed signals.

Progressive Party

Closer to the lead than usual after a half-mile in most recent race and the strategy resulted in a diploma; like this barn more with horses older than 2.

continued

Loves Pure Light
Own: My Jolee Stables
$40,000
GARCIA M S (10 0 1 0 .00) 1996:(464 37 .08)

Ch. f. 2 (Jan)
Sire: Olympic Native (Raise a Native)
Dam: Tiffany's Gem (Effervescing)
Br: M Helen Smith & Georgiana D Blatz (Cal)
Tr: Stute Melvin F (7 0 0 0 .00) 1996:(364 37 .10)

120

Lifetime Record : 6 1 1 1 $17,790
1996 6 1 1 1 $17,790 | Turf 0 0 0 0
1995 0 M 0 0 | Wet 0 0 0 0
SA 2 0 0 1 $5,550 | Dist 2 0 1 0 $2,890

28Sep96-12Fpx fst 6½f :221 :462 1:121 1:184 ⒻMd 32000 66 4 1 1hd 15 16 16 Garcia M S B 116 b *.80 87-12 Loves Pure Light1166 Tahiti Tease116nk Lebec1161 Handily 10
19Sep96-6Fpx fst 6f :214 :452 :581 1:111 Ⓕ[S]Md 32000 66 8 2 33½ 34 24 23 Garcia J A B 116 b 3.30 90-09 Iza Bay1163 Loves Pure Light1163½ Abbeyside1161½ Chased winner 10
8Sep96-7Dmr fst 6f :213 :45 :572 1:103 Ⓕ[S]Md Sp Wt 35 6 2 45½ 46 610 618½ Antley C W B 118 b 25.10 67-12 Fleet Lady1184 Nature's Fury1182 Teach Only Love118½ No rally 8
11Aug96-6Dmr fst 5½f :22 :451 :572 1:034 Ⓕ[S]Md Sp Wt 45 11 1 44½ 58½ 710 714½ Solis A B 118 9.40 79-11 Kamali1184½ Tuta Niche1188 Cozzy Flyer118nk Wide, weakened 11
10Apr96-1SA fst 2f :213 Ⓕ[S]Md Sp Wt — 10 9 62¾ 63½ Douglas R R B 118 6.00 — — TheresaEileen118nk ExcellentHalf1181¾ RendiesPrimver118hd Off bit slow 10
20Mar96-6SA fst 2f :213 ⒻMd Sp Wt — 6 3 41 31 Douglas R R B 118 3.60 — — Truly June's1181 La Moza Realeza118no Loves Pure Light118½ Willingly 8
WORKOUTS: Oct3 SA 4f fst :483 H 15/33 ●Sep26 Fpx 3f fst :342 H 1/9 Sep16 SA 4f fst :473 H 7/45 Sep3 Dmr 5f fst 1:002 H 9/29 Aug29 Dmr 5f fst 1:012 H 26/68 Aug23 Dmr 5f fst 1:003 H 10/57

Small Town Blues
Own: Ito & Patterson & Tsujimoto
$40,000
DOUGLAS R R (21 4 4 1 .19) 1996:(1031 122 .12)

Dk. b or br f. 2 (Mar)
Sire: Lucky Point (What Luck)
Dam: She's Caught (Native Uproar)
Br: Walker Colvin (Tex)
Tr: Chapman James K (2 0 1 0 .00) 1996:(69 5 .07)

L 120

Lifetime Record : 2 1 0 0 $5,700
1996 2 1 0 0 $5,700 | Turf 0 0 0 0
1995 0 M 0 0 | Wet 0 0 0 0
SA 0 0 0 0 | Dist 0 0 0 0

12Jun96-8Hol fst 5½f :213 :444 :572 1:034 ⒻCinderella61k 41 8 7 86½ 77¼ 77½ 715¼ Douglas R R B 114 36.10 77-09 Starry Ice1194 Spirited Jaclyn117¾ Caprifoil116½ Wide trip 8
Previously trained by Estevez Manuel A
18May96-1Hia fst 3f :214 :324 ⒻMd 40000 — 2 1 13½ 13¾ Rivera J A II 114 3.60 98-22 Small Town Blues1143¾ Frijoles Con Garra1162 Kitty's Spirit1151½ Driving 6
WORKOUTS: Oct5 Hol 4f fst :474 Hg 3/30 Sep30 Hol 5f fst 1:02 H 12/20 ●Sep24 Hol 5f fst 1:002 H 1/20 Sep18 Hol 5f fst 1:004 H 8/33 Sep12 Hol 5f fst 1:01 H 5/24 Sep5 Hol 4f fst :50 H 10/12

Beyond Redemption
Own: Killing Time Stable
$35,000
SORENSON D (2 0 0 0 .00) 1996:(208 21 .10)

Gr/ro f. 2 (Apr)
Sire: Prospectors Gamble (Crafty Prospector)
Dam: Dainty Diplomat (Deputy Minister)
Br: Jan Mace & Samantha Siegel (Fla)
Tr: Aguirre Paul G (1 0 0 0 .00) 1996:(74 11 .15)

L 118

Lifetime Record : 4 1 1 0 $12,950
1996 4 1 1 0 $12,950 | Turf 0 0 0 0
1995 0 M 0 0 | Wet 0 0 0 0
SA 0 0 0 0 | Dist 1 1 0 0 $9,350

23Sep96-12Fpx fst 6f :223 :464 :593 1:121 ⒻMd 32000 65 8 2 12 112 13 15½ Sorenson D LB 116 b *.90 88-09 BeyondRedemption1165½ TimlyViw1162 GtuRoug116½ Drew off 2nd turn 10
22Aug96-4Dmr fst 7f :221 :453 1:114 1:26 ⒻMd 28000 42 2 4 2hd 1hd 23 24 Vergara O LB 116 b 6.20 66-13 Millbrae1184 Beyond Redemption1166 Criteria1186 Inside duel 8
Previously trained by Divine Don
10Jly96-4Hol fst 5½f :221 :461 :592 1:054 ⒻMd 32000 22 10 2 32½ 45½ 911 1013½ Valenzuela F H LB 118 9.90 69-16 ArdntMomnt1183½ Pt'sCupid118hd ThtsKnightsGl1184 Hustled, gave way 11
12Jun96-6Hol fst 4½f :22 :453 :514 ⒻMd 50000 19 10 9 65 610 614½ Valenzuela F H 118 5.50 78-09 CrisTheSwimmer1185 BeautifulFace1181 TappinHerToes1181 Wide trip 10
WORKOUTS: Oct4 Hol 4f fst :484 H 3/9 Sep17 Hol 4f fst :474 H 3/31 ●Sep11 Dmr 4f fst :472 H 1/25 Sep6 Dmr 4f fst :492 H 28/48 Sep1 Dmr 4f fst :494 H 38/44 Aug18 Dmr 5f fst 1:01 Hg 26/54

Loves Pure Light
If first-time starters are eliminated, Mel is 11 for 102 with 2yo on SA-Hol-Dmr circuit since start of '95; flew solo on the lead for much of her graduation run; sharp enough to merit consideration.

Small Town Blues
Her best Beyer has been exceeded by each of the other entrants; was overmatched in the Cinderella; perhaps combination of time off and Lasix will agree with her, but not especially eager to test that theory at the windows.

Beyond Redemption
Ran the race of her life last month; didn't feel any pace pressure and she's in for a tougher test this time; barn has acceptable record this year; neither standout nor throwout.

Tuta Niche

Own: Valpredo John

BLANC B (18 2 2 4 .11) 1996:(1022 104 .10)

Dk. b or br f. 2 (Feb)
Sire: Flying Victor (Flying Paster)
Dam: Tuta Mia (Olmaggio)
Br: Valpredo John (Cal)
Tr: Olguin Ulises (—) 1996:(150 8 .05)

$40,000

Lifetime Record: 10 2 3 1 $45,310

1996	10 2 3 1	$45,310	Turf	0 0 0 0
1995	0 M 0 0		Wet	0 0 0 0
SA	1 0 0 0	L 120	Dist	3 1 1 0	$25,035

26Sep96- 9Fpx fst 6f	:22 :45⁴ :58⁹ 1:12¹	⑨Md Sp Wt	64 7 1 4½ 3⁹ 2½ 1½	Scott J M	LB 116 b	3.20	88-12	Tuta Niche116½ Cozzy Flyer116¹ Forafella116³	Edged clear late 9
12Sep96- 6Fpx fst 6f	:22¹ :46 :59¹ 1:12³	⑨ⓈMd Sp Wt	55 4 4 3² 2⁹ 2⁹½	Toscano P R	LB 116 b	3.10	82-09	EchoesOfSpring116³½ TuNiche116½ DoubleWinner116¾	Stumbled break 9
25Aug96- 6Dmr fst 6f	:22 :45¹ :58¹ 1:12¹	⑨ⓈMd Sp Wt	55 2 1 4½ 5½ 4⁴ 4	Blanc B	LB 118 b	3.10	74-15	Chilldown118¾ Inexcessivelylucky118¼ Aquarellist118¹½	On rail to lane 9
11Aug96- 6Dmr fst 6f	:22 :45¹ :57¹ 1:03⁴	⑨ⓈMd Sp Wt	73 5 3 5⁵ 4⁷½ 3⁵½ 2⁴½	Blanc B	LB 118 b	*2.20	89-11	Kamali118¾ Tuta Niche118⁸ Cozzy Flyer118ᵒᵏ	Second best 11
29Jly96- 6Dmr fst 5½f	:22 :45¹ :57¹ 1:03²	⑨ⓈMd Sp Wt	76 7 1 2¹ 2² 2¹½ 2²	Blanc B	LB 118 b	6.60	94-10	Merry Krisoke118² Tuta Niche118⁸ Sister Jo118⁹½	Stalked, 2nd best 9
3Jly96- 6Hol fst 5f	:22¹ :45 :57 :59	⑨Md 50000	56 6 2 4¹½ 5⁹ 3⁴ 3⁹	Blanc B	LB 116 b	16.60	87-15	Silken Magic118ᵒᵏ Critical Factor118ʰᵈ Tuta Niche116²½	Lugged out 3/8 10
12Jun96- 6Hol fst 4½f	:22 :45¹ :51⁴	⑨Md 45000	36 1 6 3²½ 5⁹½ 5⁹½	Blanc B	LB 116 b	19.50	83-09	CrisTheSwimmer118⁵ BeautifulFace118¹ TppinHerToes118¹	Inside trip 10
12May96- 4Hol fst 4½f	:22¹ :45³ :51⁴	⑨Md Sp Wt	38 4 1 2½	4⁶½ 4¹0¾	Douglas R R	LB 118	22.90	82-11	Montecito118⁵ Broad Dynamite118²½ Guthrie118⁷¼	Inside trip 5
Steadied while lugging out into lane														
27Apr96- 4Hol fst 4½f	:22 :45⁹	⑨ⓈMd Sp Wt	35 3 3 7¹²	7¹0 5¹4½	Blanc B5	LB 113	44.00	80-16	Spirited Jaclyn118¹½ Excellent Half118² Jackpot Justice118¹½	No threat 7
11Apr96- 1SA fst 2f	:21⁹	⑨ⓈMd Sp Wt	— 2 5	5⁴ 10⁷½	Blanc B5	B 113	42.50	– –	RollinIntheDough118⁼ SpiritedJclyn118½ JckpotJustice118ᵒᵏ	Weakened 10

WORKOUTS: Oct4 SA 5f fst 1:01⁴ H 3/49   Sep19 Fpx 4f fst :52 H 13/13   Sep8 Fpx 3f fst 1:01³ H 6/12   Aug19 Dmr 4f fst 1:05¹ H 60/69   Aug8 Dmr 4f fst :47² H 3/52   ● Jly25 Dmr 4f fst :46² H 1/50 odds neither of these two animals could be played, but at big prices they have to be left in. Value is king.

My two top horses are Sweet and Lowdown and Sexy Fresa. The former's Beyers are unimpressive, but she, too, drops into a claimer out of a minor stakes race. She has enough early speed to be in contention and the trainer-jockey combination is a successful one. (You would have no way of knowing this solely from the chart, but that the jockey takes her back off her last race is usually a good sign.) Sexy Fresa is the only two-time winner in the field and will probably be the public choice, though she has the look of a possible Dummy God favorite. Her speed ratings are in decline from an initial high of 70, a bad sign, and her odds will be too low to justify a straight bet.

In trying to decide how to wager on this race, I have two main factors to consider: I'm alive for five in my pick-six to two horses, Sweet and Lowdown and Tuta Niche; I'm still ahead for the day about $210. Is there a play?

It's very gratifying and beneficial to the ego to be able to predict almost exactly what will happen in a horse race. As you can see from the chart on page 153, the animals ran almost like little trained dogs around a ring, finishing pretty much as I had predicted, with three of my four selections on top. Even Tuta Niche didn't disgrace herself, beaten out of fourth by only a head.

What left me with a slightly sour taste in my mouth is that I had very little to show financially for this brilliant analysis, a tour de force that turned into a farce. I had decided to start a final pick-three, but I had four horses to choose from and wanted to use only three of them. I didn't want to use both favorites, so I threw out the winner because I already had her in my pick-six.

Then, emboldened by my tidy profit for the day, I took a flyer on a trifecta, a two-dollar box using everyone *but* Sweet

SEVENTH RACE

Santa Anita

OCTOBER 10, 1996

6 FURLONGS. (1.07¹) CLAIMING. Purse $30,000. Fillies, 2–year–olds. Weight, 120 lbs. Claiming price $40,000, if for $35,000, allowed 2 lbs.

Value of Race: $30,000 Winner $16,500; second $6,000; third $4,500; fourth $2,250; fifth $750. Mutuel Pool $239,507.00 Exacta Pool $194,150.00 Trifecta Pool $259,121.00 Quinella Pool $33,675.00

Last Raced	Horse	M/Eqt. A.Wt	PP	St	¼	½	Str	Fin	Jockey	Cl'g Pr	Odds $1
18Sep96 ¹¹Fpx³	Sweet And Lowdown	LB	2 120	3	2	1hd	1hd	1hd	1 3	Pedroza M A	40000	2.80
6Sep96 ³Dmr³	Sexy Fresa	LB	2 118	4	3	2¹	2¹½	2²	2²	Espinoza V	35000	2.60
12Sep96 ⁹Fpx³	Run for B and W	LBb	2 120	1	9	5hd	4hd	3hd	3no	Toscano P R	40000	17.40
28Sep96 ¹²Fpx¹	Loves Pure Light	Bb	2 120	7	5	4¹	5²½	5³	4hd	Garcia M S	40000	8.80
26Sep96 ⁹Fpx¹	Tuta Niche	LBb	2 120	10	4	9¹½	9¹	6½	5³	Blanc B	40000	4.50
12Jun96 ⁸Hol⁷	Small Town Blues	B	2 120	8	1	3¹½	3hd	4hd	6³½	Douglas R R	40000	6.80
26Sep96 ³Fpx¹	Progressive Party	LB	2 120	6	10	10	8hd	7¹	7²½	Pincay L Jr	40000	27.80
24Sep96 ⁹Fpx¹	Hunny Now	LBb	2 120	2	7	7¹½	6hd	8hd	8¹	Hunter M T	40000	38.60
6Sep96 ⁶Dmr¹	Sparkling Ripple	LB	2 120	5	8	8hd	7²	9⁴	9⁵½	Valenzuela P A	40000	12.40
23Sep96 ¹²Fpx¹	Beyond Redemption	LBb	2 118	9	6	6½	10	¹10	10	Sorenson D	35000	20.10

OFF AT 4:00 Start Good. Won driving. Time, :22, :45², :57⁴, 1:10⁴ Track fast.

$2 Mutuel Prices:

3–SWEET AND LOWDOWN	7.60	3.80	3.40
4–SEXY FRESA		3.80	3.20
1–RUN FOR B AND W			6.40

$2 EXACTA 3–4 PAID $22.40 $2 TRIFECTA 3–4–1 PAID $175.80 $2 QUINELLA 3–4 PAID $10.00

Dk. b. or br. f, (Apr), by Stalwart–Twice Regal, by King Pellinore. Trainer Mayberry Brian A. Bred by White Oak Ranch (Cal).

SWEET AND LOWDOWN dueled inside SEXY FRESA but off the rail until past midstretch, then kicked clear under urging. SEXY FRESA vied for command outside the winner to deep stretch, then could not match that one but held the place. RUN FOR B AND W was a bit slow into stride, had a rail trip and just got the show. LOVES PURE LIGHT was close up a bit off the rail on the backstretch, raced between rivals leaving the turn and was narrowly edged for third. TUTA NICHE raced well off the rail early and outside PROGRESSIVE PARTY early on the turn, came wide into the stretch and also just missed third. SMALL TOWN BLUES attended the pace off the rail on the backstretch and three deep on the turn and could not offer the needed late response. PROGRESSIVE PARTY was bumped and steadied at the start, settled off the inside, steadied again off heels early on the turn and was not a threat. HUNNY NOW was between rivals early and inside BEYOND REDEMPTION on the turn, then weakened. SPARKLING RIPPLE was bumped at the start, angled to the inside for the turn and did not rally. BEYOND REDEMPTION broke in the air, raced outside rivals on the backstretch and turn and began to give way before completing a half mile.

Owners— 1, Busby & Plumley; 2, Granja Mexico; 3, DeLima Jose E; 4, My Jolee Stables; 5, Valpredo John; 6, Ito & Patterson & Tsujimoto; 7, Charles & Clear Valley Stables; 8, Cox Donald Lee; 9, Reinsch & Weissman; 10, Killing Time Stable

Trainers— 1, Mayberry Brian A; 2, Palma Hector O; 3, DeLima Jose E; 4, Stute Melvin F; 5, Olguin Ulises; 6, Chapman James K; 7, Shulman Sanford; 8, Dutton Jerry; 9, Orman Mike; 10, Aguirre Paul G

$3 Pick Three (1–4–3) Paid $393.90; Pick Three Pool $77,483.

and Lowdown. Why? Again because I had to choose between her and Sexy Fresa, while keeping the long shots in my action. Had either of them won, with the others in the picture, I might not have needed a Brink's truck to get home, but perhaps a small satchel and an armed guard.

It didn't happen. I had wound up with Sexy Fresa on the

basis of her superior Beyers, but ignored her decline. I paid for that mistake in judgment, losing forty-eight dollars on the race, with nothing to show for my handicapping prowess but survival in a possible pick-five. My profit tumbled to $162.

Looking back, as one often does in this game, I don't know that I would have played it any differently. Let's just say that we can use this race as an example of how easy it is to be right about who the contenders are in any contest as opposed to how difficult it is to make that skill pay off for you. A useful discipline, as Pooh-Bah might have put it in *The Mikado*, but an irritating one. No day at the racetrack passes without its quota of minor aggravations.

This is the race we've been waiting for all afternoon, one you can build a whole day at the track around. I had told myself, when handicapping it, not to be afraid to step out and make a solid bet on it, regardless of how the rest of my action might have fared. In approaching it now, I do so from the strong position of still being ahead and also alive for a pick-five. Let's look at pages 155–158 and see why I feel so optimistic about it.

■ RACE 8: At first glance, it wouldn't seem to be a good betting race. The field is small, only six entries, and entered on the turf course, where horses get into more trouble than on the main track. But we can immediately throw out two of them, Birthday Time, a filly who clearly wants to go longer than a mile and whose two races in this country have not been impressive, and Lady Ling, who hasn't competed since last December and who is probably using this race as a conditioner for contests at longer distances later on.

We are down to a quartet, all of them potential winners. Dusty Girl has won four times at this distance and sports a series of excellent Beyers. Miss Lady Bug looks less impres-

8 Santa Anita Park

1 MILE. (Turf). (1:32^{2}) ALLLOWANCE. Purse $49,000. Fillies and mares, 3-year-olds and upward which are non-winners of $3,000 three times other than maiden or claiming or have never won four races. Weights: 3-year-olds, 120 lbs. Older, 122 lbs. Non-winners of two such races at one mile or over since August 1, allowed 3 lbs. Of such a race since September 1, 5 lbs. (Horses eligible only to the above conditions are preferred.) Rail at 30 feet.

Dusty Girl (NZ)

Own: Lima Family Trust

BLACK C A (8 1 0 0 .13) 1996:(754 69 .09)

Gr. m. 6
Sire: Pre Catalan (My Swallow)
Dam: Fleur de Joie (Bellissimo)
Br: Nearco Breeding Ltd & Co (NZ)
Tr: Carava Jack (3 0 0 2 .00) 1996:(333 53 .16)

L 117

Lifetime Record :	33	9	6	4	$160,150						
1996	8	3	2	0	$108,800	Turf	32	9	6	3	$154,150
1995	13	4	3	1	$46,261	Wet	1	0	0	1	$6,000
SA Ⓣ	2	0	1	0	$10,000	Dist Ⓣ	6	4	0	0	$55,043

2Aug96-7Dmr	fm	1 3/8	Ⓣ	$:51^{3}$	$1:17^{2}$	$1:42^{3}$	$2:18^{1}$	3↑ⒻHoney Fox H76k	96	4	2	2 1/2	2 1/2	2hd	2 1/4	Black C A	LB 116	2.50	72-22	Admise117 1 1/4 Dusty Girl116 1/2 Alyshena114 1	Game between foes lane	5
20Jun96-5Hol	fm	1 1/16	Ⓣ	$:23^{3}$	:47	$1:10^{4}$	$1:41^{3}$	4↑ⒻClm c-80000	95	6	7	6 3/4	5 3/2	4 1 3/4	1 2	Desormeaux K J	LB 119	*.70	88-12	Dusty Girl119 2 Park Valley116 1 Glorious Force116 2 1/2	Going away	7
Claimed from Feldman & Silber & Swartz, Stein Roger M Trainer																						
30May96-8Hol	fm	1	Ⓣ	$:23^{4}$	$:47^{3}$	$1:11^{1}$	$1:34^{4}$	4↑ⒻAlw 54000N3X	95	2	6	6 3	5 4	4 3 1/2	4 1 1/4	Desormeaux K J	LB 117	4.30	88-11	Call Now115 1 Se Souvenir115nk Sixieme Sens117no	Finished well	7
23May96-8Hol	fm	1 1/16	Ⓣ	$:23^{3}$	:47	$1:10^{1}$	$1:40^{1}$	3↑ⒻAlw 48000N2X	95	5	5	6 5 3/4	4 6	2 3	1 3/4	Nakatani C S	LB 116	5.70	95-09	Dusty Girl116 3/4 Jah116hd Inscrutable Dancer116nk	Closed gamely	8
5May96-4Hol	fm	1	Ⓣ	:23	$:45^{4}$	1:10	$1:34^{1}$	4↑ⒻClm 62500	95	2	5	3 5	2 1 1/2	1 2	1 2 3/4	Stevens G L	LB 116	*1.80	92-06	Dusty Girl116 2 3/4 Dell Rapids116 6 Royal Chapel108 3 1/2	Ridden out	7
6Apr96-8GG	fm	1	Ⓣ	$:23^{1}$	:47	1:11	$1:35^{4}$	3↑ⒻMissAmercaH-G3	83	5	11	11 10	9 9	7 9 1/2	6 7 1/4	Schvaneveldt C P	LB 115	50.50	84-10	Lady Lodger114 1 3/4 Tricky Code115 1 Traces Of Gold115 1/2	No rally	11
29Feb96-7SA	gd	1 1/8	Ⓣ	$:47^{2}$	1:12	$1:38^{2}$	1:52	4↑ⒻAlw 50000N2X	71	4	6	6 11	6 9 1/2	6 4 3/4	6 9	Black C A	LB 117	3.30	61-30	Nimble Mind118 2 3/4 Silverbulletlover118 1/2 Stylish Society116hd	Rail to lane	7
7Jan96-7SA	fm	1 1/8	Ⓣ	$:48^{3}$	1:13	$1:37^{4}$	$1:50^{3}$	4↑ⒻAlw 50000N2X	84	9	10	8 5 1/4	8 5	4 6	2 4 1/2	Black C A	LB 119	*3.70	72-23	Two Ninety Jones117 4 1/2 Dusty Girl119nk Encoremoi112 1/2	4 wide 2nd turn	10
24Dec95-6Hol	my	1 1/16	⊗	$:23^{1}$	$:46^{1}$	$1:10^{3}$	$1:43^{4}$	3↑ⒻAlw 40000N2X	53	3	6	6 11	4 11	3 8	3 20	Black C A	LB 119	*1.50	62-18	Aly Sweet116 4 Expensive Star116 16 Dusty Girl119 4	Awkward start	6
3Dec95-10Hol	fm	1	Ⓣ	$:23^{2}$	$:47^{2}$	$1:11^{2}$	$1:35^{1}$	3↑ⒻAlw 36000N1X	89	1	9	9 6 3/4	8 4 3/4	5 2 1/4	1 1 1/4	Black C A	LB 122	3.30	87-09	Dusty Girl122 1 1/4 Nimble Mind115 1/2 Windrifter117 1	Lacked room 1/4-1/8	10

WORKOUTS: Oct4 Hol 4f fst $:49^{1}$ H *4/9* Sep28 Hol 6f fst $1:16^{2}$ H *19/19* Sep21 Hol 6f fst $1:16^{4}$ H *9/10* Sep4 Dmr 5f fst $1:02^{2}$ H *48/67* Aug28 Dmr 4f fst $:49^{3}$ H *35/51* Jly28 Dmr 4f fst $:49^{1}$ H *43/67*

A CLOSER LOOK

8th Santa Anita

Dusty Girl

Close 2nd to Admire, who returned to win the Matching and then won the Oak Tree Turf Championship Sunday via disqualification; owns the best Beyers in the cast, loves this distance and has some okay works; barn having a solid year and Black does his best work on the turf; not sure stalker will get a solid pace to chase, but she's a threat nonetheless.

continued

Birthday Time (Ger)

Own: Stacey Sally

BLANC B (18 2 2 4 .11) 1996:(1022 104 .10)

B. f. 4
Sire: Taufan (Stop the Music)
Dam: Birthday Party*Fr (Windwurf*Ger)
Br: Eisle H (Ger)
Tr: Bunn Thomas M Jr (3 0 0 1 .00) 1996:(80 8 .10)

L 117

Lifetime Record:	10	3	2	0	$26,808						
1996	2	0	0	0	$3,000	Turf	10	3	2	0	$26,808
1995	8	3	2	0	$23,808	Wet	0	0	0	0	
SA Ⓣ	0	0	0	0		Dist Ⓣ	0	0	0	0	

8Sep96-8Dmr fm 1⅜ Ⓣ :491 1:14 1:39 2:153 3↑ ⒻMatching H76k 89 1 3 42 42 55 56½ Blanc B LB 112 38.00 80-12 Admise1192 Interim1182¾ Miss Lady Bug117hd Inside trip 8
2Aug96-7Dmr fm 1⅜ Ⓣ :513 1:172 1:423 2:181 3↑ ⒻHoney Fox H76k 89 3 3 33½ 53 54¾ 55 Blanc B B 114 12.00 68-22 Admise1171¼ Dusty Girl116½ Alyshena1141 Weakened 5
Previously trained by H Remmert
26Nov95♦ Bremen(Ger) sf *1⅜ ⓉRH 2:322 3↑ Preis von Bremen Hcp 13900 59 Eddery D 116 4.20 Prairie Blitz1131 Amaganset1291 Kasparow126hd 10 *Rated in mid-pack,never threatened*
28Oct95♦ Krefeld(Ger) gd *1½ ⓉLH 2:321 3↑ Niederrhein-Ausgleich Hcp 10800 11½ Schiergen P 114 *1.00 Birthday Time1141½ Comme Il Faut114nk Fridericus131½ 8 *Tracked in 4th,led final 16th,driving*
24Sep95♦ Cologne(Ger) gd *1½ ⓉRH 2:293 3↑ Kamiros-Rennen Hcp 14300 2½ Schindler E 106 2.60 Rosaraie118½ Birthday Time1063½ Faber117½ 8 *Tracked in 3rd,led 1f out,headed near line*
27Aug95♦ BadenBaden(Ger) gd *1¼ ⓉLH 2:08 3↑ ⒻBlanquet-Rennen Alw 14700 1hd Woodburn K 119 5.20 Birthday Time119hd Windira119¾ Molto la Gamba1141 9 *Towards rear,rallied to lead near line*
5Aug95♦ Gelsenkrchn(Ger) gd *1⅜ ⓉRH 2:172 3↑ Preis der Stadt Gelsenkirchen Hcp 7200 54¼ Nagy J 111 11.60 O'Kerry1192 Longline121hd Pepper Wind1182 10 *Well placed in 4th,lacked rally*
22Jly95♦ Mulheim(Ger) gd *1 5/16 ⓉRH 2:134 3↑ Preis der Hubertusburg Hcp 6700 22½ Eddery D 112 9.30 Penango1232½ Birthday Time112hd Gietscherroth119nk 9 *Rated in 6th,bid 2f out,just up for 2nd*
18Jun95♦ Dortmund(Ger) sf *1¼ ⓉRH 2:163 ⒻKamiros-Rennen Maiden 7300 1¾ Woodburn K 123 *.80 Birthday Time123¾ La Glamoureuse1283½ Allemagne1236 8 *4th to halfway,led 1f out,held well*
4Jun95♦ Frankfurt(Ger) gd *1¼ ⓉRH 2:14 ⒻKarl Ortlieb-Rennen Maiden 6000 713¾ Woodburn K 119 *.90 Furst Speedy123¾ Wicklow1193½ Bonmon121¾ 12 *Mid-pack,lacked room 2f out,one-paced late*

WORKOUTS: Oct5 Hol 5f fst 1:004 H *9/25* Sep3 Dmr 4f fst :473 H *3/35* Aug29 Dmr Ⓣ 6f fm 1:171 H (d)*2/2* Aug22 Dmr Ⓣ 6f fm 1:164 H (d)*4/4* Aug17 Dmr 5f fst 1:021 H *49/67* Aug10 Dmr 5f fst 1:031 H *39/46*

Birthday Time

Rolled a pair of 5s to the sizzling Admise, but note she was thumped by Dusty Girl in her U.S. bow; is 2nd-time Lasix, often known to produce top efforts in horses and should be fully cranked, 3rd try off a rest; best recent German efforts were on soft courses and this course is anything but soft; Beyers need to improve; tactical speed is a plus, but we're not sold.

Miss Lady Bug

Own: Dolan & Hinds & Hitbound Stable

SOLIS A (30 5 5 6 .17) 1996:(1087 198 .18)

B. m. 5
Sire: Rough Pearl (Tom Rolfe)
Dam: Tarabilla (Bicker)
Br: Osborne Susan (Cal)
Tr: Dolan John K (—) 1996:(34 7 .21)

L 117

Lifetime Record:	23	7	0	5	$167,264						
1996	9	3	0	3	$75,650	Turf	4	1	0	1	$29,329
1995	4	1	0	0	$21,275	Wet	2	0	0	1	$5,725
SA Ⓣ	1	0	0	0		Dist Ⓣ	1	0	0	0	$1,629

8Sep96-8Dmr fm 1⅜ Ⓣ :491 1:14 1:39 2:153 3↑ ⒻMatching H76k 92 8 2 1½ 1½ 2hd 34¼ Pincay L Jr LB 117 f 24.10 82-12 Admise1192 Interim1182¾ Miss Lady Bug117hd Game for 3rd 8
27Jun96-7Hol fm 1 3/16 Ⓣ :471 1:112 1:36 1:542 4↑ ⒻAlw 25000s 84 7 1 21 2hd 1hd 1½ Solis A LB 115 f 4.60 98-02 MissLdyBug115½ SwetButBold1153½ MjsticQun1152½ Game on rail in lane 8
5Jun96-3Hol fst 1 1/16 :231 :464 1:111 1:432 4↑ ⒻClm 40000 83 2 1 1½ 11 1hd 12½ Solis A LB 116 f *1.10 84-16 Miss Lady Bug1162½ Response116½ Ruthie Jane116 Gamely kicked clear 4
17May96-6GG wf 1 :222 :453 1:10 1:372 3↑ ⒻAlw 32000N3X 84 5 6 64½ 54½ 51¾ 31 Belvoir V T LB 118 7.60 82-19 GreatThreds118no NoCompssion1181 MissLdyBug1181½ Wide stretch run 7
18Apr96-2SA fst 1 :23 :472 1:124 1:38 4↑ ⒻClm 25000 84 5 1 1½ 2½ 12 17 Desormeaux K J LB 116 7.10 79-22 Miss Lady Bug1167 Response116½ Matra116hd Rid.out, in hand late 7
10Mar96-9SA fst 6½f :221 :451 1:092 1:154 4↑ ⒻClm 25000 76 5 5 43½ 44½ 44 47 Stevens G L LB 116 f 9.50 84-15 LadyEveningBelle1164 It'sBenFreezing1132 BintharDundt1161 No rally 8
7Feb96-3SA fst 6f :213 :45 :571 1:101 4↑ ⒻClm 32000 72 6 5 86¾ 85½ 86¾ 75¼ Pedroza M A LB 117 f 27.50 82-16 GorkySquare1171 HallelujahAngel117½ MissoulLul117nk 5 wide into lane 10
31Jan96-1SA sly 5½f :211 :433 :554 1:021 4↑ ⒻClm 40000 69 2 5 67¼ 59½ 510 511¾ Pincay L Jr LB 117 18.00 87-12 Chief Charley1175 Persistant Sal1171½ Silent Lord1192½ Rail to lane 6
1Jan96-1SA fst 6f :22 :45 :571 1:101 4↑ ⒻClm 40000 72 6 3 65½ 65¼ 45 35 Nakatani C S LB 117 f 11.40 82-14 Tiny Boots1173½ Missoula Lula1171½ Miss Lady Bug1171½ Late for 3rd 6
17Mar95-9SA fst 6½f :214 :442 1:091 1:16 4↑ ⒻClm 40000 41 8 1 63¾ 88¾ 914 919¼ Valenzuela P A LB 117 fb 15.70 72-09 Jan's Turn1141¼ Fast Reward1171 Afleet Floozie1164 Very wide trip 9

WORKOUTS: Sep29 Hol 5f fst 1:032 H *21/24* Sep22 Hol 5f fst 1:031 B *19/23* Aug31 Hol 5f fst 1:021 H *4/12* ● Aug25 Hol 4f fst :463 H *1/14* Aug13 Hol 7f fst 1:322 B *5/5* Aug7 Hol 5f fst 1:034 H *14/14*

Miss Lady Bug

Looks like the speed of the field and the much shorter distance can only help; figures to improve 2nd out off the rest and connections are having big years; not beaten that badly by Admise and did thump Birthday Time pretty good in the Matching; okay Beyers and some nice drills since; proven at this distance on dirt; the one to catch.

Two Ninety Jones

Own: Hirschmann James W III

VALENZUELA P A (33 2 5 4 .06) 1996:(491 60 .12)

Dk. b or br m. 5
Sire: Sir Harry Lewis (Alleged)
Dam: Caromist (Caro*Ire)
Br: Jones Mrs Jack G Sr (Ky)
Tr: Stute Melvin F (7 0 0 0 .00) 1996:(364 37 .10)

L 117

Lifetime Record:	27 5 3 7	$192,735			
1996	10 3 2 2	$141,075	Turf	20 5 2 5	$170,495
1995	7 1 0 4	$26,800	Wet	1 0 0 0	
SA Ⓣ	4 1 2 0	$54,800	Dist Ⓣ	8 4 1 0	$113,125

27Sep96-11Fpx	fst	1 1/16		:23	:47	1:114	1:434	3↑ ⒻLasMadrinasH100k	92	8 5	6 2¾	4 2½	4 3½	3 3	Toscano P R	LB 117	12.40	88-15	BuckrooZoo1151 LdySoroll1172 TwoNinetyJones117½	Finished strongly	9
4Sep96-4Dmr	fm	1	Ⓣ	:222	:464	1:113	1:353	3↑ ⒻClm 80000	95	3 7	7 6¾	4 3	3 1	1 3½	Valenzuela P A	LB 119	2.20	92-08	TwoNinetyJones1193½ WeeMissBe1171¼ PubRivr1171	Waited 1/4,rail rally	8
16Aug96-6Dmr	fm	1	Ⓣ	:231	:472	1:112	1:353	3↑ ⒻClm 80000	93	6 6	7 4¼	5 3½	4 2½	1 1¾	Valenzuela P A	LB 117	7.90	92-08	Two Ninety Jones1171¾ Wee MissBee117nk DellRapids1171	Closed gamely	8
1Aug96-8Dmr	fm	1	Ⓣ	:232	:474	1:124	1:37	3↑ ⒻAlw 57000N3X	88	6 4	3 1	3 1	4 3	4 4½	Valenzuela P A	LB 117	17.40	80-15	Sixieme Sens117½ Smolensk1173½ Siyah Nara117½	Just missed 3rd	6
26Jun96-7Hol	fst	7f		:223	:451	1:091	1:212	3↑ ⒻAlw 47000N3X	85	6 3	5 2½	6 1¾	5 3¾	3 6¼	Solis A	LB 116	12.40	89-16	Dixie Pearl116¾ Texinadress1185½ Two Ninety Jones116½	5 wide into lane	8
30May96-8Hol	fm	1	Ⓣ	:234	:473	1:111	1:344	4↑ ⒻAlw 54000N3X	86	6 5	3 1½	2 1	5 3¾	5 5¼	Solis A	LB 115 b	8.00	84-11	Call Now1151 Se Souvenir115nk Sixieme Sens117no	Bid, weakened	7
11Apr96-8SA	fm	1	Ⓣ	:232	:472	1:113	1:361	4↑ ⒻAlw 60000N$mY	84	6 4	4 1¼	4 2½	4 1½	4 5	Solis A	LB 116 b	*1.20	81-14	MagicFeeling116nk LadyReiko1183½ ScatteredDrems1161¼	Bid, outfinished	6
21Mar96-8SA	fm	1	Ⓣ	:241	:482	1:124	1:381	4↑ ⒻAlw 57000N3X	97	3 7	6 3	5 2¾	3 1½	2 ½	Solis A	LB 117 b	*1.60	75-24	Magic Fantasy117½ Two Ninety Jones117hd MilleNuits1172	Pinched start	8
25Jan96-7SA	fm	1⅛	Ⓣ	:493	1:134	1:383	1:504	4↑ ⒻAlw 57000N3X	98	4 2	2 ½	1hd	2hd	2 ½	Solis A	LB 119 b	7.80	75-24	Angel In My Heart116½ TwoNinetyJones1194 JoKnows112½	Game effort	6
7Jan96-7SA	fm	1⅛	Ⓣ	:483	1:13	1:374	1:503	4↑ ⒻAlw 50000N2X	94	6 4	4 1½	3 2	1 2	1 4½	Solis A	LB 117 b	15.20	77-23	Two Ninety Jones1174½ Dusty Girl119nk Encoremoi112½	Clear, driving	10

WORKOUTS: Oct4 SA 4f fst :463 H 3/33 Sep26 Fpx 3f fst :344 H 2/9 Sep21 SA 6f fst 1:134 H 10/24 Aug29 Dmr 4f fst :483 H 16/48 Aug23 Dmr 4f fst :49 H 24/46 Aug13 Dmr 4f fst :47 H 4/49

Lady Ling (Arg)

Own: Heffernan Alice

DOUGLAS R R (21 4 4 1 .19) 1996:(1031 122 .12)

Ch. m. 5
Sire: Egg Toss (Buckpasser)
Dam: La Taquilla*Arg (Estribo*Arg)
Br: Haras San Maluc SA (Arg)
Tr: Moreno Henry (4 0 3 0 .00) 1996:(133 16 .12)

117

Lifetime Record:	17 3 7 2	$95,780			
1995	9 2 5 0	$76,955	Turf	13 2 6 2	$59,778
1994	8 1 2 2	$18,825	Wet	1 0 0 0	$545
SA Ⓣ	0 0 0 0		Dist Ⓣ	1 1 0 0	$8,282

16Dec95♦ San Isidro(Arg)	fm*1⅜ ⓉLH 2:124 4↑	Clasico Cocles-Hcp (Listed) Stk 30500	5 7	Falero P	126	2.50	Sugar Jack1301½ Logia127nk Ball Roy124½	6	Tracked leader,weakened 1-1/2f out.La Malversada (114) 4th
11Nov95♦ San Isidro(Arg)	fm*1½ ⓉLH 2:252 4↑	Copa de Oro-G1 Stk 68600	6 9¾	Falero P	126	1.90	Fantasio134¾ Good Whisky1324 El Banista1323	8	Led to 2f out,weakened
25Aug95♦ San Isidro(Arg)	fm*1½ ⓉLH 2:261 4↑	ⒻGran Premio La Mission-G1 Stk 61000	2½	Falero P	132	*.55	Lucky Ness135½ Lady Ling1326 La Malversada132¾	9	Led,dueled 150y out,headed 50y out,gamely
30Jly95♦ Hipodromo(Arg)	fst*1 1/16 LH 2:354 4↑	ⒻGran Premio I & I Correas-G1 Stk 40800	1 3	Falero P	132	3.30	Lady Ling1323 Equity132½ Evelyng132nk	7	Led throughout,handily.Faldilla 4th,Lucky Ness 5th
24Jun95♦ San Isidro(Arg)	fm*1⅜ ⓉLH 2:162 3↑	ⒻClasico Federico de Alvear-G3 Stk 37700	1 6	Falero P	127	4.75	Lady Ling1276 Repartija127nk Lucky Ness133¾	10	Wire to wire,never troubled.Rapifleet 5th
24May95♦ San Isidro(Arg)	fm*1¼ ⓉLH 1:591	ⒻPremio Corbeta Uruguay Alw 11000	2 2½	Falero P	117	*1.85	Baleta1172½ Lady Ling1177 Faldilla117½	11	Led to 1f out,outfinished
6May95♦ San Isidro(Arg)	fm*1¼ ⓉLH 2:001	ⒻPremio Bon Poulain Alw 11000	2no	Falero P	117	2.30	La Malversada117no Lady Ling1171½ Galeta1171½	11	Led to 1f out,dueled,just missed in game effort
5Feb95♦ San Isidro(Arg)	fm*1⅛ ⓉLH 1:48	ⒻPremio Iris-Fan Alw 10400	2½	Paule J	117	2.00	Evelyng123½ Lady Ling1176½ Muscatin1234	6	Led to 70y out,gamely
4Jan95♦ San Isidro(Arg)	fm*1⅛ ⓉLH 1:49	ⒻPremio Karate Kid Alw 10400	2 3	Cataluna R9	114	2.95	Potrilama1233 Lady Ling1142 Fancy Flirt1237	9	Led to 2f out,chased winner home
8Dec94♦ San Isidro(Arg)	fm*1¼ ⓉLH 2:584 3↑	ⒻCopa de Plata-G1 Stk 111000	7	Vaira J	119	14.20	Tocopilla132½ De La Gorra134½ Evelyng1191	21	Mid-pack,lacked rally

WORKOUTS: Oct4 SA Ⓣ 7f fm 1:29 H (d) 1/1 Sep28 SA 7f fst 1:261 H 2/4 Sep22 SA 6f fst 1:131 H 2/14 Sep16 SA 4f fst :502 H 37/45 Sep10 Dmr 1 fst 1:403 H 3/4 Sep4 Dmr 4f fst :502 H 38/39

Two Ninety Jones

Loved the mile distance at Del Mar when winning a pair against slightly softer; Beyers are good and she exits a solid race in Pomona; unlike many, she's had some success here and is reunited with P. Val, who is coming off a big Del Mar as well; Mel won the Pomona training title (for what that's worth); closer may not get the pace she needs and that style really hasn't played that great on this course this meet; maybe.

Lady Ling

Argentine invader faced some of the best in her country with success; appears to want more ground and she also seems to have a minor award habit with 2 wins and 8 2nds, 3rds from 12 turf tries; showed speed way down south, so could be on or near the lead; solid works and good connections; watch paddock and toteboard for more clues.

continued

Molly Girl
Own: Golden Eagle Farm
MCCARRON C J (18 4 3 3 .22) 1996:(680 157 .23)

B. f. 4
Sire: Seattle Slew (Bold Reasoning)
Dam: Alydar's Promise (Alydar)
Br: Mabee Mr & Mrs John C (Ky)
Tr: Hofmans David (10 4 1 3 .40) 1996:(175 45 .26)

L 117

Lifetime Record :	8	3	2	2	$101,875						
1996	5	3	1	1	$87,050	Turf	1	1	0	0	$24,200
1995	3	M	1	1	$14,825	Wet	0	0	0	0	
SA Ⓣ	0	0	0	0		Dist Ⓣ	1	1	0	0	$24,200

9Jun96-5Hol fm 1 Ⓣ :24^{2} :48^{3} 1:11^{4} 1:35^{1} 3↑ Ⓕ Alw 44000N2X 95 6 3 2½ 1hd 1^{1} 1^{2}¾ McCarron C J LB 116 *2.70 87–11 Molly Girl116^{2}¾ Marfa Smeralda117^{4} Strumming119^{1} Steady handling 10
11May96-3Hol fst 1$\frac{1}{16}$:23 :46^{2} 1:10^{2} 1:42^{1} 3↑ Ⓕ Alw 48000N2X 91 4 2 2½ 1^{1} 2hd 3^{2}¼ Solis A LB 116 1.90 88–10 Texinadress116½ Privity116^{1}¾ Molly Girl116^{12} Led, outfinished 5
17Apr96-8SA fst 1 :23 :47 1:11 1:36^{2} 4↑ Ⓕ Alw 50000N2X 92 5 4 4^{1}¼ 2^{1}½ 2^{2}½ 2^{4}½ Solis A LB 118 2.30 82–15 Lady Sorolla116^{4}½ Molly Girl118^{2} Rhythninjava116½ 6
Off step slow; 5 wide 7/8
20Mar96-5SA fst 1 :22 :45^{2} 1:11^{2} 1:37^{1} 4↑ Alw 46000N1X 87 8 5 3^{9} 2^{2} 2^{1} 1no Solis A LB 114 *3.00 83–20 MollyGirl114no StepsInTime117^{4} MajorFunding117no Steadied 3/8, just up 9
18Jan96-4SA fst 7f :23 :46^{2} 1:10^{4} 1:23 4↑ Ⓕ Md Sp Wt 82 8 7 4^{2}½ 3^{1}½ 2hd 1^{1} Solis A LB 120 *.90 87–12 Molly Girl120^{1} Cozzenes' Princess120^{5}½ Fast Nancy120^{1} 8
Led 1/4, headed, came back
8Dec95-4Hol fst 6½f :22 :44^{2} 1:08^{3} 1:14^{3} 3↑ Md Sp Wt 88 9 8 8^{4}½ 7^{7}¼ 3^{6} 2^{5} Solis A LB 117 8.10 91–09 Knifemaker120^{5} Molly Girl117½ Uno Mas Diablo120^{3}½ Game for 2nd 11
15Feb95-2SA fst 1 :22^{4} :46^{2} 1:11^{1} 1:36^{3} Ⓕ Md Sp Wt 83 5 5 4^{4} 2hd 3^{2} 3^{3} Nakatani C S LB 117 2.20 83–17 Blushing Heiress117^{3} Taianna117no Molly Girl117^{3}½ Hung in lane 7
29Jan95-4SA fst 6f :21^{4} :44^{1} :56^{1} 1:09 Ⓕ Md Sp Wt 78 1 8 8^{15} 8^{17} 7^{12} 4^{8}½ Nakatani C S LB 117 3.90 83–09 Mri'sSheb117^{5} SecretHrbor117^{1}½ BlushingHirss117^{1}½ Bumped start, wide 8

WORKOUTS: ●Oct6 Hol 6f fst 1:12^{3} H *1/6* Oct1 Hol 6f fst 1:15^{2} H *11/17* Sep25 Hol 5f fst 1:03^{4} H *27/30* Sep18 Hol 5f fst 1:01^{1} H *13/33* Sep5 Dmr 5f fst 1:02^{2} H *39/46* ●Aug30 Dmr 4f fst :46^{3} H *1/36*

Molly Girl

Hofmans is among the best with fresh runners and this gal has shown a few times she can fire fresh; owns good speed, a plus in a race that does not seem to have much zip; good Beyers and her turf win was at this distance; bullet for return, keeps McCarron, and she looks like a major player.

– Stan Granch

sive to me, but her last effort was excellent and she may love the shorter distance, as she likes to run on or near the lead. Molly Girl runs well off layoffs, has won her only start on the grass in good time, and also shows a win over colts on the dirt back in March. Two Ninety Jones has won four out of eight at a mile on the turf and has strong Beyer figs at the distance.

With four legitimate potential winners in a short field of six, what is there to be enthusiastic about? Let's take a closer look. Out of the four contenders, two of them, Miss Lady Bug and Molly Girl, want to run forwardly, which ought to guarantee fast early fractions. Dusty Girl has been away two months and didn't fire after the only other previous layoff on her chart. Two Ninety Jones's best races, on the other hand, come at this distance, when she is taken back off the pace and asked for one explosive move about three eighths of a mile from home. She's in excellent form and her rider has won with her two out of the three times he has ridden her in exactly this kind of race. Why isn't she going to win here?

The other factor that makes this an interesting betting race is the certainty that both Dusty Girl and Molly Girl will go off at low odds. Miss Lady Bug should draw some action as well. Two Ninety Jones, most recently a loser at Fairplex on the dirt, may be no better than the fourth choice in the race, at four or five to one. She will be the value play of the afternoon, the reason I singled her in my pick-six.

We'd approach any race like this looking first of all to make a solid straight bet.

Well, so much for my famous handicapping prowess. The result here turned out to be favorable to me, but not because I had correctly analyzed how the race would be run. Miss Lady Bug did go to the front, but all by herself, and set the sort of moderate early fractions that threatened to make her a winner.

EIGHTH RACE	1 MILE. (Turf)(1.32²) ALLLOWANCE. Purse $49,000. Fillies and mares, 3-year-olds and upward which
Santa Anita	are non-winners of $3,000 three times other than maiden or claiming or have never won four races. Weights: 3-year-olds, 120 lbs. Older, 122 lbs. Non-winners of two such races at one mile or over since
OCTOBER 10, 1996	August 1, allowed 3 lbs. Of such a race since September 1, 5 lbs. (Horses eligible only to the above conditions are preferred.) Rail at 30 feet.

Value of Race: $49,000 Winner $26,950; second $9,800; third $7,350; fourth $3,675; fifth $1,225. Mutuel Pool $274,059.30 Exacta Pool $277,390.00 Quinella Pool $39,058.00

Last Raced	Horse	M/Eqt. A.Wt	PP	St	¼	½	¾	Str	Fin	Jockey	Odds $1
27Sep96 11Fpx³	Two Ninety Jones	LB	5 117	4	3	2hd	2½	2¹	1hd	1nk	Valenzuela P A	2.70
8Sep96 8Dmr³	Miss Lady Bug	LBf	5 117	3	1	1¹½	1¹	1½	2¹	2²	Solis A	6.70
9Jun96 5Hol¹	Molly Girl	LB	4 117	6	5	5½	5¹½	4²½	4³	3⁴	McCarron C J	1.40
8Sep96 8Dmr⁵	Birthday Time-GE	LB	4 117	2	6	6	6	5hd	5¹½	4²½	Blanc B	29.20
16Dec95 SI⁵	Lady Ling-AR	LB	5 117	5	4	3¹½	3¹½	6	6	5	Douglas R R	12.50
2Aug96 7Dmr²	Dusty Girl-NZ	LB	6 117	1	2	4¹	4hd	3hd	3hd	—	Black C A	2.50
Dusty Girl: Fell											

OFF AT 4:30 Start Good. Won driving. Time, :23², :46⁴, 1:10¹, 1:21⁴, 1:33⁴ Course firm.

$2 Mutuel Prices:	4-TWO NINETY JONES	7.40	3.60	2.60
	3-MISS LADY BUG		6.00	3.20
	6-MOLLY GIRL			2.40

$2 EXACTA 4-3 PAID $43.00 $2 QUINELLA 3-4 PAID $25.20

Dk. b. or br. m, by Sir Harry Lewis-Caromist, by Caro*Ire. Trainer Stute Melvin F. Bred by Jones Mrs Jack G Sr (Ky).

TWO NINETY JONES was close up inside LADY LING on the first turn and early on the backstretch, pulled her way outside MISS LADY BUG leaving the backstretch and prompted that rival's pace on the second turn, took a short lead in midstretch and proved narrowly best under urging. MISS LADY BUG sped to the early lead and the inside, dueled inside the winner leaving the backstretch and on the second turn, then continued gamely inside that one to the wire. MOLLY GIRL was outside BIRTHDAY TIME early and outside DUSTY GIRL on the backstretch, went up four wide into the second turn, loomed a threat three deep into the stretch but settled for the show. BIRTHDAY TIME saved ground to the stretch, came out and lacked the needed rally. LADY LING stalked the pace outside the winner on the first turn and backstretch, fell back on the second turn, came out and weakened. DUSTY GIRL saved ground, was in very tight along the inside in midstretch and was steadied, then clipped heels and fell.

Owners— 1, Hirschmann James W III; 2, Dolan & Hinds & Hitbound Stable; 3, Golden Eagle Farm; 4, Stacey Sally; 5, Heffernan Alice; 6, Lima Family Trust

Trainers— 1, Stute Melvin F; 2, Dolan John K; 3, Hofmans David; 4, Bunn Thomas M Jr; 5, Moreno Henry; 6, Carava Jack

---

$3 Pick Three (4-3-4) Paid $558.90; Pick Three Pool $82,430.

Luckily for me, Pat Valenzuela did not take Two Ninety Jones back to make one big move, but placed her behind the leader and close enough to be able to engage her in the run down the stretch. As you can read in the chart, Dusty Girl was in the race, but in trouble all the way and fell, the sort of accident that happens all too frequently on these narrow grass courses.

What happened to me as a bettor in these last two races is a perfect example of how fickle fate can be at the racetrack. I had envisioned almost exactly how the seventh race would be run but failed to cash a ticket. In this one, I had failed to analyze it correctly but wound up a potential winner anyway.

Two Ninety Jones was listed at five to one in the morning line, but, again to my surprise, was bet down to five to two, too low for me to risk a straight bet. At six and a half to one, Miss Lady Bug became the value play. If I hadn't been so confident about my top selection's prowess, I'd have had to box Miss Lady Bug with her in an exacta.

What I did instead was to bet Two Ninety Jones in doubles to two horses in the ninth. I didn't make any money immediately, but I had the prospect of making some out of the ninth. Two Ninety Jones had justified my faith in her, but I had allowed myself to be blinded to a value play by my enthusiasm for her chances. The two-dollar exacta combination paid forty-three dollars and I would have had it at least three or four times. A clear case of "woulda-coulda-shoulda" and another humbling reminder that what the track giveth, the track may also taketh away. Have fun, but don't count on it as a steady source of income.

The eighth and the ninth races on this card are the main reasons I thought the pick-six was playable. If you feel certain that you can isolate two singles in your parlay, then why not hope you can get lucky in the other four races and play it? Especially when you know that the pool will be huge and that even five winners will probably pay adequately. In this so-called nightcap, one horse soars up off the statistics as an almost sure winner. Can you find him on pages 162–165? A quick glance at the Beyer figs is all you need.

■ RACE 9: The probable winner, of course, is Native Desert, whose speed rating of 89 makes him at least ten lengths better than anyone else in the field. The fact that he's moving up one small notch in class is of no significance, since that

9 Santa Anita Park

6½ Furlongs (1:14) MAIDEN CLAIMING. Purse $17,000. 3-year-olds and upward bred in California. Weights: 3-year-olds, 120 lbs. Older, 122 lbs. Claiming price $32,000, if for $28,000, allowed 2 lbs.

6½ FURLONGS (START / FINISH)

Over The Limit

Own: Shepard & Wicker — $28,000
GARCIA M S (10 0 1 0 .00) 1996:(464 37 .08)

Gr/ro g. 3 (Apr)
Sire: Space Station (Mr. Prospector)
Dam: Budget Maker (Olden Times)
Br: Ellsworth Kim Rex (Cal)
Tr: Wicker Lloyd C (—) 1996:(16 0 .00)
L 118

Lifetime Record:	1 M 1 0	$2,550			
1996	1 M 1 0	$2,550	Turf	0 0 0 0	
1995	0 M 0 0		Wet	0 0 0 0	
SA	0 0 0 0		Dist	0 0 0 0	

30Sep96-13Fpx fst 6f :222 :462 :594 1:13 3↑ S Md 20000 52 1 6 810 89 67½ 21 Garcia M S LB 115 6.20 83–09 Secret Sid1201 Over The Limit1152 Best Bower1151 Flying finish 8

WORKOUTS: Sep25 SLR tr.t 4f fst :492 H 4/6 Sep19 SLR tr.t 7f fst 1:263 H 1/1 ●Sep13 SLR tr.t 5f fst 1:01 Hg 1/7 Sep3 SLR tr.t 4f fst :483 H 7/14 Aug29 SLR tr.t 5f fst 1:013 H 4/7 ●Aug23 SLR tr.t 6f fst 1:13 H 1/4

T. V. Winner

Own: Cuadra T Y T Inc — $28,000
ESPINOZA V (18 0 5 3 .00) 1996:(719 95 .13)

B. c. 3 (Apr)
Sire: Orange Sunshine (Linkage)
Dam: Cox's Road (Cox's Ridge)
Br: Cuadra T Y T Inc (Cal)
Tr: Inda Eduardo (4 1 0 1 .25) 1996:(92 12 .13)
L 118

Lifetime Record:	6 M 0 1	$4,900			
1996	5 M 0 1	$4,425	Turf	0 0 0 0	
1995	1 M 0 0	$475	Wet	0 0 0 0	
SA	0 0 0 0		Dist	3 0 0 0	$600

22Sep96-12Fpx fst 6½f :221 :462 1:12 1:184 3↑ Md 20000 42 3 3 85¾ 75¼ 75¼ 77½ Espinoza V LB 115 b *2.30 79–08 He's My Beau1204 Fahd Ya Sanayadee120no Stretch The Truth1202 10
Drifted out badly 1st turn, clipped heels, wide into stretch, weakened
31Aug96-4Dmr fst 6½f :221 :451 1:11 1:174 3↑ S Md 32000 51 9 5 53¾ 53¾ 67 78 Antley C W LB 118 2.60 74–13 Cheers N Joys118hd Jalos116½ Buster O'brien1182½ Wide into lane 9
9Aug96-4Dmr fst 6f :214 :45 :574 1:11 3↑ S Md 32000 64 10 7 96¾ 76½ 55 44¼ Antley C W LB 118 *2.80 80–14 Exit1182 Key De Mere1182 Drill Team118nk Wide, steadied 3/8 12
26Jly96-4Dmr fst 6½f :22 :444 1:102 1:17 3↑ S Md 32000 53 6 12 86½ 910 58¾ 58½ Blanc B LB 118 4.40 78–13 Dance All Day1201¼ Naturally Stan122hd Proud1165 Squeezed back start 12
Previously trained by West Ted
22Jun96-10Hol fst 6f :221 :454 :583 1:104 3↑ S Md 32000 72 9 5 75½ 42½ 1½ 3½ Blanc B LB 116 9.20 84–11 Thimbledrone122½ Run The Table116hd T. V. Winner1166½ Game effort 11
Previously trained by Jones Gary
16Aug95-4Dmr fst 6f :222 :454 :581 1:111 S Md 32000 35 5 4 41½ 42½ 45 59¾ Desormeaux K J LB 118 7.00 75–10 Romaine1185 Staged And Ready1182 Oh So Spicy1181¾ Inside, weakened 12

WORKOUTS: Oct6 SA 4f fst :474 H 8/26 Sep30 SA 4f fst :483 H 13/35 Sep17 SA tr.t 3f fst :37 H 1/3 Sep9 Dmr 3f fst :36 H 8/21 Aug24 Dmr 5f fst 1:012 H 24/61 Aug18 Dmr 3f fst :353 H 2/13

Man Mountain Dean

Own: Cooperstone & Levin — $28,000
DOUGLAS R R (21 4 4 1 .19) 1996:(1031 122 .12)

B. g. 3 (Mar)
Sire: Debonair Roger (Raja Baba)
Dam: Hey Little Sister (Don B.)
Br: Martin Cooperstone & Howard Senzell (Cal)
Tr: Bean Robert A (—) 1996:(77 1 .01)
L 118

Lifetime Record:	7 M 0 2	$6,205			
1996	7 M 0 2	$6,205	Turf	0 0 0 0	
1995	0 M 0 0		Wet	0 0 0 0	
SA	0 0 0 0		Dist	2 0 0 1	$2,040

25Sep96-12Fpx fst 6f :221 :46 :584 1:114 3↑ S Md 32000 61 8 1 73½ 31½ 31½ 32 Castro J M LB 115 fb 6.10 88–09 HeavenSent1151 BusterO'brien1151 MnMountinDen1156 Wide into lane 8
14Sep96-6Fpx fst 6½f :222 :463 1:12 1:182 3↑ Md 32000 63 8 2 2hd 2½ 32½ 35½ Castro J M LB 115 fb 18.70 83–12 Loughspring1154 FabulousHeir1201½ MnMountinDen1152 Held for show 9
7Sep96-2Dmr fst 1 1/16 :224 :464 1:122 1:443 3↑ Md 32000 32 7 3 32 42 912 925¾ Castro J M LB 118 fb 100.30 53–14 PouringDownRin1164 Alyplesur1181¼ ClssicLook118¾ Stalked, weakened 12
7Aug96-9Dmr fst 1 1/16 :23 :464 1:114 1:443 3↑ S Md 28000 59 2 3 32 32 44½ 57¼ Berrio O A LB 116 b 41.40 72–20 HonestDelight1163½ BlackPheasnt122½ NinoGtico1162¾ Inside, weakened 12
19Jly96-2Hol fst 7f :224 :46 1:111 1:234 3↑ S Md 28000 42 3 4 3½ 4½ 45½ 413¾ Garcia M S LB 115 b 87.80 69–13 Tank'sStar1202 ShermanTnk1171½ BlckPhesnt12210 Dueled between foes 8
28Jun96-9Hol fst 6½f :221 :444 1:092 1:153 3↑ S Md 28000 47 3 8 75¾ 810 714 620¼ Sanchez K A LB 114 b 87.00 68–12 Busy Little Beaver1168 Moscow Flyer1161 Liberty Town1155½ Rail trip 11
12Jun96-9Hol fst 6f :213 :443 :564 1:10 3↑ Md 28000 42 5 7 911 712 513 516 Sanchez K A B 114 b 114.90 73–09 Eolus1176½ Christmas Boy116½ Busy Little Beaver1167½ No threat 12

WORKOUTS: Oct5 Hol 4f fst :492 H 13/30 Sep21 Hol 3f fst :363 H 6/14 ●Aug17 Hol 3f fst :362 H 1/23 Aug3 Hol 3f fst :37 H 9/21 Jly27 Hol 4f fst :512 H 15/16 Jly12 SA 5f fst 1:024 H 28/32

A CLOSER LOOK

9th Santa Anita

Over The Limit

Impressed with the late finish that he displayed in his debut; unfortunately, speed wins races, especially in the maiden ranks; this one will need to show more zip if he is to be effective; didn't earn much of a Beyer for his last; mixed signals.

T. V. Winner

Draw a line through his last race; considering all his trouble, he figured to run poorly; form isn't too bad if you're willing to overlook that last fiasco; not out of the question.

Man Mountain Dean

Only in-the-money finishes came at Fpx, where the competition is obviously much softer; lacks the lofty speed figures of some of these; trainer Bean is just 1 for 77 on the year; may pick up a minor check in a best case scenario.

Buster O'Brien

Own: Hochman & Isaacs — $32,000
BLANC B (18 2 2 4 .11) 1996:(1022 104 .10)

Dk.b or br g. 3 (Apr)
Sire: Desert Wine (Damascus)
Dam: Scarlet O'Brien (Interco)
Br: Isaacs Barry S (Cal)
Tr: Palma Hector O (3 0 1 0 .00) 1996:(87 12 .14) — L 120

Lifetime Record:	5 M 3 1	$12,080		
1996	5 M 3 1	$12,080	Turf	0 0 0 0
1995	0 M 0 0		Wet	0 0 0 0
SA	0 0 0 0		Dist	1 0 0 1 $2,700

25Sep96-12Fpx fst 6f :221 :46 :584 1:114 3↑ [S]Md 32000 63 4 5 2hd 2½ 2½ 21 Espinoza V LB 115 *.80 89-09 HeavenSent1151 BusterO'brien1151 MnMountinDen1156 Battled inside 8
18Sep96-9Fpx fst 6f :214 :45 :58 1:111 3↑ Md 32000 78 9 6 35½ 34½ 21½ 2¾ Espinoza V LB 115 b *.90 92-11 Shnghn115¾ BusterO'brien1158 BettesStppingout1161½ Broke slow, hung 9
31Aug96-4Dmr fst 6½f :221 :451 1:11 1:174 3↑ [S]Md 32000 68 7 2 1hd 41¾ 22 3½ Blanc B LB 118 b *1.80 81-13 Cheers N Joys118hd Jalos116½ Buster O'brien1182½ Came back on 9
16Aug96-3Dmr fst 6f :214 :443 :57 1:091 3↑ [S]Md Sp Wt 50 3 6 64 87 89¾ 819½ Blanc B LB 118 b 15.00 74-11 Destiny's Venture1222½ Expresser1182 Light Age118nk Gave way 8
31Jly96-4Dmr fst 6f :214 :452 :58 1:11 3↑ [S]Md 32000 70 8 9 64¾ 53¼ 42 2½ Blanc B LB 118 b 6.80 83-13 Toby San118½ Buster O'brien118hd Cause I'm Unique1202¾ Steadied start 11

WORKOUTS: Oct4 SA 4f fst :50 H 30/33 Sep13 SA tr.t 4f fst :50 H 2/3 Aug24 Dmr 4f fst :482 H 7/53 Aug9 Dmr 5f fst 1:001 H 9/68 Jly28 Dmr 4f fst :48 H 15/67 Jly21 Hol 6f fst 1:131 H 5/15

Buster O'Brien

With the exception of one race, this guy has run well; has the speed to sit close to the pace but can also rally from several lengths back if necessary; possesses some of the best numbers in the field; major player.

S. S. Tell

Own: Delaplane E Edward & Paula — $28,000
HUNTER M T (18 3 0 1 .17) 1996:(403 55 .14)

B. g. 3 (Apr)
Sire: Tell (Round Table)
Dam: Karyn's Lark (Best Turn)
Br: Delaplane E Edward (Cal)
Tr: Cardiel Fidel (3 0 0 0 .00) 1996:(65 2 .03) — 118

Lifetime Record:	3 M 0 0	$3,200		
1995	3 M 0 0	$3,200	Turf	0 0 0 0
1994	0 M 0 0		Wet	0 0 0 0
SA	2 0 0 0	$875	Dist	1 0 0 0

2Dec95-6Hol fst 7f :223 :453 1:101 1:224 Md Sp Wt 60 4 3 2½ 22½ 44 412 Atkinson P B 119 fb 33.20 76-09 Fourstarattrction119½ Predictble119½ BeyondComprison11911 No match 7
13Nov95-6SA fst 6f :213 :444 :572 1:101 [S]Md Sp Wt 66 7 9 99¾ 99¾ 78 55½ Pedroza M A B 118 fb 78.60 81-08 Tobsytcll1182½ TzThWhz118nk Skywlkr'sChc118½ Bumped, forced in start 11
29Oct95-6SA fst 6½f :22 :444 1:094 1:162 Md Sp Wt 37 7 9 63¾ 66 811 819½ Atkinson P B 120 fb 74.70 71-10 Shoshoni Scout1204 Scholarship1201½ Track Goer1202 6 wide to turn 9

WORKOUTS: Oct7 Hol 4f fst :481 H 2/10 Oct1 Hol 5f fst 1:021 H 25/32 Sep25 Hol 7f fst 1:283 H 5/11 Sep19 Hol 5f fst 1:01 H 4/19 Sep13 Hol 5f fst 1:01 H 11/32 Sep7 Hol 5f fst 1:011 H 6/14

S. S. Tell

Makes his first start for a tag - usually a potent angle; unfortunately he hasn't started since Dec. of last year; may need a race before he's at full strength.

Private Reserve

Own: Cain & Guillot — $28,000
VALENZUELA F H (7 0 0 0 .00) 1996:(473 25 .05)

Dk.b or br g. 3 (Apr)
Sire: Nijinsky's Table (Nijinsky II)
Dam: Buck Step (Go Step)
Br: Sherlock Gary & Sherlock Sharon (Cal)
Tr: Guillot Eric (—) 1996:(46 3 .07) — L 118

Lifetime Record:	4 M 0 0	$1,050		
1996	4 M 0 0	$1,050	Turf	0 0 0 0
1995	0 M 0 0		Wet	0 0 0 0
SA	0 0 0 0		Dist	0 0 0 0

30Sep96-13Fpx fst 6f :222 :462 :594 1:13 3↑ [S]Md 20000 44 7 7 43 41½ 42½ 44 Valenzuela F H LB 115 b 5.20 80-09 Secret Sid1201 Over The Limit1152 Best Bower1151 Wide 1st turn 8
12Jly96-4Hol fst 1 1/16 :232 :463 1:12 1:461 3↑ [S]Md 28000 — 10 2 22 714 1143 — Almeida G F LB 114 b 10.20 — 30 Work 'n' Man1146 Acivdarb120½ Nino Gatico1161 11
Bumped, wide 7 1/2; stopped, eased Previously trained by Lukas D Wayne
22Jun96-10Hol fst 6f :221 :454 :583 1:104 3↑ [S]Md 32000 32 11 2 41 2½ 54 816½ Douglas R R LB 116 b 19.00 69-11 Thimbledrone122½ RunTheTble116hd T.V.Winnr1166½ Wide early, rail lane 11
31May96-6Hol fst 7f :221 :45 1:091 1:223 3↑ [S]Md 32000 6 4 12 1010 1012 1127 1134¼ Pincay L Jr LB 117 b 28.00 55-11 Touchdown Miami1154½ Absolut Ruler1174 Ogata Be Good1223½ 12
Bumped, jostled, steadied sharply start

WORKOUTS: Sep22 Hol 6f fst 1:144 H 5/15 Sep15 Hol 6f fst 1:163 H 9/11 Sep9 Hol 5f fst 1:001 H 3/9 Sep3 Hol 4f fst :492 H 4/12 Aug27 Hol 3f fst :381 H 8/10

Private Reserve

Ran easily the best race of his life Sept. 30, but that was mainly due to the overall weak nature of that field; appears to lack the necessary talent.

Glad You Asked

Own: Lickhalter & Richardson & Roe — $32,000
VALENZUELA P A (33 2 5 4 .06) 1996:(491 60 .12)

Ch. g. 3 (Apr)
Sire: Olympic Native (Raise a Native)
Dam: Precipitory (Rainy Lake)
Br: Sutton Place Inc (Cal)
Tr: Chapman James K (2 0 1 0 .00) 1996:(69 5 .07) — L 120

Lifetime Record:	3 M 0 1	$4,415		
1996	3 M 0 1	$4,415	Turf	0 0 0 0
1995	0 M 0 0		Wet	0 0 0 0
SA	0 0 0 0		Dist	1 0 0 0 $1,190

19Sep96-9Fpx fst 6½f :213 :451 1:104 1:172 3↑ [S]Md 32000 68 8 8 910 711 57 46½ Valenzuela F H LB 115 2.80 87-09 Start Your Engines1153½ Lord Boswell1152½ Valid Tizzy120½ Wide 1st turn 9
7Sep96-10Dmr fst 5½f :221 :453 :581 1:043 3↑ [S]Md 32000 64 4 7 77¾ 77¼ 74½ 54¼ Maese A LB 120 - 86-12 NturllyStn1201 ForthAndOn1202 SoftshoRhythm1201 Hopped, off slow 7
Rocking Chair Derby - Exhibition race for retired riders
23Aug96-6Dmr fst 6f :22 :451 :573 1:101 3↑ [S]Md 32000 66 4 8 64 52½ 43½ 37 Valenzuela P A LB 118 18.80 81-10 Keaton's Carpenter1187 Check Kite118no Glad YouAsked1182½ Inside trip 9

WORKOUTS: Oct7 Hol 3f fst :354 H 2/17 Oct1 Hol 4f fst :482 H 6/24 Sep4 Hol 3f fst :363 Hg4/9 Aug18 Hol 5f fst 1:012 Hg4/23 Aug12 Hol 5f fst 1:031 H 19/23 Aug6 Hol 5f fst 1:021 H 21/35

Glad You Asked

Didn't run too badly in his last start, suffering from a wide trip; still managed to gain ground in the lane; Beyers indicate that he can be competitive against these; benefits from the services of P.Val.

continued

Aplomado

Own: 5 C Stable $28,000
VERGARA O (3 0 0 0 .00) 1996:(236 19 .08)

Dk. b or br g. 3 (Feb)
Sire: Flying Paster (Gummo)
Dam: Course (Unconscious)
Br: Seeligson & Bass (Cal)
Tr: Polanco Marcelo (—) 1996:(53 4 .08)

L 118

Lifetime Record:	7 M 1 2	$9,450			
1996	7 M 1 2	$9,450	Turf	0 0 0 0	
1995	0 M 0 0		Wet	0 0 0 0	
SA	0 0 0 0		Dist	1 0 0 0	$900

29Aug96- 2Dmr fst 6f :221 :453 :581 1:112 3↑ Md 28000 34 6 1 21 31 44½ 814¾ Vergara O LB 116 b 5.40 67–14 Rajawood1184 Captain's Bars122¾ Drill116nk Weakened 9
29Jly96- 4Dmr fst 7f :214 :443 1:094 1:23 3↑ Md 25000 16 3 5 2½ 42 1019 1027¼ Black C A LB 118 b 6.60 58–10 Try Jory118½ Slash The Price116no Native Two Spins1223½ Gave way 11
18Jly96- 4Hol fst 5½f :214 :451 :572 1:034 3↑ [S]Md 32000 68 4 3 31½ 31½ 32 34 Black C A LB 117 b 3.30 88–12 Accountsreceivable117½ Deed Of Trust1173½ Aplomado1172 Best of rest 8
5Jly96- 6Hol fst 7½f :22 :452 1:11 1:314 3↑ [S]Md 32000 58 2 4 2hd 1½ 13 32¾ Black C A LB 117 1.70 72–15 Run The Table1171¾ Jalos1151 Aplomado117½ Weakened late 8
12Jun96- 2Hol fst 1 1/16 :223 :454 1:112 1:44 3↑ Md 40000 — 2 1 19 710 730 — Black C A LB 116 b 3.90 — 13 Armidale1162 Absolut Ruler1171½ Black Pheasant1236 7
Lugged out, stopped, eased
18May96- 4Hol fst 6f :22 :451 :573 1:104 3↑ [S]Md c-32000 73 9 4 11 11½ 12 21¼ Pincay L Jr LB 117 b 2.80 84–13 Dream Hunter1161¼ Aplomado1172½ Shanghana1153 Overtaken late 12
Claimed from Bass & Seeligson Jr, Mandella Richard Trainer
4May96- 1Hol fst 6½f :213 :441 1:094 1:16 3↑ [S]Md Sp Wt 36 3 2 1hd 13 53¾ 523 Pincay L Jr LB 117 b 6.20 63–12 Caribbean Pirate1102½ Moonjay1163 Skysrai11610 Speed inside, tired 6

WORKOUTS: Oct4 SA 5f fst 1:01 H 20/49 ●Sep28 SA 5f fst :583 H 1/43 Sep22 SA 5f fst 1:014 H 31/46 Sep16 SA 4f fst :50 H 33/45 Sep9 Dmr 3f fst :373 H 18/21 ●Aug24 Dmr 5f fst :59 H 1/61

Aplomado
He's fast from the gate, but he's not known for his late finish; he often gives up up down the lane; should contribute to the early pace but is unlikely to take home the top prize.

Sammy Lee Grey

Own: Miller Grace A $28,000
DAVENPORT C L (—) 1996:(230 18 .08)

Gr/ro g. 3 (Mar)
Sire: In Tissar (Roberto)
Dam: Merry Dancer (Native Charger)
Br: Frank Debra K Mrs (Cal)
Tr: Miller Grace A (—) 1996:(22 1 .05)

118

Lifetime Record:	3 M 0 0	$2,310		
1996	3 M 0 0	$2,310	Turf	0 0 0 0
1995	0 M 0 0		Wet	0 0 0 0
SA	0 0 0 0		Dist	0 0 0 0

26Sep96- 7Fpx fst 1 1/16 :23 :47 1:123 1:462 3↑ [S]Md 32000 59 5 7 98¾ 79 55 45½ Davenport C L B 115 9.40 72–22 Fabulous Heir1201 It'sAScreecher1151 MyBettor1153½ Passed tiring foes 9
17Sep96- 5Fpx fst 7f :22 :461 1:121 1:26 3↑ Md 20000 56 2 6 910 99½ 67 43½ Davenport C L B 115 20.70 80–09 EasternGold1201 BarrierBreaker1162 CnHeRun120½ Very wide into lane 9
10Jly96- 9Hol fst 6f :221 :452 :574 1:104 3↑ Md 25000 47 11 7 1211 1114 1014 913¼ Davenport C L B 117 59.20 72–16 Wide Vision1204 Deep Seat Gambler1171¾ Slash The Price117nk No threat 12

WORKOUTS: Oct6 Fpx 3f fst :37 H 1/1 ●Sep9 Fpx 3f fst :344 H 1/5 Sep2 Fpx 5f fst 1:004 H 1/2 Aug25 Hol 4f fst :482 H 3/14 Aug20 Hol 5f fst 1:014 H 10/13 Aug14 Hol 3f fst :364 H 3/10

Sammy Lee Grey
Ran decently at Fairplex under Davenport; don't care for his lack of early speed or the move back to a sprint; may pass a few tired horses late.

Errant Star

Own: Larson Mr & Mrs Melvin C $28,000
ATHERTON J E (1 0 0 0 .00) 1996:(110 4 .04)

Ch. g. 5
Sire: Inherent Star (Pia Star)
Dam: Fake Fur (Singh)
Br: Larson Mr & Mrs Melvin C (Cal)
Tr: Cosme Ruben G (1 0 0 0 .00) 1996:(66 5 .08)

L 120

Lifetime Record:	12 M 0 1	$4,490		
1996	5 M 0 0	$1,940	Turf	0 0 0 0
1995	7 M 0 1	$2,550	Wet	0 0 0 0
SA	2 0 0 0		Dist	1 0 0 0

25Sep96-12Fpx fst 6f :221 :46 :584 1:114 3↑ [S]Md 32000 46 2 3 42½ 54¾ 45½ 48 Berrio O A LB 120 b 48.90 82–09 HeavenSent1151 BusterO'brien1151 MnMountinDen1156 Inside, no rally 8
17Sep96- 7Fpx fst 7f :223 :463 1:113 1:243 3↑ Md 20000 47 8 2 51¾ 64¼ 58 511 Berrio O A LB 120 b 68.10 80–09 Weatherby1206½ Asante1152 K C R's Country1201½ Broke inward, bumped 10
31Aug96- 4Dmr fst 6½f :221 :451 1:11 1:174 3↑ [S]Md 28000 40 8 7 88¾ 98¾ 912 812½ Atherton J E LB 120 b 98.40 70–13 Cheers N Joys118hd Jalos116½ Buster O'brien1182½ No rally 9
19Jly96- 2Hol fst 7f :224 :46 1:111 1:234 3↑ [S]Md 32000 34 7 7 85½ 87 79¾ 617½ Berrio O A LB 122 b 89.20 65–13 Tank'sStar1202 ShermanTank1171¾ BlackPheasnt12210 Broke in, crowded 8
5Jly96- 6Hol fst 7½f :22 :452 1:11 1:314 3↑ [S]Md 32000 21 1 8 89½ 810 716 621¼ Atherton J E LB 122 b 83.80 54–15 Run The Table1171¾ Jalos1151 Aplomado117½ No rally 8
14Jly95- 2Hol fst 6f :22 :45 :574 1:101 3↑ Md 25000 48 7 10 1110 1111 109½ 912½ Garcia M S LB 122 b 84.80 77–10 MedicineManJake1094 Kay'sDrling111nk RuhlTheMnn116½ Shut off start 11
30Jun95- 6Hol fst 7f :221 :452 1:101 1:241 3↑ Md 25000 53 1 8 99¾ 87 67½ 35½ Garcia M S LB 122 b 68.80 75–14 Wonderful Man116½ Chief Ribot1165 Errant Star1222 Along for 3rd 10
1Jun95- 6Hol fst 1 1/16 :233 :471 1:122 1:442 3↑ [S]Md 32000 29 11 9 1014 1113 1017 1027¼ Atherton J E LB 123 b 100.40 51–19 Onizuka1165½ Dawns Bounty121½ Librio1153½ No factor 11
19May95- 2Hol fst 7f :222 :452 1:102 1:233 3↑ [S]Md 32000 44 2 6 63¾ 85½ 76½ 58½ Atherton J E LB 122 b 93.50 75–08 Flying Razz115½ Deputized1171 Liberty Town1155 Rail to lane 9
7May95- 6Hol fst 6f :222 :46 :581 1:103 3↑ [S]Md 32000 34 1 5 75½ 78 68½ 617¼ Atherton J E LB 122 b 83.70 70–11 Cee Ghee1166½ Deputized1171¾ Imahiddennote115¾ Rail trip 9

WORKOUTS: ●Oct5 Fpx 4f fst :474 H 1/6 Aug24 Hol 6f fst 1:141 H 5/12 Aug16 Hol 5f fst 1:012 H 8/16 Aug10 Hol 3f fst :36 H 2/16 Jly26 Fpx 4f fst :491 H 2/2

Errant Star
Has hit the board just once in his 12-race career; shows no Beyers above a 53; training well, but that's the lone positive.

Native Desert

Own: Watarida Fred — $32,000

Dk. b or br g. 3 (Feb)
Sire: Desert Classic (Damascus)
Dam: Miss C. Native (Princely Native)
Br: Fred Watarida (Cal)
Tr: Amescua Rene (—) 1996:(148 27 .18)

SOLIS A (30 5 5 6 .17) 1996:(1087 198 .18) — L 120

Lifetime Record:	1 M 1 0	$3,000		
1996	1 M 1 0	$3,000	Turf	0 0 0 0
1995	0 M 0 0		Wet	0 0 0 0
SA	0 0 0 0		Dist	0 0 0 0

5Sep96–9Dmr fst 5½f :213 :45 :571 1:032 3↑ Md 25000 89 8 8 64½ 57 32½ 2hd Solis A LB 118 b 6.50 96–11 H'sARoylHony118hd NtvDsrt1188 StrtYorEngns1181¼ Drifted in 1/8, green 11

WORKOUTS: Oct4 SA 5f fst :591 H 3/49 Sep21 SA 6f fst 1:143 H 14/24 Sep15 SA 4f fst :49 H 14/32 Sep2 Dmr 4f fst :49 H 29/66 Aug25 BM 5f fst 1:002 Hg8/55 Aug18 Bmf 5f fst 1:011 H 7/26

My Boy Scout

Own: Forli International Inc & Lemalu St — $28,000

Ch. c. 3 (May)
Sire: Flying Victor (Flying Paster)
Dam: Lucky Blue Lady (Lucky Mike)
Br: Forli International (Cal)
Tr: Avila A C (3 0 0 0 .00) 1996:(76 8 .11)

BERRIO O A (5 0 0 0 .00) 1996:(434 25 .06) — L 118

Lifetime Record:	6 M 0 0	$625			
1996	6 M 0 0	$625	Turf	0 0 0 0	
1995	0 M 0 0		Wet	1 0 0 0	
SA	2 0 0 0	$625	Dist	1 0 0 0	$625

7Sep96–2Dmr fst 1 1/16 :224 :464 1:122 1:443 3↑ Md 28000 31 3 1 12 11 1012 1026½ Berrio O A LB 116 58.30 53–14 PouringDownRain1164 Alyplesure1181¼ ClssicLook118¾ Inside, gave way 12
28Aug96–9Dmr fst 1 :222 :461 1:121 1:372 3↑ Md 35000 25 8 9 99½ 97¾ 815 833¼ Berrio O A LB 116 36.70 50–22 EndRun11812 StrwberryPtch1182 Mr.Schppchr1187 Pulling early, outrun 9
17Aug96–2Dmr fst 7f :221 :451 1:111 1:241 3↑ [S]Md 28000 42 8 7 53 63½ 56 713½ Berrio O A LB 116 10.10 65–12 Tam's Ice116½ Main Man1184 Mr. Schappacher1185 Gave way 12
5Jly96–9Hol fst 6f :22 :452 :573 1:101 3↑ Md 32000 45 4 9 67¼ 710 913 918 Berrio O A LB 117 fb 10.00 70–15 Island Caper1172 No Quick Quack1172¾ Transonic1222½ Drifted in lane 11
31Jan96–6SA sly 6f :214 :443 :581 1:102 Md 45000 44 2 11 98½ 1010 1012 1114½ Berrio O A LB 117 b 5.80 71–12 DecorInCrystal119½ MohwkDncer1193½ StolenLooks1192 Forced in early 11
15Jan96–6SA fst 6½f :221 :453 1:103 1:171 Md 45000 58 3 2 2hd 31 32½ 58 Berrio O A LB 117 13.00 76–15 Abattleabove1193 Ky Wish1191¼ Nowhere Road119¾ Inside, weakened 9

WORKOUTS: Oct3 SA 4f fst :482 Hg14/33 Sep27 SA 4f fst :49 H 18/30 ●Sep2 Dmr 6f fst 1:124 H 1/21 ●Aug10 Dmr 4f fst :46 H 1/48 Aug4 Dmr 5f fst 1:004 Hg20/64 Jly21 Dmr 5f fst :593 H 2/34

Also Eligible:

Fandarel Classic

Own: Rerez Pedro R — $28,000

Ch. c. 3 (Apr)
Sire: Desert Wine (Damascus)
Dam: Baroness O'Dublin (Irish Ruler)
Br: Barton Heller (Cal)
Tr: Martin Francisco Jr (1 0 0 0 .00) 1996:(48 4 .08)

RAMIREZ M A (1 0 0 0 .00) 1996:(8 1 .13) — 118

Lifetime Record:	0 M 0 0		
1996	0 M 0 0	Turf	0 0 0 0
1995	0 M 0 0	Wet	0 0 0 0
SA	0 0 0 0	Dist	0 0 0 0

WORKOUTS: Sep29 Hol 5f fst 1:013 H 14/24 Sep22 Hol 6f fst 1:163 Hg12/15 Sep15 Hol 6f fst 1:154 Hg7/11 Sep9 Hol 5f fst 1:021 H 7/9 Sep3 Hol 5f fst 1:043 H 17/17 Aug28 Hol 5f fst 1:032 H 15/15
Aug21 Hol 4f fst :503 H 13/17 Aug15 Hol 4f fst :502 H 9/13 Aug9 Hol 4f fst :502 H 15/20 Aug3 Hol 3f fst :374 H 15/21

TRAINER CHANGES

Horses entered today, other than those claimed in their last start, which have a different trainer from their last race.

Horse / Prior Trainer	Horse / Prior Trainer	Horse / Prior Trainer	Horse / Prior Trainer
— Race 1 —	— Race 5 —	— Race 8 —	
Garden Of Roses / Jenda Charles J	B. T.'s Gold / Wise Kriston Von	Lady Ling / Juan Maldotll	

Native Desert

What's not to like? he's from a good barn, his debut was outstanding, and he's training super; earned an outstanding 89 Beyer for that 2nd place finish; that's a number good enough to win many special weights; kinda surprised that he didn't return in one of those; someone might take him for $32,000; the horse to beat at a short price.

My Boy Scout

Beaten 59 lengths in his last 2 starts; form is dreadful; may improve with today's shorter distance; first time gelding; a longshot nonetheless.

Fandarel Classic

The lone also eligible in the field; shows a foundation of slow works leading up to his career-debut; sire is adequate with first time starters; prefer to see a race.

—Byron King

number is high enough to make the horse competitive against open maidens as well, by which I mean animals not up for sale in a claiming affair.

Before we risk our life savings on this "mortal lock," however, we need to ask ourselves why he's running here, where he will almost certainly be taken by some other owner. No one gives anything away at the racetrack, where it is wise always to be at least a bit suspicious about such apparently good things.

One possible answer is that the horse has what the wise-guys call a hole in him, meaning that he has a bone chip in a knee, or a rough-looking ankle, or a bad-looking tendon, or a sore back; he may have no more than one or two races left in him.

The fact that he shows three works since his last effort, however, means that he can't be that unsound. It may simply be that his owner and breeder, Fred Watarida, wants to unload him. The animal is unfashionably bred, has already been gelded (which eliminates him as a potential sire), and Mr. Watarida wants to turn over a quick dollar. The longer we look at the race, the more unlikely it seems that he will lose. He evidently likes to run late, so the extra furlong and his outside post position will also work to his advantage; he is so much better than the other horses in this contest that he could go ten wide on the turn and still win.

We have to remember, though, that all horses can and do lose for reasons that have nothing to do with talent. Native Desert will go off at less than even money. Unless you are going into this race with some sort of parlay bet going or you think you can find a couple of big long shots to finish second and third behind him in an exacta or a trifecta play, you should not bet the race but head straight for the parking lot. You and the other wiseguys will beat the crowd home.

NINTH RACE **6½ FURLONGS. (1.14) MAIDEN CLAIMING. Purse $17,000. 3-year-olds and upward bred in California. Weights: 3-year-olds, 120 lbs. Older, 122 lbs. Claiming price $32,000, if for $28,000, allowed 2 lbs.**

Santa Anita

OCTOBER 10, 1996

Value of Race: $17,000 Winner $9,350; second $3,400; third $2,550; fourth $1,275; fifth $425. Mutuel Pool $233,033.20 Exacta Pool $184,147.00 Trifecta Pool $279.923.00 Quinella Pool $27,747.00

Last Raced	Horse	M/Eqt.	A.	Wt	PP	St	¼	½	Str	Fin	Jockey	Cl'g Pr	Odds $1
5Sep96 ^{9}Dmr^{2}	Native Desert	LBb	3	120	10	2	3^{hd}	2^{1}	$1^{4\frac{1}{2}}$	1^{13}	Solis A	32000	0.70
2Dec95 ^{6}Hol^{4}	S. S. Tell	Bf	3	118	4	3	2^{hd}	4^{2}	3^{hd}	$2^{1\frac{3}{4}}$	Hunter M T	28000	16.00
25Sep96 ^{12}Fpx^{2}	Buster O'Brien	LBb	3	120	3	5	$4^{\frac{1}{2}}$	$3^{\frac{1}{2}}$	2^{1}	3^{hd}	Blanc B	32000	3.10
19Sep96 ^{9}Fpx^{4}	Glad You Asked	LBb	3	120	6	11	$6^{2\frac{1}{2}}$	5^{hd}	4^{2}	4^{1}	Valenzuela P A	32000	7.90
30Sep96 ^{13}Fpx^{2}	Over The Limit	LB	3	118	1	10	10^{3}	9^{4}	7^{hd}	$5^{\frac{3}{4}}$	Garcia M S	28000	20.20
26Sep96 ^{7}Fpx^{4}	Sammy Lee Grey	B	3	118	8	9	11	$10^{2\frac{1}{2}}$	8^{1}	6^{6}	Davenport C L	28000	52.50
30Sep96 ^{13}Fpx^{4}	Private Reserve	LBb	3	118	5	6	7^{hd}	8^{1}	10^{5}	7^{1}	Valenzuela F H	28000	86.90
22Sep96 ^{12}Fpx^{7}	T. V. Winner	LBb	3	118	2	4	5^{2}	$6^{2\frac{1}{2}}$	6^{1}	8^{hd}	Espinoza V	28000	25.00
25Sep96 ^{12}Fpx^{4}	Errant Star	LBb	5	120	9	7	$8^{4\frac{1}{2}}$	7^{2}	$9^{1\frac{1}{2}}$	$9^{4\frac{1}{2}}$	Atherton J E	28000	114.90
29Aug96 ^{2}Dmr^{8}	Aplomado	LBb	3	118	7	1	$1^{1\frac{1}{2}}$	$1^{\frac{1}{2}}$	$5^{1\frac{1}{2}}$	$10^{6\frac{1}{2}}$	Vergara O	28000	13.80
	Fandarel Classic	Bf	3	118	11	8	9^{hd}	11	11	11	Ramirez Marco A	28000	79.00

OFF AT 5:04 Start Good. Won ridden out. Time, :21^{4}, :44^{4}, 1:09^{3}, 1:15^{4} Track fast.

$2 Mutuel Prices:			
11–NATIVE DESERT	3.40	2.80	2.20
5–S. S. TELL		9.00	3.60
4–BUSTER O'BRIEN			2.20

$2 EXACTA 11–5 PAID $32.00 $2 TRIFECTA 11–5–4 PAID $88.80 $2 QUINELLA 5–11 PAID $26.00

Dk. b. or br. g. (Feb), by Desert Classic–Miss C. Native, by Princely Native. Trainer Amescua Rene. Bred by Fred Watarida (Cal).

NATIVE DESERT was five wide early, bid three deep on the turn, took the lead leaving the bend and drew well clear under a brisk hand ride. S. S. TELL was bumped at the start, raced between rivals on the backstretch and early on the turn, continued off the rail, split foes again in midstretch and got the place. BUSTER O'BRIEN raced along the inside throughout and just saved the show. GLAD YOU ASKED broke a bit awkwardly, was sent between foes on the backstretch and off the inside on the turn, came four wide into the stretch and just missed third. OVER THE LIMIT broke a bit slowly, was taken well out from the rail early, came wide into the stretch and improved position. SAMMY LEE GREY was outrun off the inside on the backstretch, angled in for the turn and improved position toward the inside. PRIVATE RESERVE was in a bit tight early, raced off the rail and did not menace. T. V. WINNER saved ground to the stretch, came out and weakened. ERRANT STAR raced wide and did not rally. APLOMADO dueled four wide early, inched clear before completing a quarter mile, resisted briefly inside the winner on the turn, then gave way. FANDAREL CLASSIC raced wide early, cut to the rail nearing the turn and was done early. MAN MOUNTAIN DEAN (3) WAS REPORTED UNSOUND AT THE GATE AND WAS SCRATCHED BY THE STEWARDS ON THE ADVICE OF THE TRACK VETERINARIAN. ALL HIS REGULAR, EXACTA, QUINELLA AND TRIFECTA WAGERS WERE ORDERED REFUNDED, A CONSOLATION DOUBLE WAS PAID AND ALL HIS PICK THREE SELECTIONS, AS WELL AS PLACE PICK NINE AND PICK SIX SELECTIONS WITHOUT ALTERNATES WERE SWITCHED TO THE FAVORITE, NATIVE DESERT (11).

Owners— 1, Watarida Fred; 2, Delaplane E Edward & Paula; 3, Hochman & Isaacs; 4, Lickhalter & Richardson & Roe; 5, Shepard & Wicker; 6, Miller Grace A; 7, Cain & Guillot; 8, Cuadra T Y T Inc; 9, Larson Mr & Mrs Melvin C; 10, 5 C Stable; 11, Rerez Pedro R

Trainers—1, Amescua Rene; 2, Cardiel Fidel; 3, Palma Hector O; 4, Chapman James K; 5, Wicker Lloyd C; 6, Miller Grace A; 7, Guillot Eric; 8, Inda Eduardo; 9, Cosme Ruben G; 10, Polanco Marcelo; 11, Martin Francisco Jr

Native Desert was claimed by Rubio Miguel; trainer, Garcia Juan.

Scratched— Man Mountain Dean (25Sep96 ^{12}FPX^{3}), My Boy Scout (7Sep96 ^{2}DMR^{10})

$3 Pick Three (3–4–3/11) Paid $86.40; Pick Three Pool $98,198.
$2 Daily Double (4–11) Paid $13.00; Consolation Daily Double (4–3) Paid $7.20; Daily Double Pool $110,714. $2 Pick Six (1–1–4–3–4–3/11)
6 Correct 61 Tickets Paid $13,983.60 (including $342,122.25 Carryover);
5 Correct 1,623 Tickets Paid $209.80; Pick Six Pool $1,066,733.
$1 Place Pick All (2/6—2/8—4/5—1/7—1/4—3/4—3/4—3/4—3/5/11)
9 Correct 6 Tickets Paid $3,645.90; Place Pick All Pool $27,406.

Santa Anita Attendance: 8,334 Total Mutuel Pool: $1,880,400.40 Off Track Attendance: 13,064 Total Mutuel Pool: $7,186,124.40 Total Attendance: 21,398 Total Mutuel Pool: $9,066,524.80

Surprise, surprise, the best horse wins again! Such a disappointment to all the wiseguys and the paranoids, who cling tenaciously to a deeply rooted conviction that all is for the worst in this worst of all possible worlds. Native Desert ran exactly as he was supposed to in excellent time, looking like Secretariat against this field of plodders, and was promptly claimed. He went off at seven to ten, thus making it impossible to bet on him straight, but a sixteen-to-one shot did run a distant second, resulting in an exacta payoff of thirty-two dollars. I could not have picked S. S. Tell to finish in the money off what I saw in the *Form*, but the race did nicely by me just the same.

I had wound up investing a total of thirty dollars here in doubles from Two Ninety Jones—twenty dollars on Native Desert and ten on Aplomado, who finished next to last. Why Aplomado, a horse I haven't mentioned before?

Let's go back to the past performances. What else do we notice about the race besides Native Desert's obvious superiority? A dearth of speed. Aplomado emerged from the numbers as the horse most likely to get a clear lead. Although he had failed on seven previous occasions, finding himself all alone in front can sometimes free a speedball to run his best race, as he had back on May 18. If Native Desert went to his knees out of the starting gate or dropped his rider, the two most common ways odds-on favorites choose to eliminate themselves, then Aplomado had as solid a chance as anyone else to win. I'd have blown my pick-five, but the double would have paid more than enough to compensate for the loss. This betting tactic of mine didn't pay off here, but did in Aplomado's next race, when he enriched me by romping home all alone in front at odds of better than ten to one.

My twenty-dollar double from Two Ninety Jones to Native Desert paid $130, minus the thirty I'd invested, for a net profit of a hundred. Then the pick-five paid $209.80. We had it twice, because we had used two horses in the sixth race, the only one we lost. My profit there came out to just under a net of $186. A very nice ending to a very pleasant day at the races. I went home that evening with a betting profit of $448.

ONE OF THE biggest traps you can fall into at the races is to imagine that every day can be this successful. I've chosen to take you through one of my better afternoons, but I hope I've made it clear that it could just as easily have been a losing one. I made a number of mistakes, but luckily they didn't cost me the day. I passed up Provide in the second; I neglected to bet straight on Tres Paraiso in the third; I wagered incorrectly in the sixth by leaving My Sister Jane out of both my plays; I overlooked Miss Lady Bug for a value bet in the eighth. Most important, feeling as strongly as I did about Two Ninety Jones and Native Desert, and finding myself still comfortably ahead after the seventh, I should have pressed the double bets for a bigger score. All of these omissions on my part can be said to fall into the category of "woulda-coulda-shoulda" and be ignored, but it's always a good idea to try to imagine what might have been, as well as to rejoice in what was. That way you can keep your balance between the rushes of delirium and despair that can afflict all gamblers. It's a game, not a way of life.

Hazards: Numbers,
Mud, and Manners

Handicapping and betting well are essential to your happiness in this game, but the hazards to your continued success are many and require a lot of flexibility on your part.

The longer you hang around the racing scene, for example, the more aware you become of how dependent on numbers you are. The sheer preponderance of them can become suffocating. Numbers, numbers, everybody's got a number on everything. Not a day passes that somebody won't be trying to cram a number into your head. If you're not careful, you could become numb from numbers.

The horses all have a good or a bad number. The trainers and jocks have a low- or a high-percentage number. The computers flash us the numbers that are going to make us winners and download us into untold wealth. The tote board and the TV screens blink numbers. The pros spend hours deciphering the numbers for one another and the supplicants who are willing to pay for their expertise. The macho players squander thousands on losers to prove to us how humongous their numbers are. If you let it happen, it can all become ciphers, digits, fractions, integers, numerals—life at the track reduced to a number.

Those of us who go to the races regularly do have to depend in our handicapping on numbers, especially the ones that appear in the *Form* or in the statistics we pile up for ourselves from performance charts, workouts, speed ratings, etc. I started going racing in the bad old betting days when many such numbers were unavailable and the absence of accurate information provided to the public was scandalous, especially from the racetracks. And there is still room for improvement in some areas. All horseplayers have an inalienable right to life, liberty, and the endless pursuit of numbers.

That said, the trouble with numbers is not only that they aren't always accurate and can be misleading, but all by themselves they just aren't a lot of fun. Every day at the races I see people who have been betrayed by their numbers and who can't imagine why they aren't winning. Back they go to their mind-boggling statistics without even bothering to glance up from their calculations long enough to look at the horses or take in the grand spectacle of the whole event itself, from the paddock to the winner's circle.

You have to remember always that there are many ways to get to a winner, all of them legitimate. Numbers alone won't do it for you. I once turned my whole meeting around at Del Mar by ignoring my top numbers in two races to bet on a horse trained by Bobby Frankel in the third and one owned by a friend of mine named Gary Bisantz in the fifth. Why? Because Frankel is famous for winning with horses that don't quite figure on paper, and Bisantz, one of the smartest owners around, never lets his trainers enter horses in races he doesn't think they can win.

Handicapping well is only part of the story at the track. There will always be winners that don't figure at all. Flukes? Fixed races? Don't you believe it. It's called life. Nowhere is it written that virtue in the form of doing anything strictly by the numbers, at the track or elsewhere, will inevitably be rewarded. Ever hear the one about the two pals, Manny and Willie, who go to the races together for months? Manny is a numbers guy; Willie wants to have fun. Manny studies ten hours a day to come up with his numbers; Willie never spends more than an hour or so on the *Form*. Manny hasn't cashed a ticket in weeks; Willie is wallowing in winners, dates beautiful women, and drives a Testarossa.

Finally, Manny can't stand it any longer. He asks Willie how he does it. Willie takes out his program and says, "See these two horses in here, the two and the four?" "Yeah, what about them?" Manny answers. "Bet the eight," Willie says. "What do you mean, bet the eight?" Manny barks. "Two and four is six." Willie shakes his head in sorrow as he heads for a window to cash. "There you go with those numbers again," he calls back.

What's the moral of this tale? That Willie is just lucky and Manny isn't? That's not my interpretation. Maybe Willie doesn't need more than an hour to come up with his winners. Maybe he's more relaxed, more open to other important elements, such as how the horses look in the post parade or changes in equipment and medication. What is certain is that he pays attention to value. He never makes a bet that isn't going to reward him handsomely when it hits.

You need to rely to a considerable extent on your numbers, but you should be able to enjoy a day at the races without having to involve yourself in the sort of mind-numbing calculations that would have given Albert Einstein a headache. If you can't simply open the *Daily Racing Form* and immediately get some idea of how each race will be run and who the true contenders are, don't be disappointed. That will come with time. Until then, a few simple procedures will put you on the right track. For easy reference, you can always check back to the *Form*'s "past-performance explanation" for Tobin Ruler.

What essentially did we learn from it? First of all, based on recent form, that Tobin Ruler is capable of an 86 Beyer fig on the dirt. (Do not concern yourself with speed ratings earned a year or more earlier; only very rarely will a horse win coming off that long a layoff or after that many months of poor performances.) In this case that speed rating was earned in a sprint, but to me it almost always makes no difference whether the race is long or short. From the sprint distances up to a mile and one eighth, the Beyer fig is a reliable indicator of an animal's overall speed. In longer races, especially on grass, class becomes an important factor, but you can and should pass a lot of those races. You can very profitably confine your main betting action to the less glamorous events, in which horses like Tobin Ruler can enrich you by romping in at $21.80, as he did in his very next outing.

After you've isolated the contenders based on the figs, then take a look at the second most important statistics available, those regarding trainers and jockeys. If you feel you need more detailed information about trainer-jockey combinations than you can glean from the *Form*'s "pps," there are publications sold at the track, including some of the programs, that will provide it. I've never found the need to refer to them because I believe firmly in architect Mies van der Rohe's famous dictum that "less is more." You can generally get a pretty good feel for a trainer-jockey relationship from the number of times they've already collaborated over the last ten races.

Pay some attention to medication and equipment changes, especially the addition of Lasix, blinkers, and front bandages. Note the comments on the horse's most recent races, but be skeptical of them. What's important in them is information concerning any trouble the animal may have had, not opinions such as "weakened," which might have kept you from betting on Tobin Ruler in his next and winning race.

Other important handicapping factors to consider are the conditions of the race (racing surface, type of race, post position, class) weight (especially if the horse is being asked to carry 120 pounds or more for the first time or five pounds more than he has ever been asked to carry before), and workouts since the horse's last race. The latter not so much for speed, but in relation to the number of other animals working at the same distance that morning.

Another important aspect of the game that we have only touched on is what to do when it rains and the racing surface comes up muddy, sloppy, slow, heavy, or merely wet. (In this country, most races are taken off the turf on rainy days, in which case you will want to handicap only on the basis of the horses' dirt ratings.) You will see in the *Form* that statistics on the subject are readily available and can be helpful. Some Thoroughbreds, especially those with sensitive feet, relish the slop and will skim over it like water beetles. You'll note from the Beyer figs that they'll move up ten points or so on such occasions.

It will pay off not to ignore that factor. (Ha, numbers

again!) In fact, many of the regulars, especially the wiseguys always looking for an edge, make a big deal out of days when the track is off because of bad weather. They study breeding closely, looking for animals descended from sires and dams who relished the mud, and they keep statistics going back several years on this aspect of their action. They also note carefully whether the horses in such a race have been equipped with "stickers," shoes with some sort of cleat or rim designed to help the animals cope with unsteady or slippery footing. You won't be told about such changes of equipment until just before the race itself, but you'd be amazed at the significance the pros attach to such information.

My advice? Pay some attention to these factors, but don't waste a lot of time on them. I mostly ignore the sticker information; a good trainer puts the right shoes on his horses. And the track superintendents, who take care of the racing surfaces, have become far more adept in recent years at keeping the footing solid, even when the track is covered by several inches of water. In fact, on "sloppy" days, the pure speed horses are likely to do even better than usual, partly because they can wing out alone on the lead, leaving the rest of the field to cope with all that water and mud being kicked up in their faces.

In short, you can best deal with such situations by factoring into your calculations whatever you can glean from the past-performance information available in the *Form;* the same handicapping and betting strategies that serve you well in fair weather will see you through in foul. Or, if you don't feel comfortable with that assessment, you can just stay home or go to a movie. Unless it's one of racing's great days, Kentucky Derby time or some other major event, why would you want to attend when it's pouring and an icy wind is cutting into your bones as you cross the parking lot? In most parts of the country they race at least five days a week all year round. On so-called dark days, when the live horses aren't competing, you can watch races on television, either at home or at some nearby betting facility, and wager in comfort. The idea is to have a good time, isn't it?

As a frequent visitor to any racetrack, as opposed to wagering from a reserved seat at an offtrack facility or from the sanctity of your living room, the biggest hazard you'll face to your continued well-being is other people. The social aspect of a day at the races is for me one of its major attractions, but it can seriously interfere with your betting action. This is why it's important for you not to show up at the track unprepared. If you know before you get there exactly what horses you are planning to build your day around, your only concern on the premises will be *how* to bet on them, not *what* to bet on. You'll have enough time to enjoy the experience of a racing day without allowing its complementary delights and the behavior of your fellow players to distract you from your main purpose—finding the right horse and betting on him correctly.

"A man who has not an opinion of his own and the ability to stick to it in the face of all kinds of arguments . . . has not one chance in a million to beat the races for any length of time." Those lines were spoken by a legendary horseplayer nicknamed Pittsburgh Phil, who flourished around the turn of the century. His real name was George E. Smith and by the time he allowed himself to be interviewed in 1908 by a turf writer named Edward Cole he had amassed the very sizable fortune in those days of well over a million and a half dollars.

Pittsburgh Phil was very strict on the subject of socializing. He believed that distraction and interference are the great enemies of concentration. A horseplayer intent on winning has no time to waste on convivial conversation or to listen endlessly to the funny stories with which the track abounds. Above all, Pittsburgh Phil warned, a man should avoid the pitfalls posed by the presence on the premises of attractive members of the opposite sex. Women are "an addition and an adornment to a beautiful scene" and should always be made welcome, but not if the man involved is planning "to make a business of betting." For this reason, Pittsburgh Phil never even took his mother to the races, except "upon very rare occasions" at Saratoga, where presumably the graciousness of the scene overwhelmed his spartan soul.

My late friend, the movie director Martin Ritt, would never allow his concentration to be disrupted. An old pal once persuaded him to allow him to bring along his new girlfriend for an afternoon of sport at Santa Anita. She turned out to be an asset in every way. She kept quiet, asked no questions, laughed at the men's jokes, and fetched them drinks and tidbits. Everybody loved her. The next day Marty was asked by his friend what he thought of her. "She's a wonderful woman," Marty said. "Don't bring her again."

Women at the track have their own crosses to bear, not the least of which is the misbehavior caused by what my wife calls the testosterone factor. This is a disease that afflicts male horseplayers exclusively. They swagger about the premises entranced by their own expertise and the size of their bankrolls, which they equate with sexual potency. They boast about their triumphs at the windows and regard those of us who bet only modest sums as an inferior breed not worthy of consideration in the great panoply of powerful players. In some perverse way, they regard even their huge losses as affirmation of their wondrous potency. Watching them try to impress one another, especially in the presence of females, is not unlike tuning in to one of those nature documentaries on the mating habits of partridges and other pompous birds. The nasty side of their behavior is their competitiveness and their insensitivity to others. A victim of the testosterone factor will regard his own wins as his due, the inevitable result of his superior expertise, his losses as the inexplicable malignity of chance. He will revel in his triumphs and trumpet them abroad, but never condescend to congratulate anyone else on his or hers. The only way to cope with these boors is to avoid them, which unfortunately is not always easy.

I once made a list of all the people at the racetrack I could do without, then decided to set it to music. I offer it here, with apologies to the Messrs. W. S. Gilbert and Arthur Sullivan, who wrote the original for their immortal operetta, *The Mikado:*

The Executioner's Song

As someday it may happen
   that a victim must be found,
I've got a little list—I've got a little list
Of racetrack offenders
   who might well be underground,
And who never would be missed—
        who never would be missed!
There's the pestilential nuisances
        who want to know your picks—
The wiseguys in the clubhouse
        who think every race is fixed—
The experts who are up on stats
        and correct you when you're wrong—

The bettors who at post time at the windows linger long—
And the tipsters who on touting favorites insist—
They'd none of 'em be missed—they'd none of 'em be
    missed!

CHORUS OF HORSEPLAYERS
All these clowns have had their day—
        so please send them on their way;
And they'll none of 'em be missed—
            so don't wait and don't desist!

There's the liar who will tell you that he hasn't lost a race—
It's so easy, he'll insist—I've got him on the list!
And the louts with winning tickets
        who flaunt them in your face,
They never would be missed—they never would be missed!
Then the idiot who roots with enthusiastic tone
For every odds-on favorite and every selection but your own;
And the lady with her handbag who gets ahead of you in line,
Who can't seem to find her money even at post time,
And that ignorant phenomenon, the TV analyst—
I don't think he'd be missed—I'm sure he'd not be missed!

CHORUS
Oh, yes, let's get rid of them today—
        when they're gone we'll shout hooray!
They're not going to be missed—shoot them, we insist!

And the incompetent officials who can't seem to do their
    jobs,
The stewards and the starter—I've got them on the list!
The complainers, the excusers,
        the brain-pickers and the slobs—
They'd none of 'em be missed—they'd none of 'em be
    missed.

And the thieving politicians of a compromising kind,
The IRS, the OTB, the managements that rob you blind,
And columnists and pundits and touts of every hue,
The job of making up the list I'd rather leave to you.
But it really doesn't matter which bums are on the list,
They'll none of 'em be missed—they'd none of 'em be
    missed!

CHORUS
You can bet your bottom dollar—
       when they go you'll hear 'em holler!
But they'll none of 'em be missed—
       please make sure they're on the list!

The Right Horse:
Living It Up and
Doing It Live

chapter 12

If you begin attending the races on a more
or less regular basis, you'll quickly discover
that your having a good time there has at last
become a major industry concern. As I've already indicated, the racing associations for
years pretty much ignored their customers
and catered mainly to wealthy owners and
the well-heeled swells who could afford to
join their private turf clubs and subscribe
to seasonal boxes. For them that was the
golden era of horse racing, when it was
the only game in town. Everything changed
with the advent of television and, soon after,
the enormous increase in competition for the
sporting dollar. It took quite a while for the
industry to wake up to this new reality and
it is still paying for its lack of foresight. At a

time when it should have been clear to everyone that television and technology in general would forever alter the social, sporting, and entertainment scenes, the New York Racing Association tore down the charming old Belmont Park grandstand and built a huge supermarket capable of accommodating up to ninety thousand fans. Today, even for the sport's most popular events, no more than a quarter of this space is ever occupied, and on normal race days a relative handful of hardy souls rattles around in there like marbles in a shoebox.

What has saved racing economically is the proliferation of offtrack betting and the ongoing increase in the simulcasting of racing everywhere on closed-circuit, cable, and satellite television. Customers can now drop in to some conveniently located facility to bet on horses running out of state, as well as at the local hippodromes. In some areas they can also open so-called turf accounts, phone in their bets, and watch the races at home. At the tracks themselves, bettors can wager on as many as five or six other venues, and races are now being piped in from as far away as Australia and Hong Kong. It is all happening in a highly disorganized and dismayingly capricious manner, with no national racing authority overseeing its development and with every state and independent racing association pretty much making up its own laws and rules as it bumbles along.

Currently there's a movement afoot to take over the administration of the sport nationally by a group of wealthy owners, who believe, quite rightly, that the racing associations have pretty much fumbled the job. They're trying to remodel the sport to emulate the way the pro golf tour is run, but they'll have to cope not only with state gaming laws but with entrenched local interests and politicians. Where and how it will all end nobody is quite sure, but that's all in accordance

with the self-interested, chaotic approach typical of the enterprise capitalism that we Americans regard as an inalienable
right. What does seem likely is that eventually, after an inevitable series of bankruptcies and mergers, there will be fewer
racetracks, less live racing, and more and more offtrack wagering sites.

That's the bad news. The good news, as far as you're
concerned, is that you have now become a valued commodity
to the racing associations. With the possible exception of New
York City, where people at the Off-Track Betting (OTB) par-
lors are still treated as if they were vermin, it has become possible to go to the races and be welcomed as if you mattered,
which, of course, you do. At the major tracks there are information booths staffed by usually cheerful employees, closed-circuit TV screens everywhere, gift shops, infield playgrounds
for the kiddies, picnic areas, eateries of all sorts, special events
such as concerts and handicapping seminars, and, most important, video facilities at which you can call up races from the
past for immediate screening—a useful tool if you want to see
for yourself what sort of trip your horse had in a race indicating
trouble of some sort. Even the programs are now packed with
information and advice. All you have to do is ask for what you
want these days and you're likely to be granted it. A wonderful
thing, competition.

The whole idea is to make the racing day an enjoyable
one. For that, no betting facility, however luxurious and/or
conveniently located, can begin to compete with the track itself. I live near Del Mar, California, which means that, for all
but seven weeks of the year, I have to drive two hours each
way to get to either Santa Anita or Hollywood Park, up in the
Los Angeles area. The result is I now watch most of my races
on a TV screen at my local offtrack wagering site, on the fair-

grounds at Del Mar, where the track itself is located. It's comfortable, pleasant, and convenient, about four easy driving miles from my house. But I miss the live scene and I try to arrange my racing life so that I can be at Santa Anita or Hollywood for the big racing days. During the seven weeks of the Del Mar meet itself, I'm in daily attendance there and, as the summer season nears, I begin to count down the days to that glorious afternoon in late July when I can be on hand for that first parade to the post under the blue sky of a Southern California summer. Give yourself that treat when you decide to go racing. Watching horses run on a TV screen bears the same relation to the real experience as masturbation does to sex.

ALL SET to go? Tuck this book into your pocket and take it along for easy reference. You ought to have something to read at the racetrack besides the *Daily Racing Form*. And if you get into trouble, here's my list of Golden Rules to bet by, fifteen of them. Not as definitive as the Ten Commandments Charlton Heston brought back from the Mount, but merely designed to keep you cheerful and solvent at the racetrack, one of God's minor playgrounds:

1. Do your homework *before* you go to the track.

2. Once you get there, don't pay for anything you can get free, don't be afraid to ask questions, and insist on being treated well.

3. Value is the name of the game. Bet small to win big, not big to win small.

4. Take only what you can afford to lose. Don't borrow money, don't lend it, and stay away from the ATM machines.

5. Every bet you make in any one race must show a net profit. Never bet merely to get your money back or to cut your losses.

6. If your top horse is four to one or better, you must have a straight bet on him to win.

7. Don't bet every race on the card. Make it a rule to pass at least one or two a day. This will take pressure off you and give you time to do some socializing.

8. Avoid the sucker bets. In poker, you wouldn't draw to an inside straight, so why throw away money on the superfecta or the pick-nine?

9. Never listen to tips from any source, especially trainers, jockeys, jockeys' agents, stable help, and owners.

10. Never allow anyone to talk you off the horse you like.

11. Do not head for a betting window or a ticket machine until you know exactly what and how you are going to bet.

12. Always check your tickets before leaving the window. Clerks make mistakes and they're almost never in your favor.

13. Never bet on a horse to do something in a race it has already proved convincingly it cannot do.

14. Bet less when you are losing, more when you are winning.

15. If you're not having a good time, leave. Don't chase your money. Remember, there's always tomorrow.

BIBLIOGRAPHY

FUNDAMENTAL KNOWLEDGE, BASIC METHODS

Ainslie, Tom. *Ainslie's Complete Guide to Thoroughbred Racing*, rev. ed. New York: Simon & Schuster, 1986.

Cole, Edward. *Racing Maxims and Methods of Pittsburgh Phil*. Las Vegas: Gambler's Book Club, 1968.

Davidowitz, Steven. *Betting Thoroughbreds*, rev. ed. New York: E. P. Dutton, 1995.

Quinn, James. *Recreational Handicapping*. New York;/William Morrow & Co., 1990.

SPEED HANDICAPPING

Beyer, Andrew. *Picking Winners*. Boston: Houghton Mifflin Co., 1975.

——. *Beyer on Speed*. Boston: Houghton Mifflin Co., 1993.

Quirin, William L. *Winning at the Races: Computer Discoveries in Thoroughbred Handicapping.* New York: William Morrow & Co., 1979.

CLASS EVALUATION

Quinn, James. *The Handicapper's Condition Book*, rev. ed. New York: William Morrow & Co., 1986.

Davidowitz, Steven. Ibid.

PACE ANALYSIS

Brohamer, Tom. *Modern Pace Handicapping.* New York: William Morrow & Co., 1991.

Quinn, James. *Figure Handicapping.* New York: William Morrow & Co., 1992.

FORM ANALYSIS

Ainslie, Tom. Ibid.

Cramer, Mark. *Thoroughbred Cycles.* New York: William Morrow & Co., 1990.

Scott, William L. *How Will Your Horse Run Today?* Baltimore: Amicus Press, 1984.

MONEY MANAGEMENT
AND BETTING STRATEGY

Meadow, Barry. *Money Secrets at the Racetrack.* Anaheim, Ca.: TR Publishing, 1990.

Mitchell, Dick. *Commonsense Betting.* New York: William Morrow & Co., 1994.

INDEX